PRINCIPLES OF CHINESE CRIMINAL PROCEDURE

This book presents a short history and timeline of criminal procedure legislation in China. First, it addresses the status of Human Rights Conventions and the challenges resulting from human rights standards for Chinese criminal procedural law and practice. The discussion then moves on to explore the fundaments of Chinese criminal procedure such as the applicable law found in the Chinese CPL (Criminal Procedure Law) and legal institutions.

The book covers relevant actors in the Chinese Criminal Justice System (ie judges, prosecutors, police, defence councils) as well as the relationships between them. It also includes topics relating to the victims of crime and their role in criminal proceedings. Starting with pre-trial investigations (extending in particular to coercive measures and discretionary powers in the implementation of non-prosecution policies) the book continues to guide through the basic principles of criminal trial, standards of evidence and rules related to conviction. Appeals and the issue of reopening criminal proceedings are also considered, with the book making particular reference to a number of special procedures (including juvenile delinquency) in the closing chapter.

Volume 20 in the series Studies in International and Comparative Criminal Law

Principles of Chinese Criminal Procedure

Liling Yue

•HART•
OXFORD • LONDON • NEW YORK • NEW DELHI • SYDNEY

HART PUBLISHING

Bloomsbury Publishing Plc

Kemp House, Chawley Park, Cumnor Hill, Oxford, OX2 9PH, UK

1385 Broadway, New York, NY 10018, USA

29 Earlsfort Terrace, Dublin 2, Ireland

HART PUBLISHING, the Hart/Stag logo, BLOOMSBURY and the Diana logo are trademarks of Bloomsbury Publishing Plc

First published in Great Britain 2021

A catalogue record for this book is available from the British Library.

Library of Congress Cataloging-in-Publication data

Names: Yue, Liling, author.

Title: Principles of Chinese criminal procedure / Liling Yue.

Description: Oxford ; New York : Hart, 2021. | Series: Studies in international and comparative criminal law; volume 20 | Includes bibliographical references and index.

Identifiers: LCCN 2021026027 (print) | LCCN 2021026028 (ebook) | ISBN 9781509934911 (hardback) | ISBN 9781509953998 (paperback) | ISBN 9781509934935 (pdf) | ISBN 9781509934928 (Epub)

Subjects: LCSH: Criminal procedure—China.

Classification: LCC KNQ4610.Y94 2021 (print) | LCC KNQ4610 (ebook) | DDC 345.51/05—dc23

LC record available at https://lccn.loc.gov/2021026027

LC ebook record available at https://lccn.loc.gov/2021026028

ISBN: HB: 978-1-50993-491-1
ePDF: 978-1-50993-493-5
ePub: 978-1-50993-492-8

Typeset by Compuscript Ltd, Shannon

To Prof. Dr. Hans-Jörg Albrecht, Freiburg, Germany

PREFACE

I am pleased to have the opportunity to write and publish this book. This is the first English language book to provide a comprehensive introduction to China's modern criminal procedure law, its development and main procedures. From a legal scholar's perspective, this text explores the advances of China's Criminal Procedure Law (CPL) and its implementation, while discussing the problems which remain even after three sets of amendments to the CPL since its first enactment in 1979. In this book, I have also clarified and corrected some errors and misunderstandings caused by translating Chinese legal terms into English, a problem which has dragged on for decades, in the hope that the corrections given will be helpful for international scholars who are interested in the study of Chinese law.

First of all, I would like to thank Professor Michael Bohlander, the General Editor of this series on international and comparative criminal law. He invited me to join the Editorial Committee of the series more than ten years ago. By reading the books published in this series and reviewing some of them, my knowledge of international and comparative criminal law has been greatly expanded. Professor Bohlander supported me in developing the structure of this book before I started writing and I appreciate his thoughtful advice.

Second, I would like to dedicate this book to Professor Hans-Jörg Albrecht, who made great contributions to China's reform of its criminal justice policies during his 25 years as a director of the Max Planck Institute of Criminal Law in Freiburg, Germany. With funding from the European Union, the Freiburg Max Planck Institute has conducted research on sentencing, legal aid, and especially capital punishment jointly with Chinese research institutions and universities, and has contributed enormously to promoting the reduction and abolition of the death penalty in China.

I am very grateful to the Freiburg Max Planck Institute for Criminal Law for providing me with office space, and access to its library and other resources during the Covid-19 pandemic. I owe special thanks to the head of the library of the Max Planck Institute, Elisabeth Martin, for her effective support in obtaining access to the relevant literature.

I am also very grateful to my Chinese colleagues. Professor Chen Yongsheng, Professor Chen Xuequan, Professor Guo Shuo, Associate Professor Su Mingyue, Associate Professor Tian Linan, Associate Professor Wu Hongqi, Professor Wu Hongyao, Ms Wang Yijia and Professor Zheng Xi (listed alphabetically by (Pinyin) surname) provided most valuable help by sending me scanned versions of their work and opinions on important issues when I was unable to return to China because of Covid-19 travel restrictions.

In addition, I would like to express my deep gratitude to Hart Publishing for accepting this book and allowing it to be included in this series. I take this opportunity to thank Richard Hart again for giving me the book 'Presumption of Innocence' when I wrote a book on 'Criminal Trial and Human Rights Protection' in Chinese more than ten years ago. I appreciate the patience and understanding that the staff at Hart Publishing have shown at all stages of the production process.

Whilst I was writing this book, the Chinese criminal justice institutions revised their implementation rules for the CPL. In particular, in February 2021 the Supreme People's Court announced amendments to the interpretation of the CPL 2018, which necessitated some late revisions to the manuscript.

Liling Yue
Freiburg, Germany
April 2021

CONTENTS

LIST OF ABBREVIATIONS

CCCP	Central Committee of the Communist Party
CP	Communist Party
CPC	Communist Party of China
CPL	Criminal Procedure Law
CUPL	China University of Political Science and Law
DCL	Detention Center Law
ECHR	European Convention on Human Rights
Guiding Opinions of Leniency System	Guiding Opinions on the Application of the Leniency System for Guilty Plea and Accepting Punishment
Guiding Opinions on Sentencing	Guiding Opinions on Sentencing Procedures of the People's Courts
guilty plea and leniency	Leniency system of admitting guilt and accepting punishment
ICCPR	International Covenant on Civil and Political Rights
ICESCR	United Nations International Covenant on Economic Social and Cultural Rights
JL	Judges Law
LAC	Legislative Affairs Committee
LL	Lawyers Law
MoJ	Ministry of Justice
MPS	Ministry of Public Security
MPS Provisions	Provisions on the Procedures of Handling Criminal Cases by Public Security Organs
MSS	Ministry of State Security
NHRAP	National Human Rights Action Plan
NJE	National Judicial Examination
NPC	National People's Congress

NPCSC	National People's Congress Standing Committee
NSC	National Supervision Commission
OLC	Organic Law of the People's Court
OLP	Organic Law of the People's Procuratorate
Opinions on Death Penalty Cases	Opinions on Strengthening Handling Cases in Strict Accordance with Law and Guaranteeing the Quality of Handling Death Penalty Cases
OSP	Opinions on Several Issues Concerning the Regulation of Sentencing Procedures
PAL	People's Assessor Law
PL	People's Police Law
Provisions on Confiscation	Provisions of the SPC and the SPP on Several Issues concerning the Application of the Confiscation Procedures for Illegal Income in a Case Where a Criminal Suspect or Defendant Escapes or Dies
Provisions on Evidence for Death Penalty Cases	Provisions on Several Issues Concerning the Examination and Judgment of Evidence in Death Penalty Cases (2010)
Provisions of Guiding Cases	Provisions of the SPC Concerning Work on Guiding Cases
PSO	Public Security Organs
Provisions on Exclusion of Illegal Evidence	Provisions on Several Issues concerning the Strict Exclusion of Illegally Collected Evidence in the Handling of Criminal Cases
Provision on Electronic Data	Provisions on Several Issues concerning the Collection, Taking, Examination, and Judgment of Electronic Data in the Handling of Criminal Cases
PPL	Public Prosecutor Law of the PRC
PRC	People's Republic of China
Rules for Court Investigation	Rules for Court Investigation in First-Instance Ordinary Procedure in the Handling of Criminal Cases by People's Courts
Rules for Pre-trial Conferences	Rules for Pretrial Conferences in the Handling of Criminal Cases by People's Courts

Several Provisions on Defence	SPC and the MJ, Several Provisions on Sufficiently Guaranteeing Lawyer's Performance of the Defence Duty According to Law to Ensure the Quality of Handling Death Penalty Cases
SL	Supervision Law
SPC	Supreme People's Court
SPC Interpretation	Supreme People's Court's Interpretation on the Implementation of Criminal Procedure Law
SPC Rules for Exclusion of Illegal Evidence	Rules for the People's Courts Handling Criminal Cases to Exclude Illegally Obtained Evidence
SPC Rules for Pre-trial Conferences	Rules for Pretrial Conferences in the Handling of Criminal Cases by People's Courts
SPP Regulations on Juvenile Cases	Procuratorate Regulations on Handling Juvenile Criminal Cases
SPP Rules	Supreme People's Procuratorate Rules for Criminal Procedure
SSC	State Supervision Commission
SSO	State Security Organs
UNCAT	United Nations Convention against Torture
UNCRC	United Nations Convention on the Rights of the Child

1

Introduction

I. Subject Matter

Writing and publishing a book on Chinese criminal procedure law amounts to a very challenging task, for various reasons. To begin with, this book is the first comprehensive introduction to modern Chinese criminal procedural law and practice in the English language. While numerous articles in foreign academic journals have dealt with individual issues of Chinese criminal proceedings, a systematic and complete presentation of Chinese criminal procedural law accessible to foreign scholars has so far been lacking. Also, the modern era of Chinese criminal procedure law started just four decades ago, when 1979 the first Criminal Procedure Law (CPL) came into force. The enactment of the CPL coincided with the beginning of a rapid and profound economic and social transformation of Chinese society. The CPL (and the Criminal Law) expresses also the political will to build a criminal justice system which is based on systematic codification. Although the CPL may be considered but a small part in a codification enterprise which involves a multitude of legal areas, the particular emphasis and attention placed on the reform of criminal investigation and proceedings in China cannot be explained solely by the generally sensitive nature of criminal punishment. Issues about criminal proceedings and controversially discussed criminal cases have increasingly attracted public interest in China, not least fuelled by the arrival of social media. Public interest and opinion in China have focused on miscarriage of justice cases. At the time of writing, a serial murderer and rapist, Wang Shujin, who had confessed to six rape murders, was executed after his case had been through seven years of appeals and retrials. Before the death penalty was finally approved by the Supreme People's Court (SPC), it turned out that Wang Shujin had also confessed to a murder for which – some 25 years ago – another, evidently innocent, person had been sentenced to death and executed. The family of the innocent man applied for a re-trial, which took place and resulted in an acquittal of the executed person and compensation for the family. It is publicly debated cases like this, which show advances in the normative framework of criminal proceedings, that have driven procedural law reform in China and contributed to slowly moving away from crime control and towards an understanding of criminal procedural law which emphasises the protection of the rights of suspects and defendants.

A close relationship between criminal procedure law and the protection of human rights is indisputable. Invoking issues of fundamental rights in the reform of criminal procedure law, voicing criticism of law enforcement practices that sideline the rights of suspects and defendants, and making proposals for reforms to implement internationally recognised standards of criminal proceedings are no longer taboo in China. Evidence of highly controversial issues debated among legal scholars, practitioners and politicians is on display in a rapidly growing body of criminal justice literature. This reflects not only the growing influence of a younger generation of Chinese lawyers who received their academic degrees in Europe, North America or Australia, but also a burgeoning interest in actively participating in international debates on procedure law and putting forth Chinese perspectives. In this book, room has been given to fundamental rights and the proper balancing of these rights with the effective implementation of criminal law in criminal proceedings. As well as human rights instruments created by the United Nations, the European Convention on Human Rights (ECHR) and its implementation by the European Court of Human Rights are also considered, with a view to elaborating on the need for further and future criminal procedure reform in China.

This book differs from conventional Chinese criminal procedure textbooks. Differences manifest themselves first in the structure of the book. China's major criminal procedure textbooks more or less retain a structure which was borrowed from former Soviet Union scholarship. This book tends to follow a structure adopted in countries with a civil law tradition, especially in Germany. In addition, the substance of the book is not restricted to a simple presentation and explanation of the statutory law: the text also attempts to introduce disputes and discourses on key procedural issues in legislative and academic circles. And in particular, socio-legal research and empirical evidence (as far as possible) are considered in order to contrast statutory law and practices. The execution of criminal sentences is not included in this book, because enforcement of criminal penalties is usually dealt with in the subject matter of penology and involves issues of substantive criminal law, especially the system of criminal sanctions and sentencing.

In Chinese legal terminology, there is no concept equivalent to 'criminal justice system' as used in common law countries to point to the interdependencies between substantive criminal law, criminal procedure law, institutions and practices. These components of the system are studied and analysed in China as independent subjects. Having said that, it should be noted that statutory law, jurisprudence, legal doctrines and discourses are all heavily influenced by history, culture and the political constitution. Beyond that, law is always inextricably linked with the language of a country, and translation to another language may not be capable of fully capturing the meaning carried by the original wording. The translation may also act as a barrier, imposing a sense of distance and distinctness between the reader and the original text.

II. Chinese Legal Sources and Materials

Apart from the CPL, and as described further in Chapter 3, Chinese criminal proceedings are guided by a second layer of rules, called 'Interpretations'.

Interpretations have been issued by the main institutional actors in Chinese criminal proceedings:

(1) Supreme Peoples' Court's (SPC) Interpretation on the Implementation of Criminal Procedure Law (SPC Interpretation) 2021;
(2) Supreme Peoples' Procuratorate's (SPP) Rules for Criminal Procedure (SPP Rules) 2019;
(3) The Ministry of Public Security's (MPS) Provisions on the Procedures for Handling Criminal Cases (MPS Provisions).

Interpretations serve important functions. First, they aim to clarify the sometimes vague formulations found in the CPL. Second, they aim to reduce the wide margins of interpretation and discretion that are characteristic of Chinese legislative technique, in order to achieve more uniformity in the application of statutory law.

Important sources of information on criminal procedure law, discourses and practices can be found in the internet-based collection of Chinese jurisprudence.[1] Chinese academic literature can be drawn from two databases: the China National Knowledge Infrastructure[2] and the Peking University Magic,[3] both major sources of legal literature.

III. Form of Citations

The modes of citation in this book basically follow Hart Publishing's style guidelines, but there are some exceptions. For example, Chinese names are displayed in Pinyin according to the order in the original work. Codes are cited in accordance with the number of the article and its subordinate sections, for example: Article 56(2) CPL, which is read as the second paragraph of Article 56 of the Criminal Procedure Code. Sometimes the year in which the criminal procedural law was amended is added.

IV. Content: An Overview

Chapter 2 introduces the various stages of development of China's CPL, starting with the revision of the CPL in the late Qing Dynasty and ending with the most recent amendment of the CPL in 2018. While portraying the main revisions of criminal procedure law, it also briefly presents the background to the CPL reforms.

Chapter 3 delves into the most fundamental issues in China's criminal procedure. This includes the statutory aims and tasks of criminal proceedings; the main normative sources, especially the 'soft law' with Chinese characteristics. The latter

[1] Available at wenshu.court.gov.cn.
[2] See www.cnki.net.
[3] See www.pkulaw.cn.

concerns 'Interpretations' or implementation rules issued by legislative bodies, the judiciary and law enforcement agencies. Following this, the main stages of criminal procedure are addressed. A significant part of Chapter 3 is devoted to the clarification of Chinese legal terms relating to criminal procedure and problems associated with translating these terms into English. Finally, Chapter 3 introduces several principles that govern Chinese criminal proceedings, especially the policy of 'Guilty plea and leniency' added to the CPL in 2018.

Chapter 4 deals with the institutional actors involved in the criminal process, their powers and their role in criminal proceedings. In particular, it introduces the Supervision Committee (SC) established in 2018 and the Supervision Law (SL), and explains the SC's relationship with criminal proceedings.

Chapter 5 explains the procedural rights and duties of criminal suspects, defendants, defence council, and victims.

The focus of Chapter 6 is on pre-trial criminal investigations. It covers the commencement of investigations, and compulsory and investigative measures. Here, technical measures of criminal investigations receive particular attention. Finally, decision-making on the part of investigative agencies after the completion of investigations is discussed, and its consequences for the further processing of a case are outlined.

Chapter 7 consists of two parts. The first part deals with procedural options of the procuratorate (the official term for the prosecution service in China) and the second part addresses the trial procedure at first instance. In the prosecution section, prosecution standards and the power of prosecutors to dismiss a case are analysed. The Chinese have recently adopted, although in a limited way, a non-prosecution policy, taking up the idea of diversion as an alternative to a conventional trial. The section on first instance trials covers the trial preparation procedure, specific steps at the court trial, subsidiary civil action, private prosecution, summary trial and expedited procedures.

Chapter 8 focuses on criminal evidence, especially on the statutory evidence forms and exclusionary rules pertaining to illegally obtained evidence. Other evidence-related rules, such as the standard of proof and the burden of proof, are briefly discussed in the context of presenting the principle of the presumption of innocence.

Chapter 9 deals with legal remedies after a verdict at the end of the first-instance trial. These include ordinary remedies (appeals), and special remedies, looking in particular at the re-opening of finalised criminal proceedings and death penalty review procedures.

Chapter 10 provides information on four so-called special procedures. The CPL provides special rules on juvenile criminal proceedings, reconciliation procedures in public prosecution cases, trial procedures in absentia, procedures for the confiscation of illegal proceeds in cases where a criminal suspect, defendant escapes or dies and, finally, procedures for involuntary medical treatment where mentally ill offenders are legally exempted from criminal liability.

2

The Development of Criminal Procedure Law

I. The Statutes before 1979

A. The First Draft Code of CPL in the Qing Dynasty

In the last years of the Qing Dynasty,[1] the Qing government faced internal and external pressures. Externally, China's defeat in the Sino-British Opium War of 1840 resulted in the Qing government signing a series of unequal treaties with Western countries. Subsequently, the Beijing and Hebei areas were invaded by eight countries.[2] On the domestic front, the conservative forces of the Qing government suppressed the reformists, creating a paradoxical situation. In order to alleviate these contradictions and continue its rule, the Qing government decided to reform the legal system, and appointed two officials, Shen Jiaben and Wu Tingfang, to be responsible for the legislative work of revising the procedural laws.

The first draft of Great Qing Criminal and Civil Procedure Law, completed in April 1906, was the first separation of procedural law from substantive law in the history of ancient Chinese legislation. This 'Draft' consists of five chapters and 260 articles.[3] After it was submitted to the emperor (Guangxu), he did not immediately approve the promulgation of the law. Instead, it was sent to local government and military officials for discussion, which caused great controversy in the local areas. The main disputes included whether to completely abolish torture; whether arrest should take into account Chinese national conditions; how to establish the legal principle of *nulla poena sine lege* (no penalty without law) and how to establish a lawyer's defence and jury system. These disputes reflect the conflicts between the legal values of China and the West, as well as the different motivations and purposes of the legislators and local officials. In the end, the 'Draft' was neither promulgated nor implemented.[4]

[1] Qing Dynasty (1636–1912).

[2] This was also known as 'The Eight-Nation Alliance', from 10 June 1900 to 7 September 1901. The countries involved were: Great Britain, the United States, France, the German Empire, Russia, Japan, Italy, Austria-Hungary.

[3] Wu Hongyao and Zhong Songzhi (eds), *One Hundred Years of Chinese Criminal Procedure Code* (Beijing, China University of Political Science and Law Press, 2012) 3–37.

[4] Hu Han, 'Controversy over Draft Criminal and Civil Procedure Law of the Qing Dynasty' (2010) 4 *Journal of Shanxi Institute of Technology (Social Science Edition)* 56–60.

In December 1910, Shen Jiaben submitted a new Draft, called 'The Draft of a Procedure Law for Criminal Matters of the Great Qing' (大清刑事诉讼律草案, *Da Qing Xing Shi Su Song Lu Cao An*) to the Emperor. It consisted of six parts, and contained a total of 515 articles. It was the first time in Chinese legislative history that the CPL had been separated from civil procedure law, but unfortunately when it was published in 1911, the Qing Dynasty collapsed and the Law was never implemented. It did, however, become the model for subsequent modern CPLs.[5]

B. Republican Period and Wartime (1912–1949)

In October 1911, the Xinhai Revolution (辛亥革命)[6] led by Dr Sun Yat-sen overthrew the Qing government, ended the imperial system that had lasted for 2132 years,[7] and established a republican system. Sun Yat-sen was elected as the temporary president, but his presidency lasted only a few months. He was replaced by Yuan Shikai, who enjoyed military leadership; he formed the Beiyang government in Beijing and became the first president of the Republic of China. During the reign of the Beiyang government, a series of laws were enacted on the basis of the laws formulated by the original Qing government, including the 'Interim New CPL' of 1914. The 'Regulation of Criminal Procedure' was promulgated on 14 November 1921. The law consisted of 8 parts and 514 articles and came into effect on 1 July 1922. It was the first CPL to be formally put into effect in modern Chinese legislative history.[8]

In the 1920s, China had two major political parties: the National Party (Kuomintang), established in 1919; and the Communist Party of China, established in 1921. These two political parties operated in different regions and were based on different legislative guiding principles. The legislation presided over by the National Party was mainly based on the laws of the late Qing Dynasty and merely modernised them. Its representative law was the 'Regulations on the Implementation of the CPL of the Republic of China' which was promulgated on 28 July 1928, and later on 1 January 1935. The revised 'Code of CPL of the Republic of China' was formally effective, which included nine parts and 516 articles.[9] The legislation presided over by the Communist Party was based on the laws of the former Soviet Union. In 1931, the Chinese Soviet Republic's Interim Rule No 6 on the 'Disposition of Counterrevolutionary Cases and Establishment of Justice Organs' was promulgated. Thereafter, in 1932, the 'Provisional Organisation Regulations of the Chinese Soviet Military Tribunal' and the 1934 'Judicial Procedure of

[5] Wu Hongyao and Zhong Songzhi (eds), *One Hundred Years of Chinese Criminal Procedure Code* (Beijing, China University of Political Science and Law Press, 2012) 103–222.

[6] It was also called the Revolution of 1911.

[7] Since 221 BC, Qin Dynasty.

[8] Wu Hongyao and Zhong Songzhi (eds), *One Hundred Years of Chinese Criminal Procedure Code* (Beijing, China University of Political Science and Law Press, 2012) 269–331.

[9] ibid, 332–454.

the Chinese Soviet' were promulgated.[10] From the Second World War until the founding of the People's Republic of China (PRC) in 1949, in the Shanxi, Gansu, and Ningxia border areas led by the Communist Party of China, the legislation of the CPL was roughly divided into two stages. The first stage was from 1937 to 1942, when the draft law was enacted. The legislative guiding ideology of the Communist Party was to abandon the 'Six Laws' at the end of the Qing Dynasty, and use Soviet law as a blueprint. In 1941, the 'Criminal Procedure Bill' had six chapters and 76 articles. The second stage was the trial stage of the Draft, from 1942 to 1949. Four amendments were made during this period, but the law was not formally promulgated and implemented until the establishment of the PRC.[11]

C. The Foundation of PRC to the End of the Cultural Revolution (1949–1979)

After the founding of the PRC, the new government, led by the Communist Party, abandoned the 'Six Laws' that had been formulated by the Kuomintang-led government and followed instead the Soviet Union's model to build a new legal system and legal institutions. The landmark moment was the designation and promulgation of the first Constitution in 1954.[12] The sixth section of the Constitution was entitled 'the Court and Procuratorate'. This section provided details of: the levels of the courts; the composition of trial courts; a lay assessor system; and several trial principles, such as the public trial, the defendant's right to counsel,[13] and a centerpiece was the provision proclaiming the independence of the judiciary in Article 78: 'The court exercises its judicial power independently and only obeys the laws'. This expression is slightly different from subsequent constitutional amendments and the expressions in the Criminal Procedure Code. In the civil rights section of the Constitution, when setting out the right to personal liberty, it is clearly stipulated that 'citizens are not subject to arrest without the decision of the court and the approval of the prosecutor's office';[14] and that a person's house or home is inviolable.[15] In the same year, the Organic Law of the Court (OLC)[16] and the Organic Law of the Procuratorate (OLP) were also promulgated and implemented. These laws and the structure of the legal institutions all followed the model in the then Soviet Union, close to the model of the civil law system. But the nature of the procuratorate is slightly different from the jurisdictions of the civil law tradition, as it does not have much association with legal administrative agencies, such as

[10] Yang Honglie, *History of Chinese Legal Development* (Shanghai, Shanghai Bookstore, 1990).

[11] Yang, Yonghua and Fang, Keqin, *Law History Draft of Shan-Gan-Ning Border Area – Litigation and Prison Administration* (Beijing, Law Press, 1990).

[12] The National People's Congress on 21 September 1954, adopted at the first meeting.

[13] Art 76 of the 1954 Constitution.

[14] Art 89 of the 1954 Constitution.

[15] Art 90 of the 1954 Constitution.

[16] 21 September 1954.

the ministry of justice. Instead, it is an independent legal institution. A further characteristic is that the Constitution grants the procuratorate the power to supervise the implementation of law. During this period, although the CPL had not yet been devised, the system of courts and procuratorates played an important role in handling criminal cases. In addition to the laws, the legislative Committee also enacted several other regulations, such as the 'Regulation on Arrest and Detention',[17] which made arrest and pre-trial detention legitimate. In 1957, the National People's Congress (NPC) had begun preparations for the formulation of the CPL and entrusted the SPC to draft it. In May 1957, the SPC drafted a total of 7 parts, 16 chapters, and 325 articles. This draft was revised in June 1957 and was renamed 'The First Draft of the CPL'.[18] In this draft the principle of the presumption of innocence was clearly stipulated. This was marvellous, given the historical and political conditions at that time. It was unfortunate that the anti-rightist political movement which gained momentum in 1957 interrupted the process of formulating the CPL. In 1963, the process of formulating the law was resumed. After six revisions, the final draft remained as seven parts but added two chapters and the number of articles in total was reduced to 200.[19] Regrettably, several political movements occurred, which again interrupted the process of amending the law. The most disastrous was 'the Cultural Revolution', which started in 1966 and lasted until 1976. During these ten years, procuratorates were closed up, the establishment of the lawyer system was suspended, and even the law schools were closed; the construction of the legal system was at a standstill.

II. The First Effected Modern Code of Criminal Procedure in 1979

Following the end of the Cultural Revolution, some leaders who had been persecuted during that political movement reached a consensus on rebuilding the legal system. Their aim was to prevent the recurrence of such incidents of arbitrary trials, convictions and punishment as had come about during the Cultural Revolution. The legislative Commission was established under the Standing Committee of the NPC in February 1979. This Commission drafted the first and second drafts of the CPL based on the draft CPL of 1963. This draft law has 164 articles in four parts and was adopted at the NPC on 1 July 1979. It came into effect on 1 January 1980. The provisions and contents of this law were relatively roughly sketched, but the overall framework still established some basic principles of the CPL, such as the independent exercise of the judicial power of the court, the prohibition on obtaining confessions by illegal means, the right to a public trial, etc. Also, the basic

[17] It was promulgated in December 1954.

[18] Wu Hongyao and Zhong Songzhi (eds), *Centenary of the Chinese CPL*, vol 2 (Beijing, Peking University Press, 2005).

[19] ibid.

jurisdiction of criminal cases was established, in addition to rudimentary structures of the criminal defence system and the lay assessor system. This CPL marked the beginning of China's due process of punishment of crimes and the protection of participants in proceedings.[20] This was the first CPL to actually be implemented after the demise of the Qing Dynasty, so it was an important milestone.

The implementation of the CPL in 1979 has important significance in the history of the development of modern Chinese criminal procedure. After the promulgation of the CPL in 1979, the Central Committee of the Communist Party (CCCP) of China in September 1979 issued the 'Instructions of the CCCP of China on Resolutely Guaranteeing the Effective Implementation of the Criminal Law and CPL'. This document is also known as Document No 64. In this directive, the concept of a 'socialist rule of law' was first proposed, which displayed a realisation that the relationship between the party's leadership and judicial independence had not been well established over the past 30 years. Additionally, the Directive abolished the conventional practice of past decades by which the judgments in criminal cases were approved by the party committee. In the three years following the implementation of the CPL, the courts re-examined the 1.2 million criminal cases decided in the 10 years of the Cultural Revolution and corrected 301,000 cases of miscarriages of justice. This enabled 326,000 innocent people who had been convicted and punished to seek redress.[21] It could not be denied that the implementation of the Criminal Law and the CPL of 1979 brought China on track in adhering to the Rule of Law.

However, the implementation process of the CPL was not as smooth as expected. If we examine the reasons for this, it becomes evident that the social and political environment at that time determined the success of the implementation of CPL. In the late 1970s and early 1980s, Chinese society was in a transition period after the Cultural Revolution. On the one hand, the policy of reform and transparency had brought social progress and rapid economic development, but on the other hand, it had also brought certain crimes back, for example, drug crimes. During the Cultural Revolution, China closed its borders and drug-related crimes basically disappeared. When the opening policy began to take effect, control of the borders was relaxed, especially in Yunnan Province, near the 'Golden Triangle', where the number of drug users and the crime of drug trafficking began to reemerge and increase. According to rough statistics, in Yunnan Province alone, from 1982 to 1989, there were 20,845 drug addicts, and the number of drug trafficking suspects reached 33,294.[22] Under such circumstances, the Standing Committee of the NPC formulated the 'Decision on Drug Control' in December 1990. In this decision, the penalties for drug trafficking crimes stipulated in the 1979 Criminal Law was raised from a lighter term of imprisonment to a maximum of the death penalty. This

[20] Chen Guangzhong and Zeng Xinhua, '40 Years Legislation of China's CPL', www.aisixiang.com.
[21] ibid.
[22] Gao Wei, *30 years of Drug Prohibition in China – with Criminal Rules as the Main Line* (Shanghai, Shanghai Social Sciences Publishing House, 2017).

move towards toughening criminal law-based responses to drug problems coincides with profound international concern about drug trafficking and organised crime, reflected in the UN Convention against Illicit Traffic in Narcotic Drugs and Psychotropic Substances of 1988 which was ratified by China in 1989. At the same time, other types of crime proliferated, especially violent crime. In 1980, there were 750,000 criminal cases filed, and the number had reached 890,000 in 1981.[23] The phenomenon of these crimes was related to the social and political background before and after the Cultural Revolution. During the Cultural Revolution, young people were incited by ideology, and many actively joined this misleading political movement; at the same time, many graduates lost their jobs. In accordance with the theory of socialism at that time, China's leaders believed that a socialist system could not experience unemployment, as unemployment could only be part of a capitalist system. At that time, national leader Mao Zedong proposed to solve the problems of young people, and let junior high school, high school, and university graduates go to the countryside to be 're-educated by the poor and lower-middle peasants'.[24] Until the end of this movement in 1978, approximately 16 million young people were sent to work in the countryside during this 10-year period. When these young people returned to the cities at the end of the Cultural Revolution, they had lost their educational opportunities. Only a handful of them entered university after returning to the college entrance examination in 1977, and there were 20 million young people who were still unemployed. All of these problems resulted in an unstable security in society and a rise in serious violent crimes. Deng Xiaoping, the leader at the time, decided to severely crack down on serious crimes. He suggested that the sentences for crimes should be harsher and the process of execution of punishment should be faster. On 2 September 1983, the Standing Committee of the NPC issued two decisions. The first was from the perspective of the substantive criminal law: to stipulate the scope of severely cracking down on crimes and provide guidelines for the application of penalties. Following this decision, more than a dozen crimes, such as hooliganism,[25] could be punished on a scale from the criminal law's maximum term of imprisonment to the death penalty. The second decision made by the Standing Committee resulted in 'The Decision on Procedures Related to the Speedy Trial of Criminals who Seriously Endanger the Social Security',[26] and 'Supplementary Regulations on the Time Limit of Handling Criminal Cases' (7 July 1984). These decisions began the 'strike hard' campaign. In two decisions relating to the CPL, it was stipulated

[23] Tao Ying, 'The Storm of Strike Hard 30 Years Ago' (2013) 9 *Culture and the History Vision* 5–10.

[24] *People's Daily*, 22 December 1968.

[25] Hooliganism is a crime stipulated in Art 160 of the Criminal Law of 1979. It is an offence which is very general and difficult to determine. It was addressed as a catch-all offence (in China known as 'a pocket offence'). It was deleted when the criminal law was revised in 1997. The former offence of hooliganism was broken down into indecency, insulting women, indecency with children, congregating for prostitution, congregation for fighting, and provoking trouble.

[26] 20 September 1983.

that during the period of 'strike hard', the time limits for delivering case files and appeals would no longer be subject to the restrictions set out in Article 110 of the 1979 CPL. In the legal field, this movement is considered to be the 'end of the political movement',[27] which was a manifestation of China's traditional state governance approach of 'governing the country with severe law in troubled times' (乱世用重典, *luan shi yong zhong dian*). According to academic surveys, the effect of the 'strike hard' policy did not meet the expectations of decision makers, and the crime rate did not decline.[28] In terms of the CPL, only four years after the law became effective, it was modified very quickly. This indicates that the concept of political struggle left over from the Cultural Revolution had profoundly affected the thinking patterns of legal policy makers. Additionally, it demonstrates a tendency to use the law as a tool to combat crime, while ignoring the important role of the procedural law in ensuring the parties' right to a fair trial, and the basic principles of the law in pursuit of stability, which were modified and damaged somewhat by the 'strike hard' campaign.

III. The Revision of the CPL in 1996

In the 1990s, under the policy of 'reform and opening up', the depth of China's market economy developed. This development brought about social transformation, making more intense the need for a sound legal system, which guaranteed equality and the right to a fair trial. Legal scholars and practitioners gradually realised that the CPL of 1979 was inadequate for the protection of due process and human rights. From a technical point of view, the law in general was relatively roughly sketched and the operability was relatively poor, so when the law was first implemented, various related legal institutions promulgated a great number of rules, decisions, and judicial interpretations.[29] In this situation, if a party did not have a lawyer's assistance, the party would not understand the regulations, and their rights could easily be violated.

During the transitional period for Chinese society in the 1980s and 1990s, new forms of crime emerged. The government and legal institutions used a political movement model to deal with crime, for example by way of the aforementioned 'Decision on the Issues Related to the Verification of Death Penalty Cases'. The final review of death penalty cases for several serious crimes under the CPL was

[27] Yang Jintao and Tian Quanhua, 'Strike Hard' Social Background Analysis, www.guancha.cn.

[28] Tao Ying, 'The Storm of Strike Hard 30 Years Ago' (2013) 9 *Culture and the History Vision* 5–10.

[29] The Standing Committee of the NPC promulgated three major decisions supplementing the Criminal Procedure Code of 1979: (1) Decision on the Issues Related to the Verification of Capital Punishment Cases (10 June 1981); (2) Decision on Procedures Related to the Speedy Trial of Criminals who Seriously Endanger the Social Security (20 September 1983) (initiating the 'Strike Hard' campaign), and (3) Supplementary Regulations on the Time Limit of Handling Criminal Cases (7 July 1984).

transferred from the SPC to the provincial High Courts. In practice, the situation was that the appeal procedure and the review procedure of the death penalty were combined into one, so that the death penalty review procedure was actually abolished. Some scholars believe that the aforementioned 'strike hard' campaign in 1983 also 'caused the loss of the rights protection mechanism of the CPL'.[30] All of these issues drew the attention of the government and the legislator, who quickly realised that additional revisions to the law would be needed.

In addition to the rapidly changing economic, political and social climate that emerged following the enactment of the 1979 CPL, other factors contributed to its revision. One of the most important factors was the re-establishment of a Chinese community of legal practitioners and scholars. In the mid-1980s, when the 1979 CPL was being developed, many of China's most respected legal scholars were still in the process of moving back from the countryside where they had been assigned to do manual labour during the Cultural Revolution. Although legal education in China resumed in 1977, few law schools existed at that time and the students who had been admitted to these schools were just beginning their studies. As law schools began to re-emerge, a small number of law reviews resumed the publication of scholarly articles. Around this time, a few scholars and students went to other countries to study, which helped to reintroduce into China the study of comparative law. Although some of these developments came too late to influence the CPL 1979, all played a major role in the discussions that followed.

It was not until 1978 that the legal profession itself resumed the practice of law, and thereafter the profession developed rapidly. Despite the fact that at the beginning there were only a few thousand lawyers in the whole of China, by the end of 1996 there were 100,148 attorneys and more than 10,000 law firms.[31] Although much of the work that these lawyers and firms did focused on economic matters, the legal profession also played an important part in the criminal justice system. In 1998, for example, Chinese lawyers defended nearly 250,000 criminal cases. This was, in part, as a result of the introduction of a bar examination during this period[32] which improved the quality of the legal profession. The rapid growth of law firms and the legal profession had a number of significant effects. It made legal assistance more accessible to criminal defendants, and it also played a role in encouraging change in the legal profession, as well as encouraging lawyers to seek to enhance their role in the criminal process.

Another important factor in the growing realisation that the 1979 CPL needed to be updated was China's increasing involvement with international developments in criminal justice. In 1988, for example, China ratified the UN Convention

[30] Chen Weidong, '40 years of criminal procedure rule of law: review and prospect', www.procedurallaw.cn.

[31] *China Law Yearbook* (China Law Yearbook Press, 1997) 1074.

[32] China introduced a bar examination in 1986 and used this system until 2000. In 2002, the bar examination was replaced by State Law Examination.

Against Torture (UNCAT) and in 1991 it ratified the UN Convention on the Rights of the Child (UNCRC).[33]

All these factors led the Standing Committee of the Eighth NPC to consider revising the CPL of 1979 and brought it into the revision plan in 1988. To assist in this revision, in 1993 a Legislative Affairs Working Committee initiated a survey on the implementation of the CPL 1979. The Working Committee solicited the opinion of legal institutions, as well as legal scholars, on the need to revise the CPL 1979. Soon thereafter the Standing Committee's Legislative Affairs Office authorised the China University of Political Science and Law (CUPL) to draft a revision of the CPL 1979.[34] By the Autumn of 1995, the Legislative Affairs Working Committee had prepared a 'draft for comment' of an amended Criminal Procedure Code.[35] On 20 December 1995, the Committee presented its draft to the Standing Committee for preliminary review. Following this preliminary review, the Standing Committee invited all the relevant governmental departments to a special meeting for the purpose of discussing the revision and addressing an important set of controversial issues that had been raised. After a thorough discussion, the Standing Committee presented its revision to the Fourth Session of the Eighth NPC, where many delegates made suggestions and proposed new provisions. On 17 March 1996, the Congress adopted a collection of amendments entitled the 'Decision on Amending the CPL of the PRC'. The President of the State, Jiang Zemin, signed the revised Code into law later that same day and the amended law became effective on 1 January 1997.

The 1996 amendment significantly altered the 1979 CPL. It was a relatively comprehensive revision, which increased the previous 164 articles to 225 and introduced 110 changes in the law. Some of the main important changes are discussed below.

A. Establishing a Principle Similar to the Presumption of Innocence in Western CPLs

After debates lasting almost a century, ultimately a principle similar to the presumption of innocence was set out in the 1996 CPL,[36] which stated that 'No one shall be convicted without a verdict rendered by people's court according to law'. Although this has been debated for a further two decades in China with regard to whether the provision is an accurate expression of the principle of the presumption of innocence, nonetheless, it is significant progress to have this principle stipulated

[33] UN Convention Against Torture and Other Cruel, Inhuman or Degrading Treatment or Punishment. The Convention was adopted on 10 December 1984 and came into force on 26 June 1987. The UNCRC was adopted on 20 November 1989 and came into force on 2 September 1990.

[34] The author was invited by the head of drafting group, Professor Chen Guang Zhong, to participate in the research and drafting.

[35] In pinyin, this is called '*zheng qiu yi jian gao*' (征求意见稿).

[36] Art 12 of the 1996 CPL.

in the CPL. What does it mean in Chinese law? Has this principle been integrally expressed in the law and implemented in practice? These details are discussed in Chapter 3 on basic concepts.

B. Increasing the Role of Criminal Defence Lawyers and Establishing the Legal Aid System

Under the 1979 CPL, defence lawyers became involved in criminal proceedings and in offering assistance to the accused only very late in the process, and only after the case files had been transferred from the prosecutor's office to the court. Following this, the court had an obligation to inform the accused of the right to retain defenders seven days before the trial commenced.[37] During the 'strike hard' period, this seven-day limit for notification of the right was shortened to just three days.[38] This temporary provision and the situation in practice may have constituted a violation of the right to a fair trial in the UN International Covenant on Civil and Political Rights (ICCPR). Article 14.3(b) of the ICCPR states that a defendant has the right 'to have adequate time and the facilities for the preparation of his defense and to communicate with counsel of his own choosing'. The amendments of the 1996 CPL made efforts to change the situation by permitting defence lawyers to be involved in criminal proceedings and giving them the opportunity to offer legal assistance to suspects during the investigation. Article 96 of 1996 CPL stated that:

> After the criminal suspect is interrogated by an investigation organ for the first time or from the day on which compulsory measures are adopted against him, he may appoint a lawyer to provide him with legal advice and to file petitions and complaints on his behalf.

As progress, this was limited, as the status of defence lawyers during the investigation was tricky: they could offer legal advice to their clients, but they did not hold a position as a formal defender, therefore they could not access case files and could not collect evidence by themselves. Further, the time specified for assistance from lawyers was 'after the criminal suspect is interrogated by an investigation organ for the first time or from the day on which compulsory measures are adopted against him', which meant that suspects would already have made a confession before they had a chance to receive advice from their defence lawyers. However, the progress made in 1996 still improved the situation in practice, as it at least built up links between suspects, their family members, and the lawyers, so that if the suspects were under arrest, the defence lawyer could liaise with the family and apply for other non-custodial coercive measures on behalf of the suspects.

[37] Art 110 of 1979 CPL.

[38] Art 1 of Decision of the Standing Committee of the NPC Regarding the Procedure for Prompt Adjudication of Cases Involving Criminals Who Seriously Endanger Public Security, 2 September 1983.

Under the 1979 CPL, mandatory defence lawyers were available in limited cases, ie in cases of public prosecution, and for those accused who were blind, deaf, mute, or minors. In these cases, the trial courts would appoint a defender for them.[39] The 1996 CPL made tremendous progress in revising the criminal defence system. Defence lawyers were mandated, besides those for disabled defendants, also for those accused who were facing the death penalty.[40] Prior to the 1996 revision, under the law, defence lawyer's assistance to the accused who were facing the death penalty was discretionary; it became mandatory in practice by the 1996 revision to the CPL. As regards poor defendants, the 1996 amendment provided that 'if a defendant failed to retain a defender because of financial difficulties or other reasons, the people's court may appoint a lawyer who is obligated to provide legal aid to serve as a defender'.[41] This was the first time that the concept of 'legal aid' had been expressed in the law. Prior to this, the legal aid system had not been established and therefore the 1996 CPL was a milestone development in China's legal system. Detail of this development are discussed in the following chapters.

IV. The Revision of 2012

After the implementation of the second amendment to the 1996 CPL, during the years from 1997 to 2012, China's legal reforms resulted in far-reaching and essential changes. This change was first manifested in the updating of certain legal concepts. In 1999, the phrase 'ruled by law' (依法治国, *yifazhiguo*) was added by a Constitutional amendment. However, its official English translation was different from the Western 'rule of law'. The amended Constitution[42] provides that: 'the PRC governs the country according to law and makes it a socialist country ruled by law'.[43] Since then, these two different phrases have caused huge confusion and controversy among legal scholars in China and abroad. On the one hand, this confusion stems from the fact that these two English translations are one phrase in the Chinese expression (依法治国, *yifazhiguo*), but they are made different by the use of the two prepositions 'of' and 'by' in the English translation. The other confusion is the political meanings of 'rule of law' and 'rule by law'. Until now, this topic has not been widely or deeply discussed in China. At the time of its introduction, legal scholars were generally more interested in the significance of the phrase

[39] Art 27 of the 1979 CPL.

[40] Art 34 of the 1996 CPL.

[41] ibid.

[42] When the amendment was translated by the Legislative Affairs Office, the author was consulted by a colleague charged with the translation of the law, about whether the proper translation of the term was 'rule of law' or 'ruled by law'. The author explained the difference between the two phrases. Years later, the official version of the translation has been published as 'ruled by law'.

[43] Compiled by the Legislative Affairs Commission of the Standing Committee of the NPC of the PRC, *The Law of the PRC 1999* (Beijing, Law Press, 2000) Art 13 of the amendment.

'ruled by law' (依法治国, *yifazhiguo*) being added to the Constitution. But its exact connotation and specific standards have not aroused widespread academic concern. When explaining its meaning, one higher official mainly emphasised that it was to be construed as abandoning the 'rule by man'[44] approach. Under these circumstances, to what extent the concept of 'rule by law' affected the revision of the CPL in 2012 has not yet seen a detailed analysis.

After the revision of the Constitution in 1999, the CP, the government and legislator gradually recognised that China has an important role to play in the international community, and several positive steps were taken towards this. In 1997, China signed the UN International Covenant on Economic, Social and Cultural Rights (ICESCR)[45] and in 1998 it signed the International Covenant on Civil and Political Rights (ICCPR).[46] Although 23 years have passed since it signed, China has not yet ratified the ICCPR. Nevertheless, the act of signing in 1998 showed at least a willingness to accept international standards for human rights protection which are closely related to criminal justice, and the criminal process. Until now, four steps of The National Human Rights Action Plan (NHRAP) have been elaborated, and corresponding evaluation reports have also been published in both Chinese and English. It is especially important to note that in 2004 the principle of 'respecting and protecting human rights' was inserted for the first time into the Constitution. It may be that this will draw more attention to the balance between crime control and basic rights protection in the criminal process. All of these changes made by the legislator and the government were positive, and had strong impacts on the revision of the CPL in 2012.

The Chinese media also played a role in raising the public's legal awareness through publishing details of miscarriage of justice cases. Prior to the reform of the CPL, a high-profile case in the public eye was the wrongful conviction case of She Xianglin and Zhao Zuohai.[47] These wrongful conviction cases caused a public outcry as well as a dramatic drop in public confidence in the judicial system.[48] The release of these miscarriage of justice cases to the public may be one of the factors

[44] Han Dayuan, 'Analysis of the "Rule of Law" Norm in the Text of the Chinese Constitution', www.cityu.edu.hk.

[45] The Convention was adopted on 16 December 1966 and came into force on 3 January 1976.

[46] The Covenant was adopted on 16 December 1966 and came into force on 23 March 1976.

[47] *Legal Daily*, 1 April 2005, www.baik.baidu. The case began when an unidentified body was found in a Jingshan township reservoir. Coincidentally, Mr She's wife, Ms Zhang, disappeared in January 1994. Later investigation showed that before Ms Zhang left, she and Mr She had a quarrel, and she had a slight mental disorder. The local police arranged for members of Ms Zhang's family to identify the body, but no DNA test was carried out because, at that time, small city police stations had no capability to perform such tests. Ms Zhang's family members confirmed that the body was Ms Zhang. Mr She became the prime suspect, and was arrested in April 1994. The media reports showed that he was tortured by the police. Mr She was convicted of murder and at the first instance trial he was sentenced to the death penalty. Later the jurisdiction of the case was changed. Mr She appealed in 1998 and his final sentence was reduced to 15 years' imprisonment, because the higher court's judges doubted his confession and other evidence. While Mr She served his sentence, after 11 years in the prison, his former 'dead' wife's memory had recovered and she came back to the village. In April 2005, the case was reopened, and Mr She was acquitted. He later received compensation from the court.

[48] Hugo Winckler, 'Reforming China's CPL', *China Perspectives* 2012.

that led to main legal institutions to promulgate several regulations relating to the rules on collection and evaluation of evidence.[49] These regulations established the principles of evidence collection and evaluation in the following CPL reform and the author believes that they also played a role in reducing the number of death penalty sentences handed down by the courts, and hence a reduction in the number of executions as well.

A direct and urgent ground for updating the 1996 CPL was the revision of the Lawyers Law of the PRC (LL) in 2007. In the amended version of the LL there were several provisions which conflicted with the 1996 CPL. For instance, Article 33 of the 2007 LL provides that:

> as of the date of first interrogation of or adoption of a compulsory measures on a criminal suspect by the criminal investigative organ, an authorised lawyer shall have the right to meet the criminal suspect or defendant and learn information related to the case, by presenting his lawyer's practicing certificate, certificate of his law firm and power of attorney or official legal aid papers.

This provision shows that, since its implementation on 1 June 2018, if lawyers would like to meet their clients, they do not need additional permission from legal institutions such as the police, prosecutorial offices or courts, so long as they satisfy the requirements mentioned by the LL. However, on the first day that the LL became effective (1 June 2018) when lawyers went to detention centres to meet with their clients, carrying the appropriate documents, the police who worked at those detention centres prevented them from doing so, on the basis that the police had not received confirmation from their superiors that this was permitted. The CPL had not yet been revised to reflect the new LL, and the police continued to follow the law as set out in the CPL.[50] These problems with implementing the LL in practice led the NPC to suggest that the CPL be revised so as to resolve these conflicts.[51]

After recognising that the 1996 CPL would eventually require revision, the Tenth NPC in 2003 scheduled a revision for 2008. Although much preliminary work had been done by 2008, the issues under consideration proved to be controversial. This led to several postponements. In 2009, a motion to amend the CPL was formally filed again. The Legislative Affairs Committee (LAC) of the NPC organised a series of discussions among NPC deputies, legal practitioners, and legal scholars. Ultimately a draft was completed and submitted to the 22nd meeting of the 11th NPC Standing Committee. Following this, the Committee held discussions and afterwards, the full text of the draft was published through the

[49] SPC, SPP, MPS, MJ and MSS in October 2010 jointly promulgated 'The Regulations on the Exclusion of Illegally Obtained Evidence in Criminal Cases', 'The Regulations on the Examination and Evaluation of Evidence in Death Penalty Cases'.

[50] Tian Wenchang, 'Conflict between the New LL and CPL: Interaction and Connection', 7 May 2009, www.proceduallaw.

[51] See eg NPC, Draft Amendments to Criminal Procedure Code, Explanatory Notes, indicating that 'there are several improper problems in criminal procedure'.

NPC website to solicit opinions from the wider public. This was the first time in China's modern legislative history that a proposed amendment to the law had been made available to the whole public, where any individual had the right to participate and submit comments or suggestions for amendments to the LAC of the NPC before the prescribed deadline.[52] The NPC passed the amendments on 14 March 2012 and the new code became effective on 1 January 2013.

The 2012 CPL contains 290 articles compared to the 1996 CPL's 225 articles, and more than half of the articles are either new or amended. An official explanation published by the NPC[53] indicates that the new CPL addresses eight major issues. The following text summarises the major points; the details are discussed in the following chapters.

A. Improvement of Criminal Defence and Legal Aid

Updating the provisions on criminal defence was a major element of the 2012 CPL revision. The state of practice after the CPL revision in 1996 showed that it was not easy for defence lawyers to become involved in criminal proceedings smoothly and to protect their clients' right to a fair trial, especially at the investigation stage. In practice, lawyers or scholars often referred to this as the 'trilemma' (三难, *sannan*), ie difficulties: meeting and interviewing their clients; with accessing case files; and investigating and collecting evidence by themselves. The LL revision in 2007 made some progress to improve this situation. The 2012 CPL amendments confirmed and consolidated the results of the LL revision and eased the 'trilemma' situation to some extent.

Legal aid assistance in criminal proceedings was also improved. First, suspects and defendants could now receive legal aid assistance at an earlier stage in proceedings. Under the 1996 CPL, if the defendants met the legal requirements and needed assistance from legal aid lawyers, the courts could designate a lawyer when the case entered the trial stage, The 2012 CPL amendment brought this forward, to the investigation stage. Second, the category of legal aid services was expanded further in comparison to the 1996 CPL. In relation to the treatment of persons with disabilities, the 1996 CPL afforded the assistance of legal aid lawyers only when the suspect or the defendant was blind, deaf or mute. However, the 2012 amendment added a new category for those who suffer from mental health problems. If they do not have a defender, the related legal institutions shall inform the legal aid agencies to designate a legal aid lawyer for them and provide assistance.[54] Regarding the

[52] Since the China University of Political Science and Law (CUPL) is the leading university to do research in the CPL area, the Legislative Affairs Committee authorised the CUPL to organise a group discussion and submit group comments and suggestions. The author participated in the intensive discussion and submitted written comments to the organiser of the group meeting.

[53] Criminal Law Department, Legal Committee of Standing Committee of NPC, *Comparative Form of Criminal Procedure Code* (Beijing, People's Court Publisher, 2012).

[54] Art 34 of the 2012 CPL.

requirement for potential penalties, the 1996 CPL was limited to offering assistance for defendants who were at risk of being sentenced to death. The 2012 amendment reduced the penalty requirement to life imprisonment. Although this is still some way from the international human rights requirements, legislators believe that the principle of gradual and orderly progress has been adopted in accordance with national conditions.[55]

B. Improvement of Evidence Rules and Establishment of Exclusionary Rules

The provisions on prohibiting the collection of evidence by illegal means were stipulated in the 1979 CPL and in the 1996 CPL. The 1996 CPL stated: 'It is strictly forbidden to extract confessions by torture and collect evidence by threats, inducements, deception and other illegal methods'. However, observations of judicial practice prior to the 2012 CPL revision suggest that the situation of heavy reliance on the suspect or defendant's confession in criminal procedures was not controlled. One reason for this was that legislators and legal practitioners preferred the crime control model, and tended to focus their efforts on finding the truth and punishing criminals. Although there is nothing intrinsically wrong with this aim of criminal procedure, when the aim is over-emphasised, the balance between crime control and due process will be lost. And then, as mentioned above, miscarriage of justice cases will be the result. The legislator recognised this and in the 2012 revision added half of a sentence to stipulate that 'no one may be forced to prove his own guilt'.[56] The legislators also pointed out the significance of the addition of this sentence when interpreting this revised clause, believing that:

(1) this provision captures the nature of the principle of CPL and has an important role in guiding the implementation of the law;
(2) from the perspective of principles and ideology, it explains the reasons for the prohibition of torture to extract a confession;
(3) it is connected with the relevant international conventions.[57]

Although the legislators' purpose is clear from their interpretation of this amendment, unfortunately, this important clause was not placed in the part of the CPL dealing with principles, but in the evidence part. The clause is also in contradiction with Article 118 of the 2012 CPL: 'The criminal suspect should answer the investigators' questions truthfully', which shows that the criminal suspect has actually

[55] Lang Sheng, *Revision and Application of the CPL of the People's Republic of China* (Beijing, Xinhua Press, 2012) 86.
[56] Art 50 of the 2012 CPL.
[57] Lang Sheng, *Revision and Application of the CPL of the People's Republic of China* (Beijing, Xinhua Press, 2012) 116.

not been given the right to silence. A detailed discussed on this is contained in the following chapters.

A technical flaw in the 1996 CPL which prohibited illegally obtained evidence was another major reason for the ineffectiveness of this prohibition in practice. Article 43 of the 1996 CPL stated that:

> Judges, prosecutors, and investigators must, in accordance with the legally prescribed process, collect various kinds of evidence that can prove the criminal suspects or defendants' guilt or innocence and the gravity of his crime. It shall be strictly forbidden by threat, enticement, deceit or other unlawful means.

It should be noted that this clause only set out the prohibition against using illegal means to collect evidence. However, when illegal behaviour occurs, there was an absence of regulation as to: how to define the illegally obtained evidence; whether or not such illegally obtained evidence could be used as a basis for conviction; whether a defendant or his defence lawyer could make a complaint to exclude the evidence; and what the proper proceedings were in which to apply for the evidence to be excluded. As noted above, legislators realised the necessity of establishing rules to exclude illegally obtained evidence prior to the 2012 CPL revision. In 2010, the SPC, SPP, MPS, MoJ, and MSS jointly promulgated the 'Regulations on the Issues Concerning the Exclusion of Illegally obtained Evidence in Criminal Cases' and the 'Regulations on the Examination and Evaluation of Evidence in Death Penalty Cases'. These rules and regulations were implemented in practice. In 2012, a reasonable part of the regulations were actually absorbed into the 2012 CPL, and the provisions on illegally obtained evidence were divided into two groups. The first category is verbal evidence obtained by illegal means, such as: the suspects or defendant's confession, the witness's testimony and the victim's statement. The second category is illegally obtained non-verbal evidence, such as physical or documentary evidences, etc.[58] Following the 2012 CPL amendments, relatively comprehensive procedures were added for excluding these two types of evidence.[59]

Between the first CPL in 1979 and the revision of the 1996 CPL, the substance of the standard of proof, that 'the evidence is reliable and sufficient' had not changed much. There was much controversy over this standard of proof among judges and academics. The author believes that the statement in the CPL uses objective truth as the standard of proof, and further is of the opinion that such a stance is incompatible with our general knowledge of philosophy. Furthermore, the standards of 'clearness' and 'sufficiency' may vary from case to case, and it is difficult to grasp a unified and measurable standard of proof, which means that the standard lacks operability. In practice, some judges adopted 'beyond reasonable doubt' as the standard of proof.[60] Fortunately, in the 2012 CPL amendment,

[58] Art 54 of the 2012 CPL.

[59] Arts 55–58 of the 2012 CPL.

[60] Liling Yue, *Criminal Trial and Human Rights Protection* (Beijing, Law Press, 2010) 136.

an attempt was made to improve this standard. Three conditions were added to 'the evidence is reliable and sufficient', especially the third condition, which introduced the consensus statement in other jurisdictions. Section 3 of Article 53 states that: 'the facts are proved beyond reasonable doubts based on the evaluation of all evidence'. There are, though, still controversies surrounding the new standard of proof in theory and practice. In any case, this amendment is a step forward in the reform of the rules of evidence.

C. Changes to Coercive Measures (Sometimes Called 'Compulsory Measures')

The term 'coercive measures' is not a legal phrase that is used in common law jurisdictions. Rather, it is used in continental law jurisdictions, such as Germany or Italy. It is a collective term to describe measures that limit or infringe upon criminal suspects or defendants' basic rights, such as arrest, pre-trial detention, search and seizure, and most other measures used during criminal investigations. However, as is described in the following chapters, the term 'coercive measures' (强制措施, *qiang zhi cuoshi*) in Chinese criminal procedure differs from the term in European continental jurisdictions. In China, it refers only to measures that deprive suspects and the accused of their liberty. In the 1996 CPL, there were five coercive measures provided by law which could be used to deprive suspects or the accused of liberty during investigations or trials. These measures are:

(1) summons for questioning (sometimes called 'compelled appearance') (拘传, *ju chuan*);
(2) obtaining a guarantor pending trial, (sometimes called 'bail') (取保候审, *qu bao hou shen*);
(3) residential surveillance (监视居住, *jian shi ju zhu*);
(4) arrest (拘留, *ju liu*); and
(5) pre-trial detention (逮捕, *dai bu*).[61]

Several coercive measures are controversial following the 2012 CPL revision. The first issue concerns 'residential surveillance'. This measure was part of the 1979 CPL, and the 1996 CPL retained it as an alternative measure to bail, where the suspects or defendants could not find a guarantor or could not pay the fee to be released on bail. From the wording of the 1996 CPL, the law permitted the use of designated residential surveillance,[62] whereby suspects could be detained in designated guesthouses and kept under surveillance. Suspects who are migrant workers may not have a 'residence' (domicile), so they could be placed in a specially designated guesthouse instead. However, in practice, sometimes police or prosecutors

[61] The detailed points are discussed in the chapters that follow; the discussion here is limited to the amendments' issues in relation to the coercive measures.

[62] Art 57 of the 1996 CPL.

misused this measure to give themselves more time for investigation by detaining suspected public officials in designated guesthouses, and to avoid the requirements for formal arrest or pre-trial detention.[63] Designated residence surveillance has been heavily criticised and even the legislator described it as a 'disguised detention'.[64]

In the 2012 CPL revision, the legislator decided to retain the measure of residential surveillance but made several changes. The first positive change is that, in the related provisions, the nature of residential surveillance as an alternative for pre-trial detention has been clarified, providing in the first condition that:

> For the criminal suspects or defendants who meet the conditions of pre-trial detention but also fall into following circumstances, ... may be placed under residential surveillance.[65]

The second positive change is that the amendments added several provisions to strengthen management of the measure, through providing monitoring measures and obligations for persons who are under surveillance.[66] The third positive change is that the period of designated residential surveillance will decrease the length of the term of imprisonment if the defendant is sentenced. However, the detailed computation method for this must be discussed in each case. The law stipulates that 'for the offenders who are sentenced to criminal detention or imprisonment, the jail terms can be reduced by one day for every two days under residential surveillance'.[67] The legislator explained this as follows:

> considering that although designated residences is not a measure of custody, the degree of restriction and deprivation of personal liberty of citizens is stronger than that of ordinary residential surveillance and release on bail, so the sentence is offset.[68]

His key words mean that residential surveillance is not equivalent to arrest or pre-trial detention. This opinion is challenged fiercely by academics; some scholars argue that designated residences may have become the 'sixth type of coercive measure, showing a trend of detention in disguise'.[69] There was a more sensitive, debatable point in the first draft of the revision, about notification of family members of a person under designated residence surveillance. Article 73 of the draft CPL stipulated that:

> the family members of the person who is under a designated residential surveillance with the reason and the place of the surveillance shall be notified within 24 hours after

[63] Author's interview of prosecutors in 2011.
[64] Lang Sheng, *Revision and Application of the CPL of the People's Republic of China* (Beijing, Xinhua Press, 2012) 160.
[65] Art 72 of the 2012 CPL.
[66] Art 75 of the 2012 CPL.
[67] Art 74 of the 2012 CPL.
[68] Lang Sheng, *Revision and Application of the CPL of the People's Republic of China* (Beijing, Xinhua Press, 2012) 163.
[69] Sun Yuhua, 'Constitutional Review of Designated Residential Surveillance' (2013) 6 *Law Science* 146.

> the surveillance may be carried out at a designated location, except in circumstance where the notification could not be delivered, the case involved the crime of endangering national security or the crime of terrorism, or the notification will hinder the investigation.

After the draft was released, it caused huge panic in society, especially in the legal field. Lawyers and legal scholars became worried that if a case was deemed to be a special situation stipulated by the law, or if this rule was abused by law enforcement officials, then it would result in a situation where some criminal suspects may be subjected to clandestine arrest or abnormal disappearance, where the period of detention may be as long as six months.[70] These concerns were considered by the legislator and the final version was revised. However, the revisions are still a matter of concern at present. In the final version, the special circumstances that 'the case involved the crime of endangering national security or the crime of terrorism, or the notification will hinder the investigation' were removed and it seems that progress has been made. However, the clause 'with the reason and the place of the surveillance' had been removed as well, which means that, if a suspect was under designated surveillance, then a family member would be informed. Although this avoids the potential for abnormal disappearance, the lack of notification content may represent a shortcoming in the protection of the rights of suspects or the accused.[71] Further detail of these measures are discussed in the following chapters.

D. Special Criminal Proceedings

Further significant progress was made in the 2012 CPL revision by way of the addition of four new criminal proceedings. These are:

(1) procedures for juvenile criminal cases;
(2) procedures for reconciliation between parties in public prosecution cases;
(3) procedures for confiscating the illegal incomes of suspects or defendants who escape and hide or die;
(4) compulsory medical treatment procedures for mentally ill persons who are exempted from criminal liability according to law.

Although there are debates about the implementation of these special procedures, their addition to the CPL demonstrates the significant progress the legislature has made in protecting vulnerable groups in criminal proceedings. The detailed contents of these special procedures are discussed in related chapters.

[70] Phoenix TV, 'Art 73 of the Draft CPL was accused of or led to the abuse of secret arrest', 14 March 2012, http://service.law-star.com/cacnew/201203/1760075815.htm.

[71] Guo Shuo, 'On the Designated Residential Surveillance System as an "Extra-custodial Means"' (2016) 6 *Journal of Wuhan University* (Philosophy and Social Sciences Edition) 119.

V. The Revision in 2018

The 2018 CPL revision came about after the shortest time interval in the history of CPL revisions. According to the legislator's declaration, the direct missions for the revision were:

(1) to establish a connection between the investigation of State Supervision Commissions (SSCs) and criminal proceedings;
(2) to strengthen anti-corruption measures by the introduction of *trials in absentia* for certain crimes; and
(3) to summarise the experiences gained in the pilot schemes for the policy of leniency in guilty pleas and the expedited trial procedure, and codify practice so that it that can be replicated and incorporated into legal norms.[72]

The first mission was the most urgent because, after the SL was enacted, the SSC replaced the procuratorates in the investigation of corruption and bribery of public officials cases. That is to say that if the CPL had not been amended, the two laws would be in conflict.

The NPCSC published the draft amendments to the CPL on 24 April 2018 and solicited public comments by 7 June 2018. The Standing Committee of NPC enacted the amendments on 26 October 2018 and the amendments were effective on the same day. The main aspects of the 2018 CPL are as follows.

A. Transfer of the Authority to Investigate Corruption and Bribery Cases from the Procuratorates to Supervision Commissions

After the enactment and implementation of the SL in March 2018, the newly established NSC integrates the investigative and supervisory powers in corruption cases involving state civil servants from four agencies: the CPC Central Commission for Discipline Inspection; the Ministry of Supervision; the National Bureau of Corruption Prevention; and the procuratorate. According to the SL, the investigative power in related cases has been transferred to the NSC, so the procuratorate loses its power to investigate corruption in state official cases. However, if the Supervisory Commissions determine, after preliminary investigation, that a case constitutes a crime, the case will be transferred to the procuratorate for prosecution. If a case would not constitute a crime, it should be transferred to the administrative agencies so that administrative penalties can be imposes.[73] Discussion is ongoing about the connection between supervision procedure

[72] Shen Chunyao, Explanation on the CPL (Draft Amendment), at the second meeting of the Standing Committee of the 13th NPC on 25 April 2018, www.npc.gov.cn.
[73] Art 11(2) of SL, 'it shall conduct investigations of duty-related violations and crimes such as suspected corruption, bribery, abuse of power …'.

and criminal procedure, especially on the coercive measures and evidence. The detailed issues are discussed in the following chapters.

B. Trial in Absentia

The 2018 amendments to the CPL added a new chapter in Part Five, 'Special Procedures',[74] which addresses trial in absentia to deal with three categories of crimes:

(1) embezzlement or bribery;
(2) seriously compromising national security or terrorist activities; and
(3) those cases which require a timely trial, as confirmed by the SPP.

The procedural requirements for applying these special procedures are where:

- the suspects or defendants are outside China;
- the procuratorate confirms that the defendants shall bear the criminal liability; and
- following the court's examination, the court decides to hold a court session to hear the case.

The detailed issues are discussed in Chapter 10 on special procedures.

C. The Principle of the Guilty Plea and Leniency Policy

This policy was added to the part on principles in the CPL 2018 amendments. Article 15 provides that:

> where a criminal suspect or defendant voluntarily and truthfully confesses to his or her crime, admits to the facts of the crime that he or she is charged with, and is willing to accept punishment, the criminal suspect or defendant may be granted leniency in accordance with the law.

The policy had been applied in practice even before the law was amended, and pilots of the programme have been running since September 2016 in several provinces. After more than a year of applying the leniency policy, the SPC, SPP, MOPS, and the MOSS issued a 'Guiding Opinions on the Application of the Leniency System for Guilty Plea and Accepting Punishment (Guiding Opinions of Leniency System).[75] The issues about whether or not a guilty plea is truly voluntary, the suspects or the defendants' legal assistance from the duty-lawyer, and the degree of leniency are still under discussion. This is covered in more detail in Chapter 3 on the principles of criminal procedure law.

[74] Arts 291–297 of the 2018 CPL.
[75] It was issued on 11 October 2019.

3

Basic Concepts

I. The Aims of Criminal Procedure

The aims of criminal procedure are discussed among academic scholars and refer to what legislators and legal practitioners would expect to reach through the implementation of the law on criminal proceedings.[1] Sometimes, these aims are also expressed in the choice of various values involving criminal proceedings. However, the categorisation is distinct from one scholar to another. Some British scholars have classified the values as 'internal and external values'; the 'internal values' have been regarded as 'accurate determinations and fair procedures'.[2] One American scholar has identified three categories in which to place the fundamental values, such as human dignity, truth, and fairness.[3] Scholars have recognised the complexities present in organising these basic values and have also found, in some circumstances, that those values could conflict and overlap.[4]

In most jurisdictions, discussion and debate about the aims of criminal procedure are mainly confined to theoretical exchanges between academics. However, in some jurisdictions, these values have been articulated into codes of criminal procedure. For example, Article 1 of the Japanese Code of Criminal Procedure sets out the purpose of the Code.[5] Additionally, in the Russian Code of criminal procedure, the purpose of criminal court proceedings is stipulated in the 'Chapter of Principles'.[6] China has also articulated the mission and aims of its criminal procedure into the CPL. Article 1 sets out the general aims as follows:

> To assure that the Criminal law is correctly implemented, to punish crimes, to protect people, to safeguard national security and the public security of society, and to maintain the order of the socialist society, this law is formulated in an accordance with the Constitution.

[1] Liling Yue, 'The Development of Chinese Criminal Procedure' in Marco Fabri (ed), *Four Criminal Procedure Case Studies in Comparative Perspective: China-Italy-Russia-USA* (Staempfli, Nomos,Jan Sramek Verlag, 2016) 35.

[2] Liz Campbell et al, *The Criminal Process*, 5th edn (New York, Oxford University Press, 2019) 27.

[3] Darryl K Brown et al, *The Oxford Handbook of Criminal Process* (New York, Oxford University Press, 2019) 25.

[4] ibid.

[5] Japanese Code of Criminal Procedure 1948.

[6] Art 6 of the Russian Code of Criminal Procedure.

This article has remained unamended since 1979. It has been criticised because the expression of purpose contains a strong emphasis on combating crime and ignores the importance of human rights protection in criminal proceedings. Such a purpose affects the structure of criminal proceedings.[7] Article 1, it seems, sets out a hierarchy of levels of criminal procedure law. First, the immediate level is to implement correctly the criminal law; the second, middle level is to punish crimes and protect people; and at the final level, a general purpose is to safeguard the security of society and maintain order. At the first level, Article 1 states that the criminal law is to be 'correctly implemented'. It seems that this aim overlaps with the purposes of substantive criminal law and is a deterministic expression to the effect that criminal procedure law and process play the sole role of enforcing the substantive law. It is partly correct to state that there are connections between substantive criminal law and criminal procedure law, but the connections are pro forma and shaped technically, for instance, 'the seriousness of crimes and the punishments attached to them, also heavily influences the rules of criminal procedure'[8] such that the jurisdictions of trial courts have to be organised through criminal procedure law. In the author's opinion, whether or not the substantive criminal law could be 'correctly implemented' relies to a great extent on what kinds of wrongdoings are defined as crimes (or offences), what kinds of proper punishments could be imposed, and what kinds of criminal justice policies should be implemented in practice. In other words, criminal law has independent values and the implementation of criminal procedure cannot replace the criminal law to achieve the purposes of criminal law and sentencing policies.[9]

The middle level aim is to 'punish crimes' and 'protect people'. This a consequence of the implementation of substantive criminal law. What does the phrase 'protect people' mean? In the author's view, from its 1970s political and social background, the logical meaning is to protect the public from becoming victims of crime, rather than protecting the right to a fair trial of participants of criminal procedure, especially the rights of suspects and defendants in criminal proceedings.

The description of the tasks of CPL is set out in Article 2 in the part on the development of CPL legislation. One of the greatest steps forward in the 2012 CPL revision was that the words 'the respect and protection of human rights' were inserted into the text, which now reads as follows:

> To ensure the accurate and timely finding of facts of crimes, correct application of law, to punish criminals, to protect innocent people from criminal prosecution, to educate citizens to voluntarily obey the law, to actively fight against criminal conduct, to safeguard the socialist legal system; to respect and protect of human rights, to protect the personal rights, property rights, democratic rights of citizens, and to guarantee the smooth progress of socialist construction.

[7] Sun Weiman, 'Inquiry into the Theoretical Issues of the Purpose and Structure of Criminal Proceedings' (2016) 10 *Application of Law* 116.

[8] Jeremy Horder, *Ashworth's Principles of Criminal Law*, 9th edn (New York, Oxford University Press, 2019) 3.

[9] Liling Yue, *Criminal Trial and Human Rights Protection* (Beijing, Law Press, 2010) 11–12.

This provision is largely focused on the criminal process. It seems that 'finding of facts of crimes' is the core task, to which are added the requirements 'accurate' and 'timely'. This purpose of 'finding truth' is commonly accepted by both common law and civil law traditions, as well as by mixed model traditions. However, for decades, scholars have debated the meaning of 'truth' from philosophical and legal practice perspectives.[10] Gradually, Chinese legal scholars in the relatively younger generations recognised the distinction between 'the objective truth' and 'truth' in the legal process.[11] As a result of this, the facts in the point of law have been accepted as the standards of proof for prosecution, court decisions, and even for cases of miscarriage of justice.

II. The Main Sources of Criminal Procedure Law

The operation of criminal process in China is based on laws and also so-called 'soft laws', which are the implementation of rules and other interpretations. The legislative power rests with the NPC and the Standing Committee.[12]

A. The Constitution

At the top of the hierarchy of legislation is the Constitution. However, China's Constitution is unlike those of other jurisdictions: the SPC and other lower level courts have no judicial review power. The implementation of Constitutional principles mainly relies on substantive and procedural laws. The Constitution cannot be cited in the courts' judgments or decisions. In 2002 a special committee was created inside NPC. Called the 'NPC Constitution and Law Committee', its mission is to review the Constitution and implement it. To date, the Committee has not ruled any laws or regulations unconstitutional.

Chapter Two of the Constitution on the Fundamental Rights and Duties of Citizens stipulates certain principles and rights which directly relate to criminal procedure, and which guide legislation and practice.

Article 37 provides for the liberty and privacy of citizens, stating that: 'no citizen may be detained except by the approval or decision of a people's procuratorate or by the decision of a people's court, and that pretrial detention must be carried out by a public security organ'. Also, 'unlawful deprivation or restriction of a citizen's liberty by detention or other means is prohibited; and unlawful search of the person is prohibited'.

Article 38 provides the right to protect the personal dignity of citizens.

[10] Thomas Weigend, 'Is the Criminal Process about Truth?: A German Perspective' (2003) 26(1) *Harvard Journal of Law & Public Policy* 157.

[11] Liling Yue, *Criminal Trial and Human Rights Protection* (Beijing, Law Press, 2010) 13–17.

[12] Arts 62(3) and 67(2) of the Constitution (2018 amendment).

Article 39 protects a citizen's residence; it states that unlawful search and intrusion into a citizen's residence is prohibited. No organisation or individual may, on any ground, infringe upon a citizen's freedom and privacy of correspondence, except in cases to meet the needs of state security or of criminal investigation. Public security or procuratorial organs are permitted to intercept correspondence in accordance with procedures prescribed by law.

Article 40 provides for the protection of private correspondence. It states that 'freedom and privacy of correspondence of citizen of the PRC are protected by law'.

In Chapter Three of the Constitution, 'The Structure of the State', Section 7 provides for the Supervision Committees and the authorities it has. This section was added in the 2018 revision. Article 127 specifically says that 'supervisory organs shall, in handling duty-related violations of law or crimes, cooperate with judicial organs, procuratorial organs, and the law enforcement organs, with mutual checks'. Further, in Section 8, the courts and prosecutor's authority and obligations are detailed: Article 130 provides that all cases, including criminal cases, shall be heard in public, except in special circumstances specified by law. The same article also stipulates that the accused has the right to defence. Although these rights are not directly provided for in the part on fundamental rights, they relate to criminal proceedings.

B. The Criminal Procedure Law and Related Laws

The most important source of law on criminal procedure is the CPL. As described in Chapter 2 above, the original CPL was created in 1979 and amended in 1996 and 2012. The CPL currently in force was enacted on 26 October 2018 and has 308 articles. In China, juvenile criminal procedures are part of the special procedures of the CPL. There is no separate criminal or procedural law for juvenile offenders.

Other sources related to the CPL are:

- the Organic Law of the People's Court (OLC), which was originally enacted in 1979 and later amended in 1983, 1986, and 2006. The current version was amended in 2018, and has been effective since 1 January 2019;
- the Organic Law of the People's Procuratorate (OLP), which was originally enacted in 1979, and later amended in 1983 and 1986; the current version was amended in 2018;
- the Supervision Law (SL), which was adopted and effective in March 2018;
- the Judges Law (JL) of PRC, which was adopted originally in 1995 and amended in 2001, 2017 and 2019;
- the Public Prosecutors Law (PPL) of PRC, which was adopted originally in 1995, and then amended in 2001, 2017 and 2019;
- the People's Police Law (PL) of PRC, which was enacted in 1995 and amended in 2012;

- the Lawyers Law (LL), which was adopted for the first time in 1996, and amended in 2001, 2007, 2012 and 2017.

C. Other Implementation Rules and Interpretations

Since the promulgation of the CPL in 1979, a tradition has been formed by the Standing Committee of the NPC, SPC, SPP, and some related ministries that they formulate and issue the interpretations and rules for implementation of the CPL. This power is mainly derived from the Constitution,[13] but it only endorses the power of interpretation of the law to the Standing Committee of the NPC. In 1981, the Standing Committee of the NPC issued a 'Resolution on Strengthening the Interpretation of Laws', which authorised the Standing Committee of the NPC, as well as the SPC, SPP and the State Council to interpret laws on issues 'involving the specific application of laws and degrees'.[14] This Resolution is still effective at the time of writing. Subsequently, the Legislative Law in Chapter II, Section 4 authorises only the NPC Legal Work Committee to interpret the law, while the SPC, SPP and the State Council have the right to request interpretation of the law to the Standing Committee of NPC.

Because the 2012 CPL revision was a relatively comprehensive and important revision, the Standing Committee of the NPC and the relevant law enforcement organs all issued interpretation and implementation rules. Shortly after the coming into force of the 2012 CPL, the Standing Committee of the NPC jointly with the SPC, the SPP, the MPS and the MJ adopted a Provision on Several Issues of Implementation of Criminal Procedure Law (Provision). After the enactment of the 2018 amendment, the SPC, SPP, MPS, and the MSS jointly issued a Guiding Opinion on the Application of the Leniency System for Admitting Guilt and Accepting Punishment. After that, SPC, SPP, and MPS published their own interpretations of the CPL and the implementation rules. These are as follows:

(1) the SPC adopted a revised SPC Interpretation on 26 January 2021, which became effective on 1 March 2021. Consisting of 655 articles, it has more than doubled the original 2018 CPL (308 articles);
(2) the SPP published Draft Rules for Criminal Procedure on 22 November 2012 which contains 708 articles, again over double the number of the articles in the CPL. On 30 December 2019, the SPP revised the 2012 Rules and issued a revised Rules for Criminal Procedure (SPP Rules), where the number of articles was reduced to 684;
(3) the MPS published its 'MPS Provisions' on 13 December 2012, which has 376 articles. On 20 July 2020 the MPS published a revised version of the Provisions, which has 388 articles.

[13] Art 67(4) of the Constitution.
[14] Section 2, 3 of the 1981 Resolution.

In addition to the aforementioned judicial interpretations or implementation rules issued by legal institutions and directly related to criminal procedures, administrative agencies such as the Ministry of Justice and the MSS have also issued rules relevant to criminal procedure, such as publications on defence lawyers, legal aid, and issues related to national security.

Although the 2018 CPL amendments expanded the number of provisions to 308, the number is still relatively small compared to European countries of the continental law family.[15] The production of a large number of judicial interpretations and implementation rules shows that the CPL itself is not concrete enough, and the legal expressions are not rigorous enough, and thus it lacks operability. Therefore, under the current situation, the formulation of these judicial interpretations and implementation rules is in line with the needs of law enforcement. However, the characteristics of these judicial interpretations or implementation rules are very controversial among legal scholars. First, scholars disagree about the content of the interpretation of the law; in accordance with the 'Resolution on Strengthening the Work of Legal Interpretation' of the Standing Committee of the NPC, the interpretation of the law is limited to the specific application of laws and decrees in trial and procuratorial work. However, some scholars argue that some interpretations go beyond the scope of this authorisation and are similar to legislation or supplements/amendments to the law, for example, Article 182(2) of the 2012 CPL, concerning pre-trial meetings, Articles 277–279 on criminal reconciliation, and Article 52 concerning evidence collected by administrative agencies.[16] These issues are discussed in the following chapters.

Second, these law enforcement agencies seem to interpret the law in a similar way to the legislation, so the interpretation merely contains text duplicated from the legislation itself. For example, Article 75 of the CPL refers to one of the conditions for residential surveillance in designated residences: 'execution in the residence may hinder investigation'. The explanations issued by the SPC, SPP, MPS, MSS are almost the same and basically only repeat the words of the CPL. Third, in practice, these judicial interpretations or implementation rules seem to have a higher force than the law itself. Some judges, prosecutors, and law enforcement officers leave the CPL aside in the law enforcement process and only refer to these judicial interpretations or implementation rules.[17] Law students also regard these judicial interpretations and implementation rules as very important when preparing for the national judicial examination. It is argued that in future legal reform, the principles of legal interpretation should be further explored, especially when interpreting the CPL. Also, the protection of the rights of litigation participants

[15] The French Criminal Procedure Code (as of 2020) has 937 articles; the German Code of Criminal Procedure (as of 2019) has 499 articles; the Italian Criminal Procedure Code (as of 28 February 2021) has 746 articles: see www.brocardi.it.

[16] Wang Ming Yuan, 'A Study on the Judicial Interpretations of CPL, after the Amendment of 2012' (2015) 1 *Journal of the National Prosecutors College* 131.

[17] ibid.

should be taken as the basic principle of interpretation, and each law enforcement agency should be prevented from focusing on its own implementation procedures whilst ignoring the problem of linking procedures in various agencies.

III. The Main Stages of Criminal Procedure

The normal flow of an ordinary criminal case is illustrated by Table 1, below; the other special procedures are discussed in subsequent chapters. The Chinese manner of dividing up the stages of criminal procedure has its own characteristics: the first is that every criminal case has to pass through the 'initiation' phrase, which is known as 'filing case' (立案 *li an*), and without that the criminal investigation cannot be started. The second characteristic is that it is not divided into pre-trial and post-trial procedures. The public prosecution phase is an independent phase which is common in other jurisdictions. In each phase there are sub-procedures, which are discussed in related chapters below.

IV. Terminological Issues Related to Criminal Procedure

From the perspective of comparative law research, the definition and translation of legal terms in various jurisdictions is one of the most difficult parts of comparative research. A comparative law expert describes how a 'tangled series of definitional terminological, translation, and statistical issues confound and confuse the comparison'.[18] The following terms have been selected by the author as some of the most ambiguous in the area of criminal procedure. It is hoped that this will clarify any confusion.

A. Judiciary

The term 'judiciary', 'judicial system' and 'judicial organs' have different meanings in common law, civil law and mixed law model jurisdictions. In common law jurisdictions is the judiciary is the system of courts that interprets and applies the law in the name of State. The judiciary can also be thought of as a mechanism for the resolution of disputes. It could be argued that this term focuses on the court's activities. However, some civil law jurisdictions believe that prosecution authorities have quasi-judicial functions, and therefore prosecution authorities are seen as having 'judicial authority'.[19]

[18] Floyd Feeney and Joachim Herrmann, *One Case-Two System, A Comparative View of American and German Criminal Justice* (New York, Transnational Publishers, Inc Ardsley, 2005) 415.

Table 1 Stage of the Criminal Procedure for Ordinary Criminal Cases

Stage	Articles	Authority
Filing a Case	Arts 109–114	Public security organs, Procuratorates and courts have authority to file a case
Investigation	Arts 115–168	Public security organs and procuratorates
Initiation of Public Prosecution	Arts 169–182	Procuratorates
Trial (first instance)	Arts 183–226	Courts
Appeal (second instance)	Arts 227–245	Appellate courts
Execution of Judgments	Arts 259–276	Courts, procuratorates, public security and prisons

[19] Richard Vogler and Barbara Huber (eds), *Criminal Procedure in Europe* (Berlin, Duncker & Humboldt, 2008). In the chapter on France, it was indicated that 'the office of prosecutor is a judicial one': see 229. The chapter on Germany stated 'This office (prosecution authorities) is a judicial authority': see 326.

When the English term 'judiciary' is translated into Chinese in modern times, the term '司法' (*sifa*) is used. The adjectival form of the word is frequently used, in phrases such as 'judicial system', 'judicial authority' and 'judicial interpretation' etc. However, in ancient Chinese the 司法 (*sifa*) is a kind of official name or title for a person who is responsible for the implementation of the criminal law. This kind of official title has existed since the Han Dynasty.[20] Additionally, in China's oldest philology work '*Shuo Wen Jie Zi*' (说文解字 'discussing writing and explaining characters'),[21] 司法 (*sifa*) was divided into two characters. The '司' (*si*) was a verb which means 'responsible, in charge of, and handling', and '法' (*fa*) means 'law', which is very similar to the modern interpretation of the term. However, in modern times, there are confusions surrounding the interpretation of '司法' (*sifa*), because the Chinese term has been translated into English as 'administration of justice'.[22] One of the reasons for the confusion might be a lack of official interpretation. In the Constitution, the term 'judicial authorities' is not used, and the courts and procuratorates are listed separately. This situation is the same in the CPL. In the period around the 2012 CPL revision, the author heard that the phrase 'judicial organs' appeared in the second draft of the CPL. This would have included the public security authority, but the inclusion of the phrase met with fierce criticism from experts.[23] In the academic arena, there is no uniform interpretation. From the late 1970s until the early 1990s, some textbooks on criminal procedure law put the police (public security), the procuratorate and the courts together in a chapter entitled 'judicial authorities in criminal proceedings'. In later works, the police have been separated from the other two judicial authorities. Legal administrative authorities, such as the Ministry of Justice (MoJ), were never included in 'judicial authorities'. Nowadays, domestically in China and internationally, the term 'judiciary' and related terms, such as 'judicial system' and 'judicial interpretations', have been used in a variety of different ways and the majority of uses have included not only the court but also the procuratorate.

B. Coercive Measures

The CPL uses the collective term 强制措施 (*qiang zhi cuo shi*) to address all forms of measures to restrict or deprive the suspect or the accused of liberty during investigation or further proceedings.[24] This term has sometimes been translated as 'coercive measures'. The author recognises that there is no such legal term in common law jurisdictions. China most probably adopted this term from the former

[20] The Han Dynasty has been divided into two parts: the Western Han is from BC202 to 9, and Eastern Han is from 25–220.

[21] Written by Xu Shen, published in around 121, this was an early 2nd century Chinese dictionary.

[22] See https://zhidao.baidu.com.

[23] Interview with Professor Chen Guangzhong, who attended the discussions on the second draft of the CPL 2012.

[24] Chapter 6, Arts 66–100 of the CPL.

Soviet Union, as when the PRC was founded in 1949, the government invited Soviet experts to assist with the drafting of the CPL. The term can also be found in the current Russian Criminal Procedure Law.[25] However, Germany, another civil law jurisdiction, has a similar term in criminal procedure (*Zwangsmassname*), though it carries a different meaning from the Chinese one, and refers to all types of measures taken by the State during criminal proceedings to limit or deprive the suspect or the accused of rights which are protected by law.

The most problematic terms are 'arrest' and 'pre-trial detention' in criminal procedure. In most jurisdictions, the term 'arrest' concerns police powers, and dictates the shortest period that police can hold a suspect. However, the Chinese CPL uses the word 'detention' (拘留, *ju liu*) to describe the police power to hold suspects for short periods during the investigation, and uses 'arrest' (逮捕, *daibu*) as the term for the longer period of detention before trial. This is a complete reversal of how the two terms are used in common law jurisdictions. The author has tried to trace the origin of this usage and it appears that it may be a translation error from the former Soviet Union Criminal Procedure Code.[26] Although the author has repeatedly attempted to draw attention to this in various books, articles and lectures, this translation error is, unfortunately, barely recognised domestically or internationally. It is, therefore, widely misused in the translation of Chinese laws and in academic papers, and confuses numerous law students and researchers. This is just one example which demonstrates the difficulties of carrying out comparative research.

C. Trial

In the Chinese official translation of the third part of the CPL, 审判 (*shenpan*) is translated into English as 'trial', but the author believes that this is an inaccurate translation which in fact causes confusion in comparative legal research. The common law word 'trial' may defined in law as a coming together of parties to a dispute, to present information (in the form of evidence) in a tribunal, a formal setting with the authority to adjudicate claims or disputes. If this common law term were to be translated exactly into Chinese, it would be '法庭审理' (*fa ting shen li*), which means court hearing, and the Chinese term '审判' (*shenpan*) would be translated as 'adjudication'. As some language scholars have explained, the original term 审判 (*shenpan*) has also been translated as 'judge' and 'judgment'.[27]

It is the author's opinion that it might be more accurate to translate审判 (*shenpan*) as 'adjudication', since the Chinese adjudication phase usually includes

[25] Section 4 of the Code, 'Measures of procedural coercion'.

[26] Liling Yue, 'Thoughts about Floyd Feeney: An Excellent Scholar and a Good Friend' (2020) 53(4) *UC Davis Law Review* 1788.

[27] Sun Xun, 'The Origin of Modern Chinese Language Term of "Judgement"' (2013) 2 *Japanese Study and Research*, in which the author notes that the term '审判' (*shenpan*) appeared for the first time in the Chinese version of *Doxies of Christianity* in 1584, which was edited by an Italian missionary. Later,

several phases of proceedings, such as the preparation of a trial (public hearing), first instance trial and sometimes also the appeal. However, the author does still use the word 'trial' in later chapters, as it is a familiar term and is used in most jurisdictions throughout the world.

V. The Major Principles Governing Criminal Procedure

China is one of the few countries to have systematically articulated the principles of criminal procedure into its criminal code.[28] The title of the first chapter of the CPL is 'Tasks and Basic Principles'. The chapter contains a total of 18 articles. Except for Articles 1 and 2, which stipulate the purposes and tasks of criminal procedure, the rest of the articles might reasonably be thought to be the principles of criminal procedure. However, for decades, several theoretical issues have been debated: what are the principles of criminal procedure? How should they be formulated? What is the relationship between principles and constitutional requirements? Are principles justifiable? It is not easy to clarify these issues. Some scholars regard the central normative question as 'what principles would rational persons accept courts to use to decide cases in a society in which they are accepted to live?'[29] Further issues have been raised by Chinese scholars, and the main issue may be stated as 'What are the characteristics of the principles of criminal procedure?' The importance of this question is that, if we cannot identify the characteristics of the principles of criminal procedure, then we cannot evaluate those principles which are set out in the CPL.[30]

The primary characteristic of the principle of criminal procedure law should be that it is unique and adjusted to criminal punishment as the most intrusive measures that can be imposed on citizens. It should not be a general principle of law; neither should it be a principle shared also by other procedural laws. First, if we carefully scan the content of the CPL's chapter on 'Objective and Basic Principles', in accordance with this requirement, the terms 'based on facts and the law as the criterion'[31] and the 'law applies equally to all citizens'[32] are general principles of the law and must be applied to all laws. The second requirement, that the principle of criminal procedure should not be shared with other procedures is also difficult to establish. For example, 'The court exercises judicial power independently

in 1815, an English missionary edited a 'Dictionary', which for the first time translated '审判' (*shenpan*) as 'judge, judgement'.

[28] From the author's knowledge, the Russian and Vietnamese criminal procedure laws also articulate such principles into their Codes.

[29] Michael Bayles, 'Principles for Legal Procedure' (1986) 5 *Law and Philosophy* 33.

[30] Xie Youping and Wan Yi, 'Reflection and Reconstruction: On the Principles of Criminal Procedure Law' (2002) 2 *Criminal Law Review* 472.

[31] Art 6 of the CPL.

[32] ibid.

in accordance with the law',[33] 'Citizens of all ethnic groups have the right to use their native languages in litigation',[34] and 'The system of people's assessor in court trials'[35] are all shared principles amongst criminal and civil procedure law. Third, the principles of criminal procedure law also require that the principles of substantive criminal law be distinct from the principles of criminal procedure. For example, the 2018 CPL amendment introduces the policy of guilty plea and leniency in the chapter on principles.[36] According to the author's view, though, this is mainly a principle of substantive criminal law. Whilst discussing the implementation of the criminal law, below, we shall examine what constitutes a 'guilty plea' and what the proper reduction in punishment might be. The CPL provides only the structure to guarantee the voluntariness and fairness of the guilty plea.

A. Constitutional Principles

The Chinese Constitution sets out the basic principles involved in criminal proceedings in its chapter 'Fundamental Rights and Duties of Citizens'. These rights are:

(1) the right not to be illegally detained, which is related to arrest and pre-trial detention in criminal proceedings;[37]
(2) the right not to have one's dignity infringed,[38] which is related to issues of illegally-obtained evidence;
(3) the right not to be illegally searched;[39]
(4) the right of free communication,[40] which is related to the technical or special investigative measures;
(5) the right of an accused to a public trial;[41] and
(6) the right of an accused to defence.[42]

Since China's SPC does not have the power of judicial review and China does not have a constitutional court, the protection of these rights provided by the Constitution depends on the formulation and implementation of laws related to criminal procedure. Details on the implementation of Constitutional rights are provided in Chapters 5, 6, 7 and 8 below, as appropriate. The following text

[33] Art 5 of the CPL.
[34] Art 9 of the CPL.
[35] Art 13 of the CPL.
[36] Art 15 of the CPL.
[37] Art 37 of the Constitution.
[38] Art 38 of the Constitution.
[39] Art 37, the right of a person not to be unlawfully searched, and Art 39, the right against the unlawful search of, or intrusion into, a citizen's residence.
[40] Art 40 of the Constitution.
[41] Art 130 of the Constitution.
[42] ibid.

discusses the principle of the presumption of innocence, and new principle of guilty plea and leniency.

B. The Principle of the Presumption of Innocence

The principle of the presumption of innocence is not articulated in the Constitution, and until now debate has focused on whether Article 12 of the CPL is an indication of the principle. As noted above, Article 12 was incorporated into the CPL in 1996. This was considered to be a major step forward, and the 1996 revision remained unchanged through the 2012 and 2018 revisions. It states that: 'No person shall be found guilty without being judged so by a people's court in accordance with the law'.

Some scholars believe that, although Article 12 embodies the basic spirit of the presumption of innocence, it is not a normative expression commonly used internationally. These scholars further point out that the internationally used expression of the principle of the presumption of innocence emphasises the presumed innocent status of suspects or those accused, and the rights that they should enjoy, while the provisions of Article 12 of the Chinese CPL emphasise the court's power of conviction. From this perspective, the principle of the presumption of innocence has not been fully established in the CPL.[43] The author considers that the explanations of these scholars seems to be inferred from the literal meaning of the legal provisions, and there has been no in-depth analysis of the essence of this expression.[44] Perhaps the legislator's interpretation can be better demonstrated by fact that this provision was added to the CPL in 1996. Former Director of the Legislative Affairs Committee of the Standing Committee of the NPC, Gu Angran, gave a report on the 'Criminal Procedure Law Amendment' at the NPC. He pointed out:

> We firmly oppose the presumption of guilt, but it is also not the presumption of innocence in Western countries, but we shall take facts as the basis and the law as the criterion. The provisions of CPL and this amendment have actually borrowed from the reasonable part of the presumption of innocence, such as the burden of proof shall be in prosecution's side, and no person shall be found guilty without a judgment by the people's court. After trial by the people's court, if the evidence is insufficient and the defendant shall not be found guilty, an acquittal shall be made.[45]

It should be noted that the first half of this statement by the legislator basically confirmed that Article 12 and related provisions absorbed the 'reasonable part' of the presumption of innocence. The fact that his interpretation went beyond the

[43] Chen Guangzhong et al, 'On the Principle of Presumption of Innocence and Its Application in China' (2013) 10 *Journal of Law*.

[44] Liling Yue, *Criminal Trial and Human Rights Protection* (Beijing, Law Press, 2010) 132.

[45] *Legal Daily*, 3 February 1996.

provisions of Article 12 to some extent confirms that the burden of proof rests with the prosecution, and if the evidence is doubted, the accused will be acquitted. However, the second part of his statement, which is set out below, demonstrates his more contentious views on the presumption of innocence:

> However, the law does not stipulate that the accused or suspects should be presumed innocent by court before the final judgements have been made, because if so, why should the investigating agency conduct investigations? Why take coercive measures? Why should the procuratorate prosecute the case? Why does the court hold hearings? That is that: before the court convicts somebody, we cannot say that the accused is a criminal, nor can we say that there is no criminal suspicion.

These questionable comments show that the legislators regard the presumption of innocence as based on an assumption of objective facts, rather than legal procedural assumption. As some scholars have argued, the function of the presumption of innocence is to maintain procedural openness, which requires that the suspect or defendant cannot be treated like a criminal.[46] The compulsory investigative measures taken before the final decision are mainly of procedural significance and should not be punitive, and these measures should have a reasonable basis and comply with the principle of proportionality.[47]

For a further two decades the principle of the presumption of innocence has been debated worldwide in a bid to work out exactly what it means. Does it only mean to treat suspects or defendants as not guilty and not innocent? What does it encompass? Does it include the burden and standard of proof, and the principle in *dubio pro reo*? These questions include issues of philosophy, law, evidence law, and human rights, which are all under challenge. It is the authors' view that Directive (EU) 2016/343 of the European Parliament and the Council 'On the strengthening of certain aspects of the presumption of innocence and of the right to be present at the trial in criminal proceedings' (the Directive) and the case law of European Court of Human Rights have established a basic, applicable criterion. This implements the principle of the presumption of innocence, and its criteria could be taken in practice as a yardstick by which to review Chinese criminal procedure law and practice. With this in mind, we may notice a gap in the implementation of the principle of presumption of innocence between European jurisdictions and China.

Article 3 of the Directive defines the principle as: 'member states shall ensure that suspects and accused persons are presumed innocent until proved guilty according to law'. The wording of this article is not very different from that in China's CPL Article 12. The only difference is that the Chinese provision clearly mentions 'being judged so by a people's court', but Article 3 of the Directive does not mention who has the power to judge who is guilty. Maybe this is too obvious to mention, or it should be deemed to be included in the phrase of 'according to law'.

[46] Carl-Fridrich Stuckenberg, *Untersuchungen zur Unschuldsvermutung* (Walter de Gruyter, 1998).
[47] Liling Yue, *Criminal Trial and Human Rights Protection* (Beijing, Law Press, 2010) 133.

Article 4 of the Directive requires public authorities not to make public statements that refer to suspects or accused persons as being guilty before they have been proved guilty according to law. In China, some hotly debated issues concern media reports in some cases, where suspects have made confessions on TV. According to the regulations of the State Council of China (administrative regulations), television stations are all state-owned, and the cases are usually in the investigation process of the public security organs (police). The suspects' TV confessions should be reasonably assumed to be organised by investigator and TV stations together. The legal scholars' concern is whether the suspects were under certain pressures when they made the TV confession. If the confession is false or wrongly obtained, then it may affect the result of the court judgment. Furthermore, does a plea of guilty on TV compromise the suspect's right to privacy before the trial? Legal scholars believe that it violates the principle of presumption of innocence.[48]

Article 5 of the Directive states that appropriate measures must be taken to ensure that suspects and accused persons are not presented as being guilty, in court or in public, through the use of measures of physical restraint. For thousands of years in China, from ancient times to modern ones, most criminal suspects and the accused in custody have worn so-called 'prison uniforms' (囚服, *qiufu*). In modern times, due to the spread of the principle of the presumption of innocence, the issue of how an accused is dressed when appearing in court has prompted debate. In 2006, the MPS suggested in a document that a criminal suspect or accused in custody should wear recognisable clothing, usually a brightly coloured vest, with 'detention centre' printed on it. According to statistics, 65 per cent of those accused wear this recognisable vest to appear in court.[49] In February 2015, the SPC issued its 'Opinions on Comprehensive Deepening the Reform of the People's Court'. Paragraph 11 states that:

> it is forbidden to allow the defendant or appellant in criminal custody to wear identification uniforms, vests, prison uniforms and other clothing with the logo of the regulatory agency to appear in court.

This SPC document marked the end of the era when those accused would wear 'identifiable clothing to attend the trial'. Although this is a small step in the civilisation of justice, it is of great significance for removing criminal labelling in criminal proceedings and in respecting the dignity of the accused.

Regarding the question of whether the defendant is subject to physical restrictions on attending court trials, in 2016 the SPC promulgated in the 'People's Court Rules' that the accused or the appellant shall not be physically restrained in court proceedings. But the SPC also set out some exceptions, so physical restraint measures may be used for those deemed personally dangerous and those who might

[48] Jia Ping, 'Reasonable Limits of Criminal Cases in the Investigation Stage of Television Media Reporting' (2017) 9 *Law Science*.

[49] 'The curtain call of the prison uniform: From the change of details to realise respect for the rights and interests of the defendant', 13 May 2016, https://finance.sina.com.cn.

endanger the security of the court trial. Therefore, in news reports, those accused of serious violent crimes can often be seen attending court trials in handcuffs.

Article 6 of the Directive provides two sub-principles: one is that the burden of proof for establishing the guilt of suspects and accused persons lies with the prosecution; the second is that, when there is any doubt as to the question of guilt, this doubt must benefit the suspect or accused person.

In the 2012 Chinese CPL amendment, the burden of proof was clearly set out. The burden of proof in cases of public prosecution shall be borne by the procuratorate, and in private prosecution cases by the person who initiated the private prosecution.[50] However, in the immediately following article, the scope of the responsibility to collect evidence has been expanded, stating that 'Judges, prosecutors, and criminal investigators must under legal procedures, gather various kind of evidence that can prove the guilt or innocence of a criminal suspects or defendant and the gravity of crime'.[51] This provision reflects the goodwill and legislative purpose of the legislators, that is, to exclude criminal suspects and the accused from the burden of proof. This could be because the sentence immediately follows the prohibition on the use of illegal means to obtain evidence. Additionally, of particular significance is the addition of the prohibition on self-incrimination found in this article, in the 2012 amendments. However, in this article, neutral judges are placed alongside prosecutors and investigators. This comes not from the non-adversarial procedure model, but from an inquisitorial model, where the investigators, prosecutors, and adjudicators are in a relationship of mutual cooperation and oversight.

A debated issue which relates to the burden of proof is the reverse onus. China has no evidence law, and the evidence rules are scattered through various procedural laws, such as the CPL, civil procedure law and administrative procedure law. Research on the theories of evidence, therefore, is still relatively rare. In theory, the burden of proof has not yet been divided into persuasive (or ultimate) burdens, evidential burden, or special defence.[52] China's Criminal Law, Article 395, describes the offence of having unexplained or unknown sources of 'huge amounts of property'. It states:

> Where the property or expenditure of any state functionary obviously exceeds his legitimate income, and the difference is huge, he shall be ordered to explain the sources. If he failed to do so, the difference shall be determined as illegal income, and he shall be sentenced to fixed-term imprisonment not more than five years or criminal detention; or if the difference is extremely huge, shall be sentenced to fixed-term imprisonment not less than five years but not more than ten years. The difference of the property shall be recovered.

[50] Art 51 of the CPL.
[51] Art 52 of the CPL.
[52] Ben Emmerson et al, *Human Rights and Criminal Justice*, 3rd edn (London, Sweet & Maxwell, 2012) 668.

According to the criteria on the burden of proof, as summarised in British justice,[53] if the above offence is scrutinised, it will be noted that its burden of proof has been transferred to the suspect or the accused. It is a typical persuasive or legal burden; the presumption is mandatory, and the presumed fact is an essential element of the offence. The author believes that this kind of reverse onus may violate the principle of the presumption of innocence.[54]

As for the standard of proof before the 2012 CPL amendment, the statement in the law was always that 'the facts of the case are clear, and the evidence is reliable and sufficient'. This standard is very controversial in academic and judicial practice, and is considered to be vague and lacking operability. Progress was made in the 2012 CPL amendment. The aforementioned standards were retained, and wording covering 'reliable and sufficient evidence' was added to the law. This requires that:

(1) all facts for conviction and sentencing are supported by evidence;
(2) all evidence used to decide a case has been verified under legal procedures; and
(3) all facts found are beyond reasonable doubt based on all evidence of the case.

The significance of this supplementary provision is that it indicates that the internationally recognised standard of proof, 'beyond reasonable doubt', has been accepted, for the first time, in CPL revisions. However, some Chinese scholars think that there are differences of degree in how the 'beyond reasonable doubt' standard is understood in Chinese law and how it is interpreted in the internationally accepted standard of proof. Chinese scholars are not ready to accept the West's version of 'beyond reasonable doubt', which the Chinese interpret as requiring a very high degree of probability, ie at least 95 per cent; China's meaning of 'beyond reasonable doubt' is that it must achieve the level that, for the determination of key facts, the conclusion is unequivocal.[55] The author argues that Chinese scholars' arguments make little sense, as in 'Western' jurisdictions, the court's decision must be definitive too: guilty or not guilty. If there are other possibilities in the case, then this means that reasonable doubt exits, and therefore the accused must not be convicted.

In general, China's CPL accepts the principle of '*in dubio pro reo*'. However, Article 200 of the CPL lists three different verdicts: guilty; not guilty and non-guilty where the guilt cannot be proved because there is insufficient evidence. The author believes that this classification is logically wrong. It confuses two different classification standards: one is guilty and not guilty; the other is guilty and not guilty that can be proved, or guilty and not guilty that cannot be proved. The classification in the first of these standards distinguishes between not guilty where the guilt cannot be proved because sufficient evidence exists to refute it, and not guilty

[53] ibid, 675.

[54] Liling Yue, *Criminal Trial and Human Rights Protection* (Beijing, Law Press, 2010) 134.

[55] Chen Guangzhong et al 'On the Principle of Presumption of Innocence and Its Application in China' (2013) 10 *Journal of Law*.

where the innocence can be proved by sufficient evidence. This is more nuanced from the perspective of the presumption of innocence. Although in both scenarios the accused has obtained the result of an acquittal, this classification leaves behind the shadow of the presumption of guilt. From a comparative law perspective, the Chinese CPL's classification of verdict is not alone: there are at least another three jurisdictions which also have more than two kinds of verdicts: Scotland, Italy, and Israel.[56] After the revision of the CPL in 2012, the SPC promulgated a judicial interpretation for the implementation of the CPL, which deepened scholars' doubts about this provision. In the interpretation, Article 181(4)[57] states that:

> Based on new facts and evidence, where the people's procuratorate files a new indictment against a defendant previously found innocent according to Item 3 of Article 195 [2012 CPL; Article 200(3) of 2018 CPL], the court shall accept and hear the new indictment according to the law.

This interpretation involves another argument, namely that it may infringe upon the double jeopardy principle.

Article 7 of the Directive states that suspects and accused persons have the right to remain silent and the right not to incriminate themselves. China's Constitution and CPL do not directly guarantee the right to silence for criminal suspects and defendants. The milestone progress in the 2012 CPL was the addition of 'No one shall be forced to prove their guilt', to Article 52 on methods of collecting evidence. However, there are still controversies in academia, especially on the relationship between the right not to self-incriminate and the right to silence. Some scholars believe that this signifies the establishment of the right to silence.[58] But so far, neither legislators nor judicial officials have explained the how a suspect is to avoid self-incriminating statements. The author believes that Article 118 of the 2012 CPL (Article 120 of the 2018 CPL) on the interrogation of criminal suspects is in conflict with the right not to self-incriminate. It should be noted that criminal suspects must not only answer investigators' questions, but must also answer 'truthfully'. Although the provision further provides that where 'the question is not related to the case [a suspect] has the right to refuse to answer', the key point here is who decides whether a question is or is not related to the case. The author asked this very question when giving a lecture to practitioners. The head of a police station immediately answered, 'of course it is our decision'. This answer is, it is thought, representative of the situation in China and suggests that this supplementary provision has no operational significance: suspects are not, in substance, given a right to silence.

[56] Yaniv Vaki et al, 'Two Kinds of Acquittals-Different kinds of Doubts' (2021) 32 *Criminal Law Forum* 97.

[57] Art 219(5) of 2021 SPC Interpretation remained unchanged.

[58] He Jiahong, 'My View on the Chinese System of Right to Silence' (2013) 1 *Tribune of Political Science and Law* 107.

In the 2012 CPL amendment, provisions on the guilty plea and leniency were added. After the law was passed, the NPC Legal Work Committee held a press conference. A reporter asked: Does the provision that no one should be forced to commit self-incrimination mean the establishment of the right to silence? And is there a contradiction with the law stipulating that 'the suspect shall answer the investigator's question truthfully'? Lang Sheng, the former deputy director of the Legal Work Committee, replied that this was set out from two different perspectives. On the one hand, the CPL emphasised the prohibition on using torture to extract a confession and, on the other, established as a condition of leniency truthful answers (or a truthful confession).[59] The second paragraph of Article 118 of the 2012 CPL (Article 120 of the 2018 CPL) stipulated the right for the suspect to be informed the leniency policy for those who truthfully confess the crimes.

We further extend the legislator's idea. If, later in the proceedings, a judge finds evidence that the accused did not 'truthfully' confess during the investigation, according to the assumption from the provision, this lack of truthfulness should be detrimental to the accused when he is convicted, ie the penalty should be more severe. In fact, some judges did do this in practice. In some judgments, they pointed out that the defendant had a bad attitude to pleading guilty, and the sentence was harsher as a result of this. This was consistent with the policy slogan in the past, 'Be lenient with confession, harsher with resistance' (坦白从宽, 抗拒从严). That policy has been popular in China for many years. Evidently the legislative purpose of this provision is to require suspects to cooperate with investigators (on behalf of the State) to provide a basis for the legitimacy of state-sponsored process and judgments.[60] After all, the pursuit of the truth is one of the aims of the criminal process, but the provisions of Article 120 more or less ignore the protection of the rights of suspects. In practice, excessive use of this provision might be one cause of miscarriage of justice cases.

C. Guilty Plea and Leniency[61]

One characteristic of China's criminal justice system that is not very different from other jurisdictions is the heavy caseload of the judiciary. In 2018, China's courts received a total of 1,834,374 criminal cases, of which 1,825,835 were finalised. This number includes first instance cases (1,203,055; 1,198,383), appeal cases (155,571; 154,391), and other cases which fall into the category of special proceedings.[62] Taking Beijing courts' caseload as an example, there were 2,628 trial judges in the criminal section of the courts, with each judge handling on average 255.7 criminal

[59] See www.china.com.cn.
[60] Liling Yue, *Criminal Trial and Human Rights Protection* (Beijing, Law Press, 2010) 218.
[61] Until now, there has been no official translation of this system. Unlike a guilty plea in common law systems, the Chinese Leniency Policy requires a truthful confession in exchange for lenient punishment.
[62] *Law Yearbook of China* (Beijing, China Law Yearbook Press, 2019) 1322.

cases in the year 2017–2018.[63] The caseload pressure is obvious.[64] Reform proposals were initiated in 2014. The Standing Committee of NPC and SPC, SPP initiated a pilot project on Fast-Track Sentencing Procedure (速裁 *su cai*) in 18 regions to handle those minor criminal cases where the predicted sentence was a term of imprisonment for one year or less. Following this project, two years later, the related legal institutions initiated another pilot project on the 'Leniency system of admitting guilt and accepting punishing' (guilty plea and leniency 认罪认罚从宽). In the 2018 CPL amendment, the policy of 'guilty plea and leniency' was included in the 'tasks and principles' section of the CPL.[65] The relevant section reads:

> where a criminal suspect or defendant voluntarily and truthfully confesses to his or her crime, admits to the facts of the crime that he or she is charged with, and is willing to accept punishment, the criminal suspects or defendant may be granted leniency in accordance with the law.

After this amendment was enacted, innumerable questions and issues related to the implementation of the policy were raised by practitioners and scholars. In 2019, the SPC, the SPP, the MPS, the MSS et al issued 'Guiding Opinions on the Application of the Leniency System for Admitting Guilt and Accepting Punishment' (Guiding Opinions on the Leniency System). It has now been three years since the 2018 CPL amendment was adopted. Media reports show that in the first six months of 2019, 80 per cent of criminal cases handled by the procuratorates in China used the guilty plea and leniency process, and 90.54 per cent of sentencing suggestions were accepted by courts.[66] The rate is approaching the plea bargaining rate in US courts, and statistics shows that the guilty plea and leniency process is playing an important role in the current Chinese criminal justice system.

The underlying motivation of the detailed design of the guilty plea and the leniency system may be indicative. When the courts and the procuratorates launched the pilot projects, some scholars made a comparison with the American plea bargaining system, which they believe is driven by a cost-benefit motivation. When China's legislators made their interpretations, they only mentioned the immediate purpose of the legislation, by way of a summary of the pilot project's experiences, and were silent on its original legislative aim. One year later, the aforementioned Guiding Opinions on the Leniency System summarised their purpose as being to 'fully implement the criminal policy of tempering justice with mercy' (宽严相济). These are: to promptly and effectively punish crimes; to strengthen judicial guarantees for human rights; to optimise the allocation of justice resources; to improve the efficiency of the criminal process; to solve the social conflicts and disputes; and to enhance harmony'.[67] Scholars are more inclined to agree that the main aims

[63] *People's Court Daily*, 6 February 2018.
[64] In 2019, except for weekends and public holidays, there were 250 working days.
[65] Art 15 CPL.
[66] www.chinanews.com, 6 September 2020.
[67] The Notice by the SPC, SPP, the MPS, the MSS, et al of Issuing the Guiding Opinions on the Application of Leniency System for Admitting Guilt and Accepting Punishment.

were 'optimising the allocation of justice resources and improving the efficiency of criminal process'. One scholar explained that in China at the moment, the number of violent crimes is decreasing, and the number of minor criminal cases is increasing. In order to optimise the allocation of judicial resources, complicated, serious criminal cases need to be separated out from the minor cases, and there needs to be a re-setting of the crime-governance model.[68] There are some scholars who do not fully agree with the idea that China's 'Guilty plea and leniency' system is simply a copy of American plea bargaining; they believe that it is moving towards further simplification, and towards establishing a Chinese-style prosecution and defence negotiation mechanism.[69]

There are a number of scholars and legal practitioners in China who discuss the relationship between the system of 'guilty plea and leniency' and the fundamental principles of a fair trial. However, the mainstream view is that the design of this system is just a 'deviation' from due process, or 'normal dynamic adjustments, rather than betrayals or violations of due process principles'.[70] There are scholars in common law jurisdictions who openly challenge sentence discounting for those who plead guilty, and who think that:

> it is certainly against the spirit of the four fundamental rights and the freedoms recognized in the ECHR: the presumption of innocence, the privilege against self-incrimination, the right to equal treatment in the exercise of rights, and the right to a fair and public hearing.[71]

A summary of the main points of the Chinese 'guilty plea and leniency system' might include the following points:

(1) first of all, the scope and conditions of the application of the guilty plea and leniency system are very different from those of common law systems, such as the US plea bargaining system. However, there are similarities with civil law systems, such as sentencing negotiation in Germany. In the provisions of the CPL and the interpretations in the 'Opinions', the so-called 'admission of guilt' refers to accused and criminal suspects who voluntarily and truthfully confess their crimes without any objection to the facts of the alleged offence. The decision whether or not to accept the guilty plea and impose the discount sentence is the decision of the procuratorate and the Court. This is quite different from plea bargaining in the US, where the defendant can admit only the offence they were charged with, without making a confession of all the facts of the crime. The Chinese provisions seem to have similarities with

[68] Wu Hongyao, 'The Systematic Interpretation of the System of Guilty Plea and Leniency' (2020) 4 *Contemporary Science of Law* 55.

[69] Chen Ruihua. 'Public Cooperation Mode in Criminal Proceedings – The Rise of the Sentencing Negotiation System in China' (2019) 4 *Law Forum* 5.

[70] Zhu Xiaoqing, 'The System of Guilty Plea and Leniency from the Perspective of Due Process in Criminal process' (2020) 8 *Science of Law* 86.

[71] Liz Campbell et al, *The Criminal Process*, 5th edn (New York, Oxford University Press, 2019).

German principles in that: 'the trial court in plea bargaining proceedings is not relieved from its obligation to find the objective truth'.[72] Furthermore, when the suspect or the accused is charged with several crimes, if he or she only confesses to one offence or to part of the facts of crime, the leniency rule cannot be applied to them; the prosecutor can only propose leniency within the range of sentencing when prosecuting the case to the court. A main difference between the plea-bargaining system in the US and the Chinese system is that in the latter it is not permitted to admit only one offence among several. This situation may reduce the defence lawyer's space for negotiation in practice

In terms of the standard of proof, according to the CPL and the Opinion, it remains the case that 'clear facts of crimes and conclusive and sufficient evidence shall be achieved'.[73] It should be noted that there is no limit on the application of the guilty plea and leniency policy for serious criminal cases, when suspects or defendants enter a guilty plea.

From a process point of view, an 'admission of guilt' in China's law can be taken from the investigation stage onwards. The second paragraph of Article 120 CPL states that when investigators interrogate a criminal suspect, 'they should inform the criminal suspect of their procedural rights and the provisions of law on leniency if he or she truthfully confesses to his or her crime as well as acknowledgement of guilt and acceptance of punishment'. The result of the suspect's guilty plea will only be recorded in the interrogation record during the investigation stage. Although the Guiding Opinions on the Leniency System allow for suspects and defendants to 'receive effective legal assistance',[74] the author is concerned about the situation where, during the investigation, the suspect does not hire a defence lawyer, or does not meet the requirements for receiving legal aid services. According to the CPL and the Opinions, the public security organ (the police) or the procuratorate should notify the lawyer on duty to provide three kinds of services for the suspect or defendant: first, to provide legal advice on the crime which the suspect is accused or prosecuted of, and the relevant legal provisions, including the legal consequences of admitting guilt and accepting punishment; second, to provide suggestions on the application of such procedures. And finally, to assist in applying for modifications to coercive measures. However, in the provisions of the CPL and the Opinions, the rights of duty lawyers and defence lawyers are different. On-duty lawyers do not have the right to access case files, and cannot examine the evidence; they only have the right to meet their clients. This is a matter of concern and the author and other scholars

[72] Gwladys Gillieron, 'Comparing Plea Bargaining and Abbreviated Trial Procedures' in Darryl K Brown et al (eds), *The Oxford Handbook of Criminal Process* (New York, Oxford University Press, 2019) 712.

[73] Art 3 of the Opinion.

[74] Art 10 of the Opinions.

believe that it would be difficult to provide 'effective legal assistance' with such restrictions in place.

(2) The key point and stage of the guilty plea and leniency is the suspect or defendant not only 'admitting guilt', but also 'accepting punishment'. The Guiding Opinions on the Leniency System state that: 'accepting punishment means that the criminal suspects and defendants sincerely repent of their crimes and are willing to accept punishment'. Also, 'accepting punishment' requires different results at different stages of the process. At the investigation stage, the suspect shall show willingness to accept punishment. At the review and prosecution stage, this willingness is shown by the acceptance of the procuratorate's proposed decision to prosecute or not, and agreement to the Procuratorate's recommendations, and further signing of a 'recognition letter'. At the trial stage, it is necessary to confirm the voluntariness of signing the 'recognition letter'. From this provision, we may be able to infer that in the review and prosecution stages, the 'recognition letter' signed by the suspect or defendant is of great significance. In most cases, the court's review of this 'recognition letter' is only a formal review, not a substantive one. At present, the controversial issue among academic and practitioners is about the validity of this 'recognition letter'. According to some academics, it should be considered as a negotiation agreement between the prosecutor and the suspect or defendant. Based on this agreement, when the prosecutor commences prosecution, the proposed sentencing shall be included in the sentencing suggestion if there are no further changes from the defendants' side and it is submitted to the court. The court's role is more controversial; the CPL and the Opinions require that courts mainly review the voluntariness and legality of the guilty plea. However, in some judges' view, they have the independent power to decide the range of sentencing. This means that judges could overthrow the negotiation between the defendant and prosecutor. This possibility may come from the structure of the guilty plea and leniency system – it is not akin to the US model, where the 'bargaining' is between the defendant or defence and the prosecutor, and where the court guarantees the reliability of the agreement, Also, it is different from the German model, where the judge presides over the 'bargaining', and guarantees the legality of the agreement of negotiation. Some scholars have suggested that if China were to make further reforms to define the judge's role, it would be easier to adopt the German model.[75]

(3) The size of sentencing discount for the guilty plea is another complicated and controversial issue. Article 15 of the CPL uses the phrase 'suspects or defendants may be granted leniency' after confessing and accepting punishment. The Guiding Opinions on the Leniency System further explain that 'leniency' may

[75] Chen Ruihua, 'On the Nature and Effect of Sentencing Negotiation' (2020) 5 *Chinese and Foreign Laws*.

> include imposing lenient punishment and procedural simplicity.[76] At present, scholars and legal practitioners agree on the principle behind the guilty plea and leniency's incentive mechanism, which is to encourage suspects and defendants to make a confession at an early stage in criminal proceedings. As to what the actual incentive should be, in terms of percentage discount, senior prosecutors have suggested that if the suspect makes a reliable confession in the stage of investigation, punishment should be reduced by 30 per cent within the statutory sentence range.[77] So far, there has been no research on how the sentencing discount is implemented. In addition, there is no research available on whether the promise of a sentencing discount adds to the pressure on criminal suspects or defendants to confess. This is a situation that British scholars are worried about, ie when an incentive range exceeds a certain limit, it may cause an innocent person to submit a guilty plea in order to avoid lengthy procedures with uncertain results.[78] This is an important issue that must be considered when China reforms its incentive mechanism in the future.

The system of 'guilty plea and leniency' has begun the process of trying to rationally allocate judicial resources in China. This attempt is positive and necessary. However, after two years of the pilot project and two years of law enforcement, from the perspective of criminal procedure, there are still some issues that need to be discussed in depth.

The first is the structural issue. As noted above, the CPL did not use the term 'negotiation' to describe this criminal justice policy, and the actual situation shows that it cannot be called a 'negotiation', because for two parties to 'negotiate' they should have equal status and a fair balance of power. However, China's 'guilty plea and leniency' policy is led by the prosecutor, during the investigation stage, and the so-called 'negotiation' is held between the prosecutor and the criminal suspect. Some scholars are concerned that in China, most criminal suspects are held in custody and, although suspects can receive some certain degree of assistance from lawyers, the means of that assistance are extremely limited. In most cases, the lawyer is not present when the prosecutor meets the suspect, and under the pressure of the prosecutor, the suspect can easily make a confession or act against himself.[79] In future reform, the German experience should be referred to, and the structure of the negotiation, which should be held between the defence lawyer and the prosecutor before the prosecution must be amended. After the prosecutor brings the case to the court, there should be a judge leading and participating in the negotiation.

[76] Art 9 of the Opinion.

[77] Chen Guoqing, 'Several Issues in Sentencing Recommendations' (2019) *Chinese Journal of Criminal Law*.

[78] Liz Campbell et al, *The Criminal Process*, 5th edn (New York, Oxford University Press, 2019) 341.

[79] Chen Ruihua, 'Public Cooperation Mode in Criminal Proceedings – The Rise of the Sentencing Negotiation System in China' (2019) 4 *Law Forum* 5.

Second is the issue of the role of lawyers in the 'guilty plea and leniency' procedure. The current situation is that lawyers have extremely limited rights and means to assist suspects during the investigation stage, especially the duty lawyer, whose rights are different from those of lawyers hired by suspects or defence lawyers appointed by legal institutions. They have no right to access case files and cannot perform any investigation independently by themselves, nor can they attend the negotiation between the prosecutor and the criminal suspect, so when the suspect signs the 'recognition letter', the lawyer is only a 'witness'. It is, therefore, difficult to provide an effective defence, as required by the law. In future reforms, lawyers should be given full defence rights, especially to attend the negotiation between prosecutors and suspects, or to represent suspects in the negotiation with prosecutors.

The final issue is the transparency of 'negotiation' information and substantive review by the courts. Currently, in handling cases of guilty plea and leniency, the rate of accepting prosecutors' sentencing recommendations has reached 95 per cent. The review of the authenticity and reliability of the defendant's guilty plea has been commented on as a mere formality.[80] If the defendant is under pressure, he will not raise objections and the judge usually accepts the prosecutor's sentencing recommendations. In future reform, the court's power of substantive review should be strengthened. One possible way to achieve this would be to make the negotiation process transparent: the content of the negotiation should be included in the case file, to ensure that the court has a document on which to base its review.

[80] ibid.

4

Agencies in the Criminal Justice System

I. Investigative Authorities

In China, under the CPL and other laws, there are five types of agencies with the authority to investigate crimes. There are two police forces: the public security organs (公安机关, *gongan jiguan*), and the state security organs (国家安全机关, *guojia anquan jiguan*). Additionally, there are the procuratorates, prison and military forces.

A. The Public Security Organs

The public security organ (PSO) is the principal investigative agency for major crimes.[1] According to the Criminal Law, the amendments of Criminal Law and the internal regulations of the Ministry of Public Security (MPS), the public security police are responsible for investigating all instances of approximately 386 different criminal offences.[2]

China's public security police force is a centralised, hierarchical system which has four levels. At the top, is the MPS, which has 33 internal operational departments within the Ministry.[3] These include: criminal investigations; economic crime investigations; food and drug crime investigations; cybersecurity; counter-terrorism; and drug control, etc. These departments guide and coordinate the investigation with lower-level PSOs, especially when major criminal cases occur. Under the MPS, in each province, autonomous region, and municipality directly under the central government,[4] there is a provincial-level public security bureau. Under the provincial-level public security bureau, in provinces and autonomous regions, there are municipal and public security bureaus. In current municipalities directly under the central government, there are district and county public security bureaus. Under this level, there are numerous police stations (派出所, *paichusuo*) which are set up in larger communities, within rural and urban areas.

[1] Art 19 of the CPL states that the public security organs shall be responsible for investigating criminal cases except for those separately provided for by law.

[2] See https//baike.baidu.com.

[3] On 27 February 2019 the State Council issued 'Provisions of the Ministry of Public Security on Functional Configuration, Internal Organizations and Staffing', see https://zh.wikipedia.org.

[4] Four cities fall into this category: Beijing, Tianjing, Shanghai, and Chongqing.

These police stations are the lowest level police force and have the closest contact with citizens in the community. When the PRC was founded, according to the administrative documents of the MPS,[5] its main responsibility was to maintain public order in the jurisdiction and register the household registration permit (户口, *hukou*). For criminal cases, the only responsibility was to protect the crime scene, and there were no independent investigative powers. However, after 1988, the scope and nature of the work of the police station changed. In addition to being responsible for maintaining public order and administering household registration, the task of investigating simple criminal cases was added. These cases should not include cases that require special technical investigative methods or complicated cases.[6] In current practice, when this level of police receive reports of crimes, such as emergency 110 calls, they are the first police force to take action to protect the crime scene and notify the higher level public security bureau that has official investigative authority. Also, they have the power to apprehend criminal suspects for a short time. In practice, this situation may make up for the shortage of formal investigative officials, but on the other hand, it raises several problems, which are set out below.

The lowest-level police stations sometimes mix up administrative coercive measures with criminal coercive measures. For example, they may impose administrative detention, provided by the People's Police Law,[7] on criminal suspects instead of criminal arrests, because they do not have the power to formally arrest criminal suspects. Consequently, suspects' rights, as provided in the CPL, may be infringed upon. Second, as the lowest level police station, the lack of proper technological facilities causes issues. For example, in the collection of evidence in order to carry out interrogation, the CPL requires that such interrogation be video-taped. If police stations do not have this facility, the interrogation is illegal, and it may not be used later as evidence to convict the accused. Third, according to China's Constitution, the procuratorates have the power to supervise police organs and courts during the criminal process. Whilst the lowest level police station is not a formal investigative authority, they cannot formally register criminal cases and they have no official recorder of interrogation, which would allow the prosecutor to supervise their investigation.[8]

In China's criminal process, police investigation plays an important and dominating role. The police are entitled to impose almost all of the coercive measures to limit or remove the liberty of suspects or those accused, the only exception being pre-trial detention, which requires approval from the prosecutor. According to the CPL, the suspect or the accused and their legal representative, or defender,

[5] 'Organization of Public Security Police Station Regulations' 1954.

[6] Opinions of the Ministry of Public Security on reforming the work of urban police stations, 1988.

[7] People's Police Law of the People's Republic of China (2012 Amendment), Art 9 stipulates the police power for 'holding up the interrogated person' (留置盘查, *liuzhipancha*). The longest period for holding a suspect would be 48 hours.

[8] Chen Gang, 'Research on the Dislocation of Public Security Administrative Power and Investigation Power', 7 May 2015, www.spp.gov.cn.

have the right to apply for the alteration of coercive measures, but the review organs retain the decision-making authority.[9] This is a feature unique to China and different from other jurisdictions, as the pre-trial detention is not reviewed nor approved by a neutral judge, but by the procuratorate. This system follows the model of the former Soviet Union and Eastern Bloc socialist countries from when the first CPL was enacted in 1979. However, now, more than 40 years later, Russia and the Eastern European countries have made changes, and in those jurisdictions, arrest and pre-trial detentions are examined by judges. But in China, despite years of debate, the procuracy's system of approving pre-trial detention remains. Furthermore, the police conduct all of the investigative measures, such as search, seizure, and all other special, technical investigative measures. However, the police monitor and supervise these activities mainly through their internal mechanisms; this system is also different from other jurisdictions, where the use of intrusive investigative measures must be approved by an impartial judge. In Chinese practice, while warrants are required, these are not issued by the judge but either by the head of police or by a higher-level police force.

As for the relationship between the police and the procuratorate in criminal proceedings, it is mainly based on legal authorisation. Article 129 of the Constitution, Article 2 of the Organic Law of the Procuratorate, and Article 8 of the CPL all indicate that the procuratorate is the state organ for legal supervision. One of the crucial parts of this supervision is overseeing police investigations. The procuracy's model of supervising police investigations is unique. It differs from continental law jurisdictions, such as the German model where the prosecutor leads the criminal investigation, in law, and the police are 'auxiliary officers to the state prosecution office'.[10] The link between Chinese police and prosecutor is loose. The related Chinese laws provide four tasks for prosecutor supervision:

(1) the legality of registration of a criminal case
(2) pre-trial detention;
(3) prosecution; and
(4) the investigative activities.

The channels of supervision are mainly through examining pre-trial detention and prosecution.[11] In practice, the characteristics shown by the procuratorate's supervision have led to doubts about the effectiveness of such supervision. First, that supervision is ex post facto. In the review of pre-trial detention, when the criminal suspect or his/her attorney has filed a complaint about possible illegal arrest, the criminal suspect may have been in custody for 30 days or longer.[12] Second, the

[9] Art 97 of the CPL.
[10] Art 152 GVG (German Court Organic Act).
[11] Art 2 'SPP Rules', effective on 30 December 2019.
[12] According to Art 91 of the CPL, normally the police should submit their applications for pre-trial detention to the procuratorate within three days. Only when the suspects commit crimes across multiple regions, commit multiple crimes, or in cases of gang crimes, may the time for submitting for review

scope of supervision of the police investigation by the procuratorate is narrow. It is limited to examining whether the applications for pre-trial detention and prosecution made by the police are lawful. The supervision of the legality of investigative measures, such as search, seizure and other intrusive measures that may violate individual rights, are absent from the category of supervision; this may well be one of the main reasons why prosecutors cannot promptly detect or correct police illegal activities. Third, the supervision methods lack efficiency. When the prosecutor discovers illegal investigative activities, it issues a notice of violation to the investigation agency. The investigation agency has responsibility for reporting the corrected violations to the procuratorate. On the one hand, even if the police do report corrections, it is difficult for the prosecutor to verify such corrections. On the other hand, if the police do not report corrections, the prosecutor has no effective sanctions. Therefore, in practice, the number of corrections is small and the process is inefficient.[13]

B. Other Investigative Authorities

Another investigative authority is a special police force called 'State Security Organs' (SSO). The SSO was created in June 1983, based on the decision of the Standing Committee of the NPC on the National Security Agency's decision to exercise PSOs' power to investigate, arrest, interrogate and execute pre-trial detention. The structure of the SSO is different from the PSO as it comprises of only two levels: on the top is the Ministry of State Security and the sub-bureaux exist only in each province, autonomous region, and municipality directly under the central government. In total, there are 23 sub-bureaux. Under the provisions of Article 4 of the CPL, the National Security Organs have the power to investigate cases that endanger national security,[14] and may exercise the same powers as PSOs.

Since the National Supervision Commission (NSC) was established in March 2018, prosecutors' investigative power has been reduced. Prior to this, prosecutors investigated most crimes involving government-affiliated individuals, particularly corruption and malfeasance, but since the CPL amendment in 2018, prosecutors' investigative authority into the crimes of embezzlement and bribery has been removed, but the authority to investigate crimes of malfeasance committed by government-affiliated individuals, has remained.[15] The other

for approval of pre-trial detention be extended to 30 days. However, in practice, the latter duration would be used by the police for normal cases.

[13] Liu Jihua, 'Chinese Model of the Investigative Supervision System and Its Reform' (2014) 1 *China Law* 243.

[14] In Chinese criminal law, 12 offences are related to the 'endangering of national security'.

[15] Art 19 of the CPL, 'People's procuratorates may open a case and investigate when people's procuratorates carrying out legal oversight of procedural activities that discover crimes by judicial personnel that violate citizens' rights or harm judicial fairness, such as unlawful confinement, extortion of confessions by torture, or unlawful searches. When it is necessary for a people's procuratorate to directly accept a case in which state personnel exploited their office and powers to commit major crimes that

agencies' investigative authority is stipulated in the last, supplementary provision of the CPL.[16]

With regard to the criminal investigation of military personnel's crimes, this mainly belongs to the military. All crimes committed by soldiers and those persons working in the military force are investigated by the security departments of the military at all levels. Following the promulgation of the amended CPL in 2018, the General Political Department of the People's Liberation Army published its 'Interim Provisions on Several Issues Concerning the Implementation of the Criminal Procedure Law by the Army'.[17] This document specifies the level of investigative jurisdiction, which is mainly based on the rank of the officer. In the field of military and legal sciences, the issue of the implementation of the criminal procedure law by the military has been discussed for several years, but so far, the relevant laws are still absent. The proceedings for handling military criminal cases still have a military administrative nature, and there is no distinction between the procedures for 'wartime' or 'peaceful' periods.[18] Reform is, therefore, still required.

Article 308 of the 2018 CPL granted the power of maritime law enforcement to the Chinese Coast Guard.[19] On 20 February 2020, the SPC, the SPP and the China Coast Guard jointly issued a Notice concerning the jurisdiction of maritime criminal cases. The 'jurisdiction' here refers to the courts' trial jurisdiction, however, in the tradition of China's criminal justice system, the jurisdiction of investigation should accord with the jurisdiction of the courts' trial. The basic principle is that crimes committed in internal and territorial waters are in the jurisdiction of the site of a crime or where the defendant landed. If a foreigner commits a crime against the PRC or a Chinese citizen in the sea areas beyond the territorial waters of the PRC, they shall be punished by the courts at the place where such foreigner lands or where they entered the territory of China. The China Coast Guard shall obey these jurisdiction rules.

For crimes committed by prisoners, the police of the prison are responsible for investigation. This jurisdiction only applies to persons sentenced to imprisonment or pre-trial detention. Crimes committed by prison staff do not come under the jurisdiction of the prison, but will be investigated by the ordinary police or by the procuratorate, depending on the nature of the crime. Because the legal provisions are relatively loosely drafted, obstacles are encountered in practice, especially when a prisoner and a person outside of the prison jointly commit a crime. Here, the coordination in the investigation procedure is more difficult, and the

are in the jurisdiction of the public security organs, the people's procuratorate may file and investigate the case upon a decision of a people's procuratorate at the provincial level or above'.

[16] Art 308 of the CPL: military security departments have the power to conduct investigations of criminal cases occurring within the military. The coast guard has the authority to investigate crimes occurring at sea in performing its maritime protection and law enforcement duties. Prisons conduct investigations of crimes committed by convicts within the prisons. Relevant provisions of this law apply when the security departments of the military, the coast guard, and prisons handle criminal cases.

[17] 8 March 2020.

[18] Qin Fu, 'On the Military and Legal Nature of the Power of Criminal Investigation' (2017) 2 *Journal of Xi'an University of Political Science* 80.

[19] The China Coast Guard has been under the leadership of the People's Armed Police since 1 July 2018.

law and related codes of practice do not specify how to operate the investigative measures, such as search, seizure, etc. Therefore, although the number of cases in this part is small, there is still a need for reform.[20]

C. The Role of the Supervision Commission

In March 2018, the NPC adopted the Supervision Law (SL), and then the Supervisory Commission was established, which is completely unique. In the 'State Organ' section of Chapter 3 of the amended Constitution, an additional section was added: the 'Supervisory Commission', in juxtaposition with the state administrative, legislative, judicial and procuratorial organs. Subsequent legal interpretations emphasised that 'it is a specialised agency that exercises the national supervisory function'.[21] Subsequently, the propaganda agency of the Communist Party further explained the supervisory commission, and clarified that it is 'a political organ, not an administrative organ, nor a judicial organ'.[22]

The adoption and implementation of the SL is also one of the reasons for the amendment of the CPL in 2018. Before the adoption of the SL, corruption-related crimes involving state personnel were directly investigated by the procuratorates. However, after the SL was adopted, the investigative power for such crimes was transferred to the Supervision Commission.[23] Where the Commission considers that a crime has been committed, they may transfer the evidence and the conclusion of the investigation to the procuratorates for review in order to decide whether to prosecute. The investigative powers and measures of the Supervisory Commission were controversial both before and after the adoption of the SL. Although the word used in the SL in English is 'investigation', it is different in Chinese (调查, *diaocha*), as an 'investigation' in criminal proceedings is referred to as *zhencha* (侦查). However, both terms and the legal effects are the same as for investigative measures in criminal proceedings. According to the SL, supervisory organs could conduct the interrogation,[24] question witnesses,[25] conduct search and seizure operations, and also impound property, documents and electronic data etc.[26] The most controversial measure is the power of detention. which is provided for in Article 22. The term used for detention (留置, *liuzhi*) in the SL is different from the terms for arrest and pre-trial detention (拘留, *juliu*; 逮捕, *daibu*) in the CPL, but this makes no difference to their nature, as the measure deprives suspects

[20] Beijing Prison Administration, 'The legislation on the power of investigation in prisons needs to be improved', www.criminal law.com, 21 June 2020.

[21] 'Interpretation of the Supervision Law of the People's Republic of China' (China Founder Publishing House).

[22] 'Details on the Nature and Responsibilities of the Supervisory Commission' (2018) *Seeking Truth*.

[23] Art 11(2) of the SL.

[24] Art 20 of the SL.

[25] Art 21 of the SL.

[26] Art 25 of the SL.

of their liberty. However, the difference is that the maximum duration of supervisory detention could be six months, and is decided by the leaders of supervisory organs without any external oversight.[27] This raises additional concerns about the protection of suspects' rights. The investigatory process of supervisory organs is different from that in a formal criminal investigation, which could involve a defence lawyer. During supervisory investigation there is no form of involvement for defence lawyers, as the whole investigation process is closed. Furthermore, for criminal suspects the place of detention is fixed by the CPL, whilst for supervisory detention the law does not indicate the exact place in practice. Therefore, some investigated persons are detained in former detention places established for holding the suspects of disciplinary violations of Communist Party (CP) rules, which fall into a special regime of disciplinary investigations.[28]

II. Procuratorate and Prosecutor in Criminal Justice

A. The Nature of Prosecution Authorities

China's prosecution system is a unique one. From a historical perspective, it was originally transplanted from the former Soviet Union. Whilst the author and other academics classify the Chinese legal system as a civil law tradition, especially as the model of criminal proceedings refers to an inquisitorial system, the prosecution authorities differ from those in some civil law jurisdictions. The prosecution authority in civil law jurisdictions has been described as a 'judicial organ', or as having judicial features.[29] However, it is the author's understanding that prosecution authorities are referred to as 'judicial organs' either because both prosecutors and judges are under the same requirement to have legal education or, as in the German tradition, because the official name of prosecutor's office has been

[27] Art 43 of the SL.

[28] The predecessor of the Supervisory Commission was the disciplinary and inspection agency of the Communist Party of China. At that time, according to the party's charter, party members suspected of duty crimes had to undergo internal party investigations before they were formally investigated by the prosecutor's office. In order to prevent party members suspected of duty crimes from evading investigations, destroying evidence, colluding or fleeing, the party documents set up measures to restrict personal liberty, called 'double regulations' and the person under investigation was usually detained in the discipline inspection and supervision training centre. Due to the promulgation and implementation of the Supervision Law, the institutions and functions of disciplinary inspection and supervision have been replaced by the Supervisory Commission, so at present, most people under the supervision commission's investigation are detained in the previous disciplinary inspection and supervision detention places. See Huang Yuanyuan and Wu Yihui, 'Discussion on the Setting of Supervision Detention Sites, (2020) 5 *Legal System Expo*, se m.fx361.com; see also Chen Ruihua, 'On the Nature of the State's Prosecutorial Power' (2019) 1 *Comparative Law Studies* 1.

[29] Richard Vogler and Barbara Huber (eds), *Criminal Procedure in Europe* (Berlin, Duncker & Humboldt, 2008). In the chapter on France, it was indicated that 'the office of prosecutor is a judicial one': 229. In the chapter on Germany, it was described thus: 'This office (prosecution authorities) is a judicial authority': 326.

attached to the courts. However, these features are not vital characteristics of prosecution authorities. The fact is that most prosecution authorities are not neutral and impartial legal organs: they have inextricable links with governmental organisations such as ministries of justice and therefore they should not be described as 'judicial organs'.

Under China's Constitution,[30] details on the prosecution authority and courts are set out in Chapter 3, 'The Structure of State', Section 8: People's Courts and People's Procuratorates. The procuratorates' role is set out in the Constitution as 'organs for legal oversight of the State'.[31] Related laws, such as the Organic Law of the People's Procuratorate of the PRC and the CPL, do not define the procuratorates as 'judicial organs'. They are not affiliated with the courts, but one similar feature of the procuratorates and the courts is their independence. The procuratorate has no close link with the Ministry of Justice (MoJ), even though the State Examination of Law is organised by the MoJ and all judges, prosecutors and lawyers take the same examination to qualify in the legal profession. However, it is unusual that judges rotate into the positions of prosecutors and vice versa, as for example German judges and prosecutors do within their first years of service in the criminal justice system.

B. The Organisation and the Roles of the Procuratorate

The prosecution system in China is centralised. According to the Organic Law of Procuratorate,[32] procuratorates have been set up at four levels, corresponding with the levels of state administration and courts. The highest level is SPP, then there are lower level and special procuratorates. The SPP is located in the capital, Beijing. The second level is at the provincial level. Procuratorates are set up in every province, autonomous region and municipality; there are 33 procuratorates at this level.[33] The third level is below the provincial level, where prosecutors are located in major cities; there are 398 at this level.[34] The fourth and lowest level are in relatively smaller cities, counties and municipal districts; there are 3,214 procuratorates at this level.[35] The special procuratorates, such as the military prosecutor offices, have been included in the numbers given above, but military procuratorates have only three levels.

In 2019, the SPP carried out an unprecedented internal working bodies reform. The background to the reform was the establishment of the Supervisory Committee in 2018, which transferred to the Supervisory Committee the procuratorates' power

[30] Art 134 of the revised Constitution on 11 March 2018.
[31] ibid.
[32] Arts 12–15 of the OLP, 2018.
[33] *Law Yearbook of China, 2019*, p 1332 (data was collected until December 2018).
[34] *Law Yearbook of China, 2019*, p 1332 (data was collected until December 2018).
[35] *Law Yearbook of China, 2018*, p 1186 (data was collected until December 2017).

to investigate cases of corruption. Prior to this reform, the SPP had established internal departments that echoed the stage of criminal proceedings, which were divided into: investigation, review and approval of pre-trial detention; prosecution; supervision by prisons; and anti-corruption. In January 2019, the SPP changed its rules for organising the internal working bodies, and divided them according to the subject areas of supervision, such as criminal, civil and administrative. With regard to criminal justice, they reorganised the departments according to the types of crime. The SPP has seven departments now:

- the department for ordinary criminal cases;
- the department for major crime cases;
- the department for the duty civil servants' duty-related crime cases;
- the department for economic crime cases;
- the department for supervision of the execution of penalties;
- the department for cases of delinquency crimes; and
- the department for review of the application of the special appeal for the cases whose judgments have become final.

Meanwhile, the SPP announced a new internal working procedure, called 'combining pre-trial detention with prosecution' (捕诉合一). Prior to the reform, each criminal case would go through at least two departments: one was responsible for approving the pre-trial detention, whilst another was responsible for prosecution.

This reform has caused great controversy in academia. Prior to the reform, several scholars including the author advocated for transferring the power of review and approval of pre-trial detention from the procuratorate to a neutral judge.[36] The purpose of this would be to strengthen the legality of pre-trial detention and to better protect human rights. Unfortunately, the internal structure of the reform is mainly divided according to the severity and characteristics of the case. Thus, whilst the efficiency of handling cases may have been strengthened, internal supervision may have been further weakened, which may lead to a reduction in protection of the rights of the accused.[37] At present, the SPP has only published details of its internal working bodies. Other subordinate procuratorates at the lower levels have not yet published their internal organisation plans.

The relationship between the SPP and lower level procuratorates means that the superior leads the subordinates. This is different from the court system, in which the courts at a higher level supervise lower level courts through the appellate procedure.

Besides the working bodies, internally, at all levels each prosecutor's office is headed by a general prosecutor and several deputy prosecutors. The general

[36] Yue Liling, *United Nations International Covenant on Civil and Political Rights and Criminal Justice in China* (Beijing, Law Press, 2008).

[37] Xie Xiaojian, 'Query on the Procuratorate's Reform of "Combining the Pre-trial Detention with Prosecution"', 7 July 2020, www.iolaw.org.cn.

prosecutor is the leading person in a prosecutor's office. According to the provisions of the OLP, the general prosecutor leads the prosecutor's office and has the decision-making power in most matters,[38] except where the law provides that matters must be decided by the prosecutorial committee. Each procuratorate must establish a prosecutorial committee. The committee is composed of the chief prosecutor, deputy chief prosecutor, and some senior prosecutors. The committee deliberates on major cases and other major issues.

According to the laws on the OLP, the CPL, and other related provisions, the procuratorates' key role is to supervise the implementation of the law. The detailed roles of procuratorate in criminal proceedings can be summarised as follows:

(1) Exercise the power of prosecution. This is the most important role played by the procuratorates in criminal proceedings. Except for a few cases that can be prosecuted by individuals (private prosecution), the decision to prosecute or dismiss the majority of criminal cases must be decided by prosecutors. In 2020, in total, procuratorates prosecuted 1,572,971 persons, of which 57,000 were investigated for serious violent crimes; 142,000 were cyber crimes; 350,000 property crimes; 54,000 related to mafia and organised crime (since 2018); 41,000 financial fraud and disrupting the financial management order;[39] 12,000 infringing upon intellectual property; 15,346 duty-related crimes and corruption; and 51,000 environment-related crimes and others.[40] If the case is to be prosecuted, the prosecutor should attend the trial in support of the public prosecution. No other institutions have the power to prosecute criminal cases in China.

(2) Investigate selected crimes committed by state personnel. According to the revised 2018 CPL and the SL, only the procuratorates are responsible for investigating crimes committed by civil servants who work in the legal field and which violate citizens' rights or harm judicial fairness when they carry out legal oversight of procedural activities.[41] For crimes committed by other civil servants, which in principle are in the jurisdiction of a police investigation, it sometimes necessary for the prosecutor directly to investigate these cases as in practice the police or the head of the police may be involved in mafia-related crimes. The law is flexible in this respect, but requires that investigation of these special cases be approved by the provincial level procuratorate or above.

(3) Review the cases investigated by normal police and special police (state security) to decide whether a suspect should be under pre-trial detention and

[38] Art 29 of the OLP.

[39] The crime of disrupting the financial management order is a class of crimes in section 4 of the Criminal Law Chapter 3 (destroying the order of the socialist market economy), ranging from Art 170 to Art 191. There are about 24 crimes, such as: financial fraud, market manipulation, insider trading, money laundering, etc.

[40] China's SPP's annual work report, delivered 8 March 2021 at a plenary meeting of the fourth session of the 13th NPC in Beijing.

[41] Art 19 of the CPL.

subsequent prosecution and supervise the legality of investigative activities. In 2020, 770,561 suspects had been approved for pre-trial detention.[42]

(4) Supervise judicial activities undertaken by courts in handling criminal cases. Implement legal supervision over the enforcement of judgments, rulings, and other effective legal documents. The power of the procuratorate to supervise court trial activities in criminal proceedings and the relationship between the procuratorate and the court are highly controversial in academia. Some scholars believe that, despite this power of supervision having its basis in the Constitution and other laws, those laws do not indicate precisely the path and specific measures of supervision.[43] In theory, scholars believe that the procuratorate's supervision of the court activities should be mainly exercised through the appellate procedure, for example when a first instance court makes a judgment, if the prosecutor thinks that the judgment contains an error, they can file a counter-appeal (抗诉 *kangsu*).[44] Even after the judgment becomes final, the procuratorate can still make a special appeal if they allege that there is an error in the original judgment. In this appeal procedure, the prosecutor plays the dual role of both the party and the supervisor. It seems that the procuratorate's power to place the procuratorate above the court means that the finality of the court judgment is impaired, and the defendant's right to avoid double jeopardy is also challenged.

(5) Implement legal supervision over law enforcement activities in prisons and detention houses. In 2020, the procuratorates in total corrected 51,000 improper executions of commutation, parole and temporary placement outside prison.[45] This supervision power has been recognised by scholars as non-procedural. In other jurisdictions the prosecutor plays a similar role.

C. Qualifications of Prosecutors

According to the PPL as amended in 2019, in addition to the requirements of nationality, political attitude, and health conditions, the educational conditions for appointment as a prosecutor are as follows:

> Having a bachelor's degree or above in law from a regular institution of higher education, or a bachelor's degree or above not in law from a regular institute of higher education with any other corresponding degree and with professional knowledge of the law.[46]

[42] China's SPP's annual work report which was delivered 8 March 2021 at a plenary meeting of the fourth session of the 13th NPC in Beijing.

[43] Huang Queying, 'On the power allocation relationship between the court and the procuratorate' (2015) 3 *Journal of Fuzhou University (philosophy and Social Sciences)*.

[44] A counter-appeal is similar to an appeal, but in the Chinese language is different from an ordinary appeal, as it means an appeal only from the prosecutor side. This issue is discussed in more detail in Ch 9 on remedies.

[45] China's SPP's annual work report which was delivered 8 March 2021 at a plenary meeting of the fourth session of the 13th NPC in Beijing.

[46] Art 12(5) of the PPL.

In addition, the PPL requires that: 'Persons to be appointed as public procurators for the first time shall have passed the national uniform legal profession qualification examination and obtained the legal profession qualification'.[47] As far as the author knows, if a person who has obtained legal professional qualifications applies for a position as a prosecutor, he/she must also pass written and oral examinations organised by the procuratorate.

As the author indicated at the beginning of this chapter, based on OLP, it is the procuratorates – not the individual prosecutor – that exercise independent prosecutorial power.[48] Therefore, in accordance with the rules of working procedure, except for the general prosecutor, prosecutors may only put forward their views to be determined by the general prosecutor after approval by the head in charge of a department. The general prosecutor and the prosecutorial committee may or may not accept the views put forth by a prosecutor and may make their own decisions. The heads of department cannot change the opinion of prosecutors but may raise their own opinion and report to the general prosecutor for a decision. These kinds of work relationships create problems in practice. For example, if there is an error in a case, it would be difficult to pin down who would be responsible for any wrong decisions. To rectify this, prosecutors and judges at all levels have proposed a reform, known as the 'personnel quota system' (员额制, *yuan e zhi*), in which the prosecutorial responsibility lays with the prosecutor in charge of the prosecution.

III. Courts and Judges

China's judicial power is exercised by courts and judges. The operation of the judiciary is based mainly on the Organic Law of the People's Court (OLC) and the Judges Law (JL). The OLC was originally adopted on 1 July 1979 (effective from 1 January 1980). Since then, it has been amended four times, in 1983, 1986, 2006 and 2018. The law provides for the setup and authority of courts; composition of the trial bench; composition of court personnel; and safeguards for the courts' exercise of authority. The JL was originally adopted in 1995 and was amended in April 2019. It has six chapters, and provides for: the judges' duties; qualification and selection of judges; appointment and dismissal of judges; management of judges; evaluation, reward, and punishment of judges; and the professional safeguards which judges must comply with. In 2020, the whole court system handled 1,116,000 first instance criminal cases and sentenced 1,527,000 offenders.[49]

[47] Art 12(7) of the PPL.

[48] Art 4 of the OLP.

[49] China's SPC's annual work report which was delivered on 8 March 2021 at a plenary meeting of the fourth session of the 13th NPC in Beijing.

A. Court Structure and Jurisdiction

China's court system differs from those in other jurisdictions. It is not categorised according to the title of substantive law, as it is in Germany, for example, where the ordinary courts handle the criminal and civil cases. It also differs from continental law jurisdictions, such as France, where the criminal court is categorised according to the offence.[50] China's ordinary courts, from the basic level to the SPC, handle all categories of case. The jurisdiction of criminal cases is determined by the length of the probable sentence. The courts are divided into four levels, which correspond to the structure of the procuratorates, and every level of court deals with criminal, civil, and administrative cases.

The local courts are known as basic courts (基层法院 *ji ceng fa yuan*), and are the lowest level trial courts, located in the districts of cities or in the counties of provinces. According to the CPL and the OLC, these courts deal with most of the ordinary criminal cases, except for cases in which higher courts have jurisdiction.[51] However, the jurisdiction of the basic courts is far removed from those in other jurisdictions. It should not be assumed that they handle only minor criminal offences: they will generally deal with cases that can be punished with anything up to life imprisonment. In 2018, the courts sentenced 1,430,091 convicted persons.[52] The OLC states that criminal cases can be heard by what is referred to as a 'collegial panel' or by a single judge.[53] The collegial panel can be composed of judges, or a combination of judges and people's assessors. For first instance cases at the basic or intermediate courts, the total number of adjudicators in the panel will be three or seven, and the maximum number of professional judges to serve on a panel is three. This means that a collegial panel could be composed of three judges plus four people's assessors.[54] Only cases in which the courts apply for a summary trial procedure or expedited procedure may be heard by a single judge.[55] The CPL also requires that, for those cases where the estimated punishment might exceed three years' imprisonment, a collegial panel should be formed for trial.[56] For those cases that have major social impact, and a fixed-term imprisonment of not less than ten years, life imprisonment or the death penalty, the trial must be handled by a collegial panel with seven members.[57]

[50] Richard Vogler and Barbara Huber (eds), *Criminal Procedure in Europe* (Berlin, Dunker & Humblot, 2008).

[51] Art 20 of the CPL.

[52] *Law Yearbook of China* (Beijing, Law Yearbook of China, 2019).

[53] Art 29 of the OLC.

[54] Art 14 of the Law of People's Assessor.

[55] Art 30 of the OLC; Art 183 of the CPL.

[56] Art 216(1) of the CPL.

[57] Art 16(1) of People's Assessor's Law 2018.

The second level of court is the intermediate court, which are set up in four types of location:

(1) municipalities directly under the jurisdiction of provinces or autonomous regions;
(2) municipalities directly under the central government;
(3) autonomous prefectures; and
(4) regions in provinces or autonomous regions.

The CPL lists detailed conditions of jurisdiction only for the intermediate court as a first instance trial court, while the jurisdiction of courts of other levels are described in general terms. The intermediate courts shall handle cases with offences of endangering national security or involving terrorist activities; ordinary cases in which the accused may be sentenced by life imprisonment or death.

As mentioned above, cases at first instance are heard by a collegial panel, which is formed of three judges and four people's assessors. However, when intermediate courts handle appeal cases from the basic courts, the collegial panel is composed of three to five judges.[58] According to the OLC, besides the above mentioned first instance trial cases as prescribed explicitly by law, intermediate courts can also handle other first instance cases where requests for trial are submitted by a lower level of basic court. These include first instance cases where the jurisdiction is designated by the courts at a higher level and appellate cases judged and ruled by the basic courts. The intermediate courts can also re-open criminal proceedings for cases filed by the trial supervision procedures.[59]

The third level is the higher courts. These are set up in provinces, autonomous regions and municipalities directly under the central government, and have first instance jurisdiction over criminal cases that are prominent and affect an entire province or region. Besides these kinds of first instance cases, the higher courts can also handle first instance cases for which requests for trial are submitted by lower-level courts, first instance cases for which the jurisdiction is designated by the SPC, and appellate cases judged and ruled on by the intermediate courts. The higher courts can also reopen criminal proceeding cases filed by the trial supervision procedure; and death penalty cases for which requests are submitted by the intermediate courts for approval.[60] There are 33 higher courts in China. The collegial panel at this level may consist of three to seven professional judges or a combination panel of judges and people's assessors and three or seven adjudicators.[61]

The highest level of court is the SPC, which is located in Beijing. The SPC has sole jurisdiction as the court of first instance for prominent cases that have a major impact on the whole country. Since 1979, when the CPL was enacted, the SPC

[58] Art 183 of the CPL 2018.
[59] Art 22 of the OLC 2018.
[60] Art 20 of the OLC 2018.
[61] Art 183(2) of the CPL 2018.

has only heard one first instance case, the 'Gang of Four' case.[62] However, where the SPC hears a first instance prominent case, there is no provision to provide convicted and sentenced persons with the right of appeal. This is a contentious and debated point amongst academics. Some think that this provision violates the international human rights standards established by the international community. ICCPR Article 14(5) and other regional human rights instruments provide similar principles, ie everyone convicted of a crime shall have the right to have their conviction and sentence be reviewed by a higher tribunal according to the law.

In addition to such first instance trial cases, under the law the SPC has authority to handle appellate cases judged and ruled on by the higher courts, and special appellate cases filed by the provisions of the Standing Committee of the NPC. It also has the power to re-open criminal proceeding cases filed in accordance with the trial supervision procedures, and death penalty cases for which requests are submitted by the higher courts for approval.[63]

B. The Adjudication Committee

Every court in China has an internal institution called the 'adjudication committee'. It is not a trial body that hears cases directly nor publicly, but it can determine the outcome of certain cases. According to the current OLC, adjudication committees are mainly composed of the president of the court, the vice president and several senior judges. Although the number of members may vary at different court levels, there should always be an odd number of members. This is because when voting on the final judgment, the rules of a simple majority shall be followed.

The function and powers of the adjudication committees have been some of the most controversial topics among legal academics and judges in recent decades. The 2019 revision of the OLC details four functions:

(1) summing up the experience gained through the trial process;
(2) deliberating and deciding on the application of laws in major, difficult and complex cases;
(3) deliberating and deciding whether the judgments, rulings and mediation documents of the court that have been made should be re-tried;
(4) discussion and deciding on other major issues relevant to the trial.

[62] For more detail see A Cook, 'China's Gang of Four Trial: The Law v The Laws of History' in J Meierhenrich and D Pendas (eds), *Political Trials in Theory and History* (Cambridge, Cambridge University Press, 2017) 263. The case had four defendants, Jiang Qing (Mao Zedong's last wife), Zhang Chunqiao, Yao Wenyuan and Wang Hongwen. They were former leaders of the government during the Cultural Revolution. They were arrested on 6 October 1976, and charged with a series of crimes. The trial was commenced on 20 November 1980, handled by the 'Special Court' of the SPC. The sentences were announced on 25 January 1981.

[63] Arts 16–17 of the OLC 2018.

Among the above-listed functions, (2) is the core function. It may be noted that the 2019 revision of the OLC narrowed the scope of cases discussed by the adjudication committee and limited the scope of 'application of the law' to major, difficult, and complex cases. Before the revision, the adjudication committee could also discuss the fact-finding issues of these cases. However, following the revision of the law, some legal scholars are concerned that in practice, there will still be some cases where issues relating to the application of law and fact-finding issues become entangled and cannot be completely separated.[64] In addition to this, there are further concerns that the range of 'major, difficult, and complex cases' is still too wide and vague, resulting in the workload of the adjudicating committee, at every level of court, becoming too heavy. Shortly after the amended OLC came into force in 2019, the SPC promulgated its 'Opinions of the SPC on Improving the Work Mechanism of the Adjudication Committee of the Courts' (the 2019 Opinions). In the 2019 Opinions, the SPC refined the range of cases. It also divided the cases discussed by the adjudication committee into two groups: one is 'shall' and another is 'may'. The following cases 'shall' be submitted to the adjudication committee for discussion:

(1) sensitive cases involving national security, foreign affairs or social stability;
(2) cases requiring retrial, as there are errors in the effective judgments, rulings, decisions and mediations of the court;
(3) criminal cases for which the procuratorate at the same level files appeals under the trial supervision procedures;
(4) new tapes of cases without clear rules for the application of laws;
(5) cases in which a defendant is to be acquitted;
(6) cases in which a defendant is to be given a criminal penalty below the statutory penalty or exempted from criminal punishment;
(7) cases in which the convict is to be sentenced to the death penalty by a higher court or an intermediate court.

The following cases 'may' be submitted to the adjudication committee for discussion:

(1) cases for which the collegial panel has substantially dissenting opinions on the application of laws and it is difficult to decide the deliberation at the meeting of professional (presiding) judges;
(2) cases in which a judgment to be rendered may conflict with similar judgments of the court or its superior court;
(3) cases ordered or remanded for retrial.

How the adjudication committee operates is complicated and controversial. Prior to the 2019 amendment to the OLC, members of the adjudication committee had to attend the 'plenary' meeting. However, such members had professional

[64] The Procedural Law Research Institute, 'Consensus and Disagreement: About the Reform of the Adjudication Committee', 15 May 2015, www.procedurallaw.cn.

expertise in the daily division of the court, and there was difficultly in making accurate professional judgments in all cases. In practice, therefore, some members who attended the adjudication committee meetings could not give their professional judgments, but simply had to follow professional judges' opinions. After the 2019 OLC revision, a professional committee was added,[65] and the work process of the adjudication committee for discussing cases was also revised. If the collegiate panel or the single judge still disagrees with the professional committee's opinions after the professional committee's discussion, the adjudication committee can submit the case to the adjudication committee's plenary meeting for discussion.

The most controversial part of the judicial committee's operating mechanism is to do with the validity of decisions made by the adjudication committee. According to OLC, decisions of the adjudication committee shall be implemented by the collegiate panel.[66] For many years, legal scholars and law practitioners have criticised this mechanism for discussing related cases, which means that the collegiate panel or the single judge who directly hears the case has no right to make the final judgment. Rather, it is done by the adjudication committee, which does not directly participate in the case hearing. Although the OLC states that 'the decision of the adjudication committee in the discussion of the case and its reasons shall be disclosed in the written judgment', the final judgment still has to be signed by the trial judge. Some legal scholars believe that the judicial committee's trial mechanism is contrary to the principle of directness and oral presentation in court trials. It replaces court trials with step-by-step reports of administrative work and meetings and discussions. These scholars suggest that, in the future, the grand collegiate should replace the adjudication committee and hear the cases directly.[67]

Another controversial issue in the operation mechanism of the adjudication committee is that the chief prosecutor at the same level may participate in the discussion of individual cases as a non-voting delegate, and has status in the adjudication committee as a trial supervisor. However, the discussion of the adjudication committee is part of the trial procedure, and according to the principle of procedural structure, it should be conducted in public with the presence of all three parties, including the prosecution and the defence. The presence of the prosecutor conflates their prosecution and supervisory functions without the participation of defence lawyers. This situation violates the general rules of procedural structure and can only be resolved by the aforementioned grand chamber trial.

C. The Guiding Case System

In addition to handling cases, the OLC provides authority for the SPC to interpret 'the issues on the specific application of the law in the trial work. The SPC may

[65] Art 38 of the OLC.
[66] Art 39 of the OLC.
[67] The Procedural Law Research Institute, 'Consensus and Disagreement: About the Reform of the Adjudication Committee', 15 May 2015, www.procedurallaw.cn.

issue guiding cases', ie model cases to act as a blueprint or template for future real cases.[68] First, there is a terminology issue: during the past three decades or more, the SPC has carried out several judicial reforms which relate to 'guiding cases'. They are referred to as 'China's case guidance system', 'typical cases' and 'China's guiding case system'.[69] Currently, the SPC is implementing the Guiding Case System. This was begun in 2011, with the SPC's document the 'Provisions of the SPC Concerning Work on Guiding Cases' (Provisions on Guiding Cases) and its subsequent 'Notice of the SPC on Issuing the Rules of the Provisions Concerning Work on Guiding Cases in 2015' (the Rules).

In the Provisions on Guiding Cases, the SPC described the purpose of establishing the Guiding Case System as: 'summarizing adjudication experience, unifying the application of the law, and enhancing adjudication quality'. Before the Rules were released, the Central Committee of the Communist Party of China (CCCP) set out their goal as being to 'strengthen and standardize [the system] of judicial interpretations and case guidance, and unify the standards for the application of the law'.[70] A number of academics and legal practitioners agreement that such a system was necessary. It was noted that, in practice, the phenomena of 'same case but different adjudication and the same law but different interpretations' occur frequently, which means that parties can never be sure what their expectations are from adjudication, which in turn negatively impacts judicial credibility.[71]

In 2018, the leading researcher of the China Guiding Cases Project at Stanford Law School released an analysis of criminal guiding cases,[72] in which they listed 16 criminal cases, among a total of 96 guiding cases. The core issue of the Guiding Case System is legal effect. According to Article 7 of the Provisions on Guiding Cases, courts adjudicating subsequent cases similar to guiding cases 'shall refer to' guiding cases. The problem here is that the 2011 Provisions on Guiding Cases do not explain how judges are to determine whether a case is similar to a guiding case. The explanation in the 2015 Rules went further. Article 9 of the Rules provides that where a case being adjudicated is, in terms of the basic facts and application of law, similar to a guiding case released by the SPC, court at all levels should refer to the 'main points of the adjudication' of that relevant guiding case.[73] Thus, the 'basic facts' and 'application of the law' are crucial parts of the guiding case. The researchers of the Stanford Project evaluated the statistics and concluded that the two parts, 'basic facts' and 'reasons of adjudication' in criminal guiding cases

[68] Art 18 of the OLC 2019.

[69] Fenping Guo, 'China's Guiding Cases System as the Instrument to Improve China's Case Guidance System, Which Includes Both Guiding Cases and Typical Cases' (2017) 45(3) *International Journal of Legal Information* 230.

[70] Decision of the CCCP Central Committee on Several Major Issues Concerning the Comprehensive Promotion of the Rule of Law, passed at the Fourth Plenary Session of the 18th Central Committee of the Communist Party of China on 23 October 2014, http://www.gov.cn.

[71] Wang Lifeng, 'The Necessity and Function of China's Guiding Cases System', 15 October 2013, https://cgc.law.stanford.edu/commentaries/9.

[72] Mei Gechlik and Jennifer Ingram (2018) *Stanford Law School China Guiding Cases Project* Issue No 8.

[73] ibid.

are shorter than other guiding cases. The researchers suggested that China's courts and judges should improve further on explaining the reasons for their decisions.[74]

When the Guiding Case System was first launched it attracted widespread attention from legal scholars of both common law and civil law traditions, but especially from common law scholars who considered that the Guiding Case System has similarities with the precedent case law system. However, after observing the last nine years of judicial practice of Chinese judges and courts, most legal scholars generally believe that the Guiding Case System is essentially different from precedents in the common law traditional. This is for two main reasons: first, a guiding case is fundamentally different from a common law precedent. Technically, the guiding case is not an original judge-made 'real case': it has been edited by the judges in the SPC, and through complicated selection proceedings.[75] Second, the legal effects are different. Precedents in the common law tradition are an independent source of law and have direct binding legal effect. But the edited guiding case is not an independent source of law – it can only be referred to in part of the reasoning in rulings and judgments. Finally, the main purposes behind the establishment of the Guiding Case System, as previously described, were to promote consistency and a uniform application of laws. This is obviously not the case with common law precedents.

D. Judge

The qualifications, selection mechanism and professional security of judges in China are regulated by the JL. This law was originally created in 1995 and has been revised three times, in 2001, 2007 and 2019. Of these, the 2001 revision is the most important, as it aimed to improve the quality of judges. The 2001 amendment increased the requirements for educational qualification from a college degree to a bachelor's degree and ended the lawyer qualification exams that had been implemented since 1986. Additionally, the qualification examinations for judges and prosecutors was also cancelled and replaced by the 'National Judicial Examination' (NJE). The NJE was first taken in March 2003 and has been implemented now for 18 years. The 2001 JL revision was the first time that a 'judges quota system' (员额制 *yuan e zhi*) had been established. This refers to fixing the number of judges at all levels of courts, according to factors such as the number of cases, economic and social development, population, and the trial level of the court.[76] The 2019 amendment of the JL made further improvements: it changed the term 'adjudicatory personnel' into 'judge', and created a separate administration of posts.[77] This distinguishes the administration sequence of judges from that

[74] Mei Gechlik and Jennifer Ingram (2018) *Stanford Law School China Guiding Cases Project* Issue No 8.

[75] Chen Luming and Gong Suni, 'A Short Review of the Case Guidance System of the Chinese Judiciary', 4 September 2019, https://www.asialaw.com.

[76] Art 25 of the JL 2019.

[77] Art 26 of the JL 2019.

of ordinary civil servants.[78] The implementation of the revised law and the judge quota system was not straightforward, as the leading judge of SPC has mentioned. Before the reform, there were 210,000 'adjudication personnel'; after the reform, there are 120,000 judges, which means that 90,000 judicial officers lost their positions as judges and could no longer adjudicate on cases. In the year to 30 June 2018, the courts received 12,295,000 cases, which is an average caseload of 99.2 cases per judge per year; it seems that judges handled cases more effectively and with better quality.[79]

E. The People's Assessor System

The 'people's assessor system' is a Chinese version of a 'lay assessor system'. The author believes that it is a legal term created by civil law scholars to distinguish this system from the 'jury system' in common law jurisdictions. As early as the legal reforms in the late Qing Dynasty, legislators were influenced by the English legal system and tried to establish a jury system, but the laws were ineffective and were not implemented. After the founding of the PRC in 1949, the people's assessor system was established, following the model of the former Soviet Union. This system was legalised in 1954, by the 1978 Constitution and the 1979 OLC. Before 2018, the rules for the participation of people's assessors in trials were stipulated in the OLC and the CPL. In 2004, the Standing Committee of the NPC issued the 'Decision on Improving the People's Assessor System' (Decision). The document has legal effect because it was made by the NPC. This Decision established the framework and basic principle of the people's assessor system until the promulgation and implementation of the 'People's Assessor Law' (PAL) in 2018.

The purpose of the people's assessor system was described in the PAL 2018 as being 'to safeguard citizens' participation in trial activities according to the law, promoting judicial justice, and improving judicial credibility'.[80] It should be noted that the Chinese legislators' version of the functions and roles of laymen in participating in the judicial system is not so different from that in other jurisdictions, despite the fact that other countries may have a jury system or a mixed court system. However, the issue has been a subject of debate for centuries,[81] and the author believes that other factors are critical in examining this issue, such as laymen's participation in the judicial decision-making process, the qualification of the assessors, selection rules, the process and the rules of voting in deliberation, and so on.

[78] Zhou Qiang, 'Explanation of the SPC on the Revised Draft of the Judge Law', 22 December 2017, www.npc.gov.cn.

[79] Li Liang, the director of the Adjudication Management Office, www.court.gov.cn.

[80] Art 1 of the PAL.

[81] Alexis de Tocqueville's observations in the mid-1800s about the educational and politicising role of a jury in the democratic ethos of American society. See Neil Vidmar (ed), *World Jury Systems* (New York, Oxford University Press, 2000).

The requirements to be fulfilled before a person can be a people's assessor have been provided in the PAL as:

(1) upholding the Constitution;
(2) having reached the age of 28;
(3) observing disciplines and laws, having good ethics and being impartial and upright; and
(4) being in a proper state of health to perform functions and duties normally.

The qualifying age was raised from 23 years old, as provided for in the 2004 Decision to 28. The Vice President of the SPC, Li Shaoping, explained the reasoning behind this change in the SPC's interpretation of the draft PAL: people's assessors should have certain social and life experience before they can participate in case trials and be able to widely absorb and represent social conditions and public opinions.[82] It is also interesting to note that the requirements for educational requirements in the PAL have been reduced from a college degree or above in 2004 to a high school degree or above. Li Shaoping explained that this amendment was made to take into account the proportions of all social strata, as well as broadness and representativeness. However, according to the data report released by China's sixth population census conducted in 2010, only 22.96 per cent of the population in mainland China has a high school degree or above. Only 13 provinces exceed this rate, and Tibet's rate was less than 10 per cent.[83] Although this rate is increasing year by year, it still accounts for a relatively low proportion of the country's total population; its representativeness is questionable when compared with other jurisdictions. Therefore, the educational background required for people's assessors is still too high, which runs counter to the purpose of preserving the system of people's assessors as declared by the law.

The most substantial argument in favour of reform is the authority which people's assessors are granted by the new PAL. The powers of people's assessors are divided into two categories: for criminal cases, when people's assessors participate in three-member collegial panels to try a case, they can decide on the facts and sentence together with professional judges,[84] but when people's assessors participate in a seven-member collegial panel, for criminal cases that carry great social impacts and where the fixed-term imprisonment is not less than ten years, life imprisonment or the death penalty may be sentenced, they can only decide on the fact-finding issues and 'may make comments on the application of the law, but may not participate in the voting'.[85]

All observers need some time to witness the impact of this new law. Potentially, in the academic arena, there may need to be further debates on how to distinguish the point of fact and the point of law issues, and further, how to define those cases 'with great social impacts'.

[82] www.chinanews.com, 26 April 2015.
[83] https://zh.wikipedia.org. In China, every 10 years the government conducts a population census. The last one was conducted in November 2020.
[84] Art 21 of the PAL.
[85] Art 22 of the PAL.

5

Other Participants in Criminal Proceedings

I. The Suspect and the Accused

Before discussing the rights of the suspect and the accused in criminal proceedings, it is necessary to scrutinise changes to the relevant terms in China's CPL. These changes reflect developments in legal ideology and demonstrate progress in terms of human rights protection. Prior to the 1996 revision of the CPL, the term for a person suspected of a crime, prosecuted, tried at courts, or even convicted in criminal proceedings was 'defendant' (被告人). In textbooks on criminal procedure, and in other regulations, detainees are referred to as '人犯' (*ren fan*). Some scholars translated this Chinese term into the English word 'defendants'. The author does not agree with this translation and argues that the more general English term 'offender' might be closer to the Chinese term, ie 'a person who commits an offence against the law; a lawbreaker'.[1] This term still is used in the MPS 'Detention Center Regulations'.[2] In 2017, the MPS promulgated its Detention Center Law of the PRC (Draft for Public Comment), but until now this draft law has not been on the schedule of discussion of the NPC. In this draft of Detention Center Law, the term 'offender' has been replaced by separate categories of 'suspect,' 'the accused' and 'sentenced person' (prisoner).

A. Suspect

The 1996 CPL amendment separated the suspect from the defendant and included them as parties to the criminal proceedings at the same time. This was a milestone step taken by the legislator in the history of criminal procedure legislation, but the problem remains that, until now, neither legislative nor the judicial interpretation have defined the term 'suspect', nor do these norms stipulate at which stage of the criminal proceedings and under which conditions a person who is suspected will formally be considered a 'criminal suspect'. This is of the utmost importance though, as a suspect enjoys the rights of a criminal suspect under the law and must

[1] http://wikidiff.com.

[2] This regulation was enacted 17 March 1990, consistently using the term 'offender' (人犯, *renfan*).

be informed about these rights before being interrogated (Article 120 CPL). There is consensus in legal circles about when the term 'defendant' becomes applicable: use of this term starts at the time of the prosecution's decision to prosecute the case and ends with the court's final judgment.[3] However, the definition of 'criminal suspect' is more complicated. As described in Chapter 3 on Basic Concepts, a normal public prosecution case is split into five phases of the criminal process. These five phases concern: the filing of the case (registration); the investigation; the prosecution; the trial; and the execution of a sentence. However, in accordance with the CPL, criminal investigations cannot be initiated without going through the procedure of filing a case. At the same time, the law stipulates that only when the public security organ (police) or the procuratorate 'discover facts or criminal suspects and in accordance with the jurisdiction' can the case be opened and investigated (Article 109 CPL). This provision establishes the preconditions for filing a case, and demonstrates how it results in a dilemma created by these preconditions and the situation in practice. On the one hand, a reported case sometimes needs to be investigated to decide whether the suspicion of a criminal case is justified. This means that (preliminary) investigations should be carried out. On the other hand, the CPL does not allow the commencement of criminal investigations without facts raising suspicion of a criminal offence or a criminal suspect. Here, evidently, gaps in the law emerge and the problem arises of how to proceed in a case where the acceptable degree of suspicion based on facts cannot yet be established but nevertheless leads are available which might result in suspicion and the identification of a suspect. This problem is debated in other jurisdictions as well.[4] Sometimes a preliminary investigation stage is separated from the formal investigation process and devoted to examining leads which possibly could result in establishing the conditions necessary for opening formal proceedings. Therefore, various questions arise, such as how should potential suspects be addressed? And what kind of rights do they enjoy? Which investigative measures may be applied? In Chinese, there are two relevant terms. The pre-investigation stage is known as '调查' (*diao cha*) and the formal investigation in the criminal process is referred to as '侦查' (*zhen cha*). The problem arises that when translated into English, these two terms become the single word 'investigation'. Questions may be raised, such as: What conditions will confirm whether a reported case may result in regular investigations? And what is the nature of the preliminary investigation here? Can the individual under preliminary investigations be called a 'criminal suspect'? This final question has received particular attention with respect to cases of DNA dragnets, where requests to provide DNA samples are based on offender profiles which fit a multitude of individuals (or possible suspects). Two options are in principle

[3] Xu Zhi and Lian Biao, 'Definition and Confirmation of Criminal Suspects' (2014) 4 *Journal of Law* 107.

[4] For a summary of Swiss and German debates see Patrick von Hahn, *Ermittlungen ohne Verdacht. Rechtliche Grundlagen und Grenzen polizeilicher Vorermittlungen in der Schweiz* (Basel, Helbing Lichtenhahn Verlag, 2019).

available in the face of such preliminary investigations: either the concept of (reasonable) suspicion is widened (ultimately reflecting a fit to a reasonable or evidence-based offender profile) or investigative measures in this preliminary stage are made dependent on voluntary cooperation. These issues are controversially debated among Chinese legal scholars. The following describes the rights of suspects that are provided for in the CPL.

i. The Right to Counsel During the Investigation

The criminal suspect can retain a defence lawyer, but only after the first interrogation, or when coercive measures have been taken. The suspect shall be informed about this right while the first interrogation is carried out (Article 34 CPL). The MPS Provisions develop detailed rules about informing suspects of their rights. For example, these rules include when the suspect is to be informed. If it is found that the suspect faces financial difficulties in retaining a lawyer, suspects shall be informed of the right to apply for legal aid lawyer's support, and the fact that they have been so informed must be recorded. A further example is that if several suspects are investigated in a case and retain the same lawyer, police shall ask them to retain different lawyers.[5] The MPS Provisions also state that, if suspects are in custody, police shall inform them of their right to retain a lawyer and in addition ask guardians or close relatives to retain a lawyer for the suspect.[6] If police find that a suspect has not retained a lawyer but meets the conditions establishing a right to mandatory defence (in cases where the suspect suffers an impairment of vision, hearing, or speech or suffers from a mental condition which has not completely impaired his criminal culpability, or where the suspect may be sentenced to life imprisonment or the death penalty), then the police must notify a legal aid agency to designate a lawyer within three days.[7] In the event that a suspect has not retained a lawyer, and where the Legal Aid Agency has not designated a lawyer for them, then the police shall inform the suspects that they have the right to make an appointment with the duty lawyer in order to receive legal assistance, including access to legal advice, recommendations on the selection of procedures, application for the modification of coercive measures, and offering opinions on the handling of the case. In these circumstances, the police shall arrange a scheduled meeting with the duty lawyer and facilitate that scheduled meeting between the suspect and the duty lawyer. The provision specially requires that, when the suspect applies for the duty lawyer's assistance, the detention agency shall arrange the meeting within 24 hours (Article 36 CPL, Article 49 of the Provision). It is notable that after the investigation has been concluded and the case is to be moved to the procuratorate for examination, prior to the decision making by the prosecutor, still the term

[5] Art 43 of the Provision, Chapter Four, 'The Lawyers involved in the criminal process', amended 1 September 2020.

[6] Art 44 of the Provision.

[7] Art 35 CPL, Arts 46–48 of the Provision.

'suspect' is applied. However, the CPL provides additional rights for the defence lawyer at the prosecution review stage as the defence lawyer can consult, extract and duplicate case materials. But when other non-lawyer defenders want to exercise those rights, they must obtain permission from the court or procuratorate (Article 40 CPL).

ii. The Limited Right against Self-incrimination

Chapter 3 on Basic Concepts discussed Article 12 of the CPL, which expresses a principle similar to the presumption of innocence, and in the CPL chapter on evidence, the prohibition on 'forcing anyone to commit self-incrimination' is introduced (Article 52 CPL). However, in the author's view, the CPL does not directly or indirectly provide for the right to remain silent. Evidence supporting this conclusion is found in Article 120 of the CPL which requires that criminal suspects should truthfully answer the investigators' questions. In the newly revised Provision of the public security agency 2020, some principles for the handling of criminal cases are established. But detailed rules on how to implement the principle of the presumption of innocence are lacking. In the revision, only the prohibition of torture to extract confessions and the use of other illegal means to collect evidence are mentioned. From this circumstance, we may infer that the right against self-crimination for investigators only means that illegal methods of collecting evidence are prohibited, and it does not include the right to remain silent. This amounts to a chronic problem in the revision of the CPL, which has been dragging on now for many years.

iii. The Right to Challenge Coercive (Compulsory) Measures

Article 97 of the CPL provides that suspects, their legal representative, and their close relatives have the right to apply for the modification of coercive (compulsory) measures (defined as pre-trial detention, release on guarantee pending further investigation or residential surveillance: Article 66 CPL). Article 97 of the CPL also states that people's courts, people's procuratorates and public security organs receiving an application for modification shall issue a decision within three days. This evidently implies that a suspect placed under compulsory measures may address courts, the procuratorate and public security organs. The process of extending the duration of pre-trial detention is a sensitive and complicated issue. The public security Provision adds a special section (Section Six) to provide for rules on arrest and pre-trial detention. The CPL stipulates in Article 156 that the usual period for criminal suspects in pre-trial detention during the investigation phase is two months. However, the law provides for a multitude of exceptional extensions. In practice, the investigation of cases is only rarely finalised within two months. Thus, the right of criminal suspects, their lawyers and close relatives to apply for modification of coercive measures is very important. Further issues related to that are discussed in Chapter 6 on investigation.

B. The Accused

The Crown Prosecution Service in the UK defines 'the accused' as a person formally charged with a criminal offence.[8] In contrast, the CPL moves the suspect into the role of an accused after the procuratorate has reviewed the case and decided formally to initiate a public prosecution. Then the case will be transferred to a court which has jurisdiction over it. Furthermore, in China, and other civil law systems, a judicial review stage follows. Upon review of the file the court shall decide to open trial proceedings if the court is satisfied that the indictment presents 'a clear criminal offence' (Article 186 CPL). This corresponds to some civil law systems where the court in intermediate proceedings examines, on the basis of the case files, whether a certain probability of a conviction can be assumed and whether a trial is barred, for example by statute of limitations.[9] In addition to the rights of both the suspect and the accused, the accused is granted further rights at the stage after the investigation, especially in the trial stage. Details of the following rights are discussed in the following, related parts of the book.

(1) Right to counsel. After the trial court has accepted a case, the accused must be informed within three days of the right to retain a defence counsel. In case of financial hardship or other relevant factors, the accused or his/her close relatives have the right to apply for legal aid assistance from the local legal aid agency. However, this is a matter of discretion, because the criterion of poverty differs from region to region. Where the accused fulfils the conditions provided for by the second and third paragraphs of Article 35 CPL, and enjoys the right to receive free legal aid lawyers' assistance, the court must notify a legal aid agency.[10]

While the court prepares for the trial, the accused has the right to receive a copy of the indictment (Article 187 CPL). In the past, information about the indictment pointed to a weak area in criminal procedure law as it did not provide the accused with the right to know the details of the accusation against them. In 2017, the National Lawyers Association formulated the 'Regulations for Lawyers Handling Criminal Cases' (Regulation of Lawyers). But, the Regulations do not mention the provisions under which the client's rights can be guaranteed. Therefore, in terms of protecting defendants' rights to know the details of the prosecution case, there are still some issues to be resolved. In particular the right to sufficient time to prepare a defence following from the fair trial principle is only poorly implemented. Article 187 of the CPL states that defendant and defence counsel shall receive a copy of the indictment

[8] See www.cps.gov.uk/publication/glossary; see also Australia's Federal Prosecution Service and www.cdpp.gov.au/prosecution-process/commonly-used-terms.

[9] See for example Arts 199–211 of the German criminal procedure law.

[10] The second paragraph of Art 35 provides that where a criminal suspect or defendant suffers vision, hearing, or speech impairment, or from a mental condition which does not completely impair criminal responsibility, the legal aid organisation must be notified, and will appoint a lawyer who shall provide defence. The third paragraph provides the same for defendants who may be sentenced to life imprisonment or the death penalty.

not later than 10 days before the trial starts. Statistical data from the turn of the twenty-first century show that in nearly 40 per cent of criminal cases, the lawyer's time for preparing trial and defence amounts to less than 10 days, and in 0.3 per cent of the cases studied, lawyers received the court's notice to appear on the day of the trial.[11] More recent data in this field are not available, so it is not possible to determine whether or not the situation has improved in recent years. The aforementioned Regulation of Lawyers states that when the defence lawyer receives the notice of appearance in the court's trial less than three days before the hearing date, the lawyer can suggest that the court change the hearing date.[12] However, implementation of this rule depends on the approval of the court and no remedy is available if the court declines to move the date.

(2) The accused's right to a public trial. The right to have a public trial is guaranteed both by the Constitution[13] and the CPL (Article 188). However, the scope and nature of the right to a public trial are much discussed, both in legal doctrine and in judicial practice. The first issue in dispute is whether this right belongs to the defendant or the public. Constitutions and criminal procedure laws of various jurisdictions clearly state that the right to a public trial is an individual right granted to defendants in criminal (and civil) cases. Both the ECHR (Article 6) and the ICCPR (Article 14) hold that anyone who is charged with a criminal offence is entitled to a public hearing. However, the interpretation of the case *GA van Meurs v Netherlands*[14] by the UN Human Rights Committee concluded that it is also a right of the public, and defendants may not waive this right. Under the CPL, a criminal trial shall be held in camera if a case involves state secrets or personal private information (Article 188). Also, in cases involving juveniles and where the accused is not yet 18 years old at the time of trial, the trial will not take place in public. However, the law provides a narrowly defined exception to that principle. If the accused juvenile or the legal representative agrees, the accused's school or juvenile protection organisations can send representatives to be present (Article 285). The CPL then adds another exception to the right to a public trial. Article 188 entitles parties to apply for a closed hearing when a public trial would disclose trade secrets. From the legal provisions on publicity of trial proceedings and their implementation in China, we can conclude that the exceptions to the principle of a public trial are in line with international

[11] Ma Mingliang and Zhang Xingshui, 'An Empirical Analysis of China's Criminal Legal Aid – Also on the Impact of Legal Aid on Modern Litigation System' in Chen Ruihua (ed), *An Empirical Research of Criminal Defense System* (Beijing, Peking University Press, 2005) 158–62.

[12] Art 84 of the Regulation of Lawyers.

[13] Art 130: 'Except in special circumstances as specified by law, all cases in the people's courts are heard in public'.

[14] Communication No 215/1986, UN Doc CCPR/C/39/D/215/1986 (1990) states that suits of law are to be held in public and that is a duty upon the State that is not dependent on any request, by the interested party. Both domestic legislation and judicial practice must provide for the possibility of the public attending, if members of the public so wish.

standards: in camera trials are to be held if state secrets or privacy are at risk and in case of juvenile defendants.

(3) Other rights of the accused at the trial stage include: the right to file a recusal motion against members of the collegiate panel, court clerks, public prosecutors, expert witnesses and interpreters (Article 190; see also Articles 29–32 CPL). As China's criminal procedure model is similar to the inquisitorial model in civil law jurisdictions, there is no typical cross-examination practice, as is present in common law jury trials. Instead, the law stipulates that the accused has the right to challenge the witness's testimony and expert's evaluation opinions presented in writing which then may result in a court decision to hear the testimony of witnesses or experts (Article 192). During the course of court hearings, the accused and his/her defender have the right to apply for new witnesses to appear in court and give testimony, obtaining new physical evidence, or for a new forensic evaluation of evidence, or to replicate a crime scene investigation (Article 197). At the end of the trial hearing, the accused has the right to make a final statement (Article 198). Finally, after the first instance trial, if the accused is convicted and sentenced, he/she has the right to appeal (Article 227).

II. The Defender

The defendant's right to defence is a constitutional right, and this fundamental right is implemented through the CPL, the Lawyers Law (LL), and administrative regulations related to legal aid. As was outlined in Chapter 2 on the development of China's CPL since its enactment in 1979, three reforms (1996, 2012 and 2018) have made amendments to the criminal defence system. The reform process has faced difficult and complex challenges in recent decades and has been affected by rapidly changing political, economic, social and cultural conditions. Although there are still shortcomings in legislation and practice, overall, the direction and progress of the reforms can be judged to be positive.

A. Different Categories of Defenders

The CPL permits the suspects and the accused to defend himself/herself in person. In addition to that, the law also permits suspects or the accused to retain three categories of persons to represent them, while limiting the number of defenders to two. Article 33 classifies defenders as:

(1) lawyers;
(2) persons recommended by a people's organisation or the employer of the defendant; or
(3) guardians, relatives, or friends.

According to international human rights provisions, it is permissible for the defendant to exercise the right to defend himself or to refuse the defence of a lawyer appointed by the State. Article 14(3)d of the ICCPR describes this as the right 'to be tried in his presence, and to defend himself in person or through legal assistance of his own choosing'. In some countries, France and Spain may serve as examples, procedural law states that the defendant's free choice of defender has priority.[15] However, the UN Human Rights Committee recognises that:

> the interests of justice may sometimes require imposing counsel against the wishes of the accused, particularly in cases where the defendant is substantially and persistently obstructing the proper conduct of trial, or faces a grave charge but is unable to act in his own interest, or if it is necessary to protect vulnerable witnesses from further distress if the accused were to question them himself.[16]

An old saying, said to originate in the US, holds that 'One who represents himself has a fool for a client', and this is often apt.[17] This aphorism expresses well founded concerns with respect to defendants acting as their own defenders.

The right of an accused to exercise the right to defend himself was set out in the 1979 CPL This provision was still retained until the 2018 amendments. The author believes that the provision in the 1979 CPL was influenced by political, economic, and socio-cultural conditions. At that time, the lawyer's system was beginning to be rebuilt and there were only 212 lawyers in the whole of China.[18] This small number of lawyers was nowhere near sufficient to meet the demand for mandatory defence, so those accused were by no means discouraged from defending themselves. By the end of 2019, however, there were 473,000 practicing lawyers available nationwide. Therefore, the basic obstacle of being unable to provide legal services to the accused because of a lack of lawyers no longer exists. Rather, an uneven distribution can be observed today, with lawyers being concentrated in affluent areas and in short supply in poorer regions of the country. In addition, analysis of data collected 2017 shows the proportion of the accused who had lawyers providing assistance (retained lawyers or designated lawyers) to be 22.1 per cent, and the rate of other types of defenders stipulated by the law 22.7 per cent. Many of these defenders have a lawyer's status. In fact lawyers accounted for 97.6 per cent of the total number of defenders, and the number of non-professional defenders (including the accused defending himself in person) has declined significantly.[19] In the reform of the judicial system in 2017, the SPC and the Ministry of Justice (MoJ) initiated a pilot project, called 'Full Coverage of Criminal Defence Lawyers' (刑事辩护全覆盖). The basic aim of this project, which is still ongoing, is to place

[15] William A Schabas, *UN International Covenant on Civil and Political Rights – Nowak's CCPR Commentary*, 3rd edn (Kiel, NP Engel, 2019) 399.

[16] ibid, 400.

[17] Hamid R Kusha, *Defendant Rights – A Reference Handbook* (ABC-CLIO Inc, 2004) 35.

[18] 2012–2016 Chinese Law Firm In-Depth Research and Investment Forecast Analysis Report.

[19] Wang Lusheng, 'On the Symbolic Legislation of Criminal Procedure and Its Consequences-Based on the Mining of 3.03 Million Judgments' (2018) 6 *Tsinghua Law Science* 124.

an obligation on the court to ensure that a legal aid lawyer is appointed in all first-instance and second-instance cases that apply ordinary procedures, and for cases tried in re-opened criminal proceedings where the defendant has not already appointed a defender. It may well be that, in the near future, the priority of obtaining a defence lawyer's assistance for an accused might be added to the CPL, and cases of the accused defending themselves would be the exception, and subject to strict legal restrictions.

B. The Role of Defenders in Criminal Proceedings

China's criminal procedural model is similar to the inquisitorial model of the civil law tradition. 'Finding the truth' is one of its main procedural objectives. The involvement of defence lawyers, especially in the investigative stage, has been debated internationally and concerns have arisen that the involvement of defence lawyers may interfere with that objective.[20] This concern may be the source of problems which have delayed progress related to a defendant's right to counsel. The reform of the criminal defence system is a major part of the reform of China's criminal procedure. The following text describes the situation of the right to counsel at various stages of the criminal process.

i. The Defender's Role before the Trial Stage

In the 1979 CPL, the defender (including professional defence lawyers) could only become involved in criminal proceedings at the trial stage. Quite often the defender became involved in cases only three days before the court hearings began. The 1996 amendments to the CPL changed this situation significantly: defence lawyers were allowed to be involved in the criminal investigative stage, but they did not have the status of defenders and could only offer limited legal assistance to criminal suspects.

The 2012 revision of the CPL may have been influenced by the 'human rights protection' clause which was written into the Constitution, as similar wording was also added to the CPL section on principles. Lawyers' involvement in criminal proceedings as defender was moved to the investigative stage. But the time for informing the suspect about the right to retain a lawyer was set as the first interrogation by investigators, or the day when coercive measures were imposed.

The CPL sets out the rights of lawyers at the investigative stage, including: providing legal assistance for criminal suspects; filing petitions on behalf of a criminal suspect; applying for the modification of a coercive measure; asking the

[20] ED Cape, 'Defense Rights, Duties, Norms, and Practice in Common law and Civil Law Jurisdictions' in Darryl K Brown et al (eds), *The Oxford Handbook of Criminal Process* (New York, Oxford University Press, 2019) 200.

investigative authority about the criminal charges and case-related information; and providing opinions.

The lawyer's right to meet with a client has been substantially improved. Before the CPL 2012 revision, especially before the LL was amended in 2007, a meeting with clients had to be approved by the investigative authorities, such as the police and the procuratorate. The LL changed that. Article 33 provides that a meeting with clients in custody or under residential surveillance may take place providing that the lawyer presents certain documents (ie his lawyers practising licence, an employment certification letter issued by his law firm, and the power of lawyer or official appointment letter issued by a legal aid agency – these are often known as the 'three certificates', 三证). It also specified that meetings between the defence lawyer and his client should not be monitored.[21] However, when the LL came into force on 1 June 2008, some lawyers took those three certificates and tried to meet with their clients at detention centres. But their demands were rejected by the detention authorities. Various excuses were given for this non-compliance with the law, such as: the CPL had not yet been amended; instructions from superiors had not been received; there were a limited number of meeting rooms; lawyers should inform the detention authority before the meeting with their clients and so forth.

Due to the conflict and disparities between the LL and the CPL, the LL was not implemented smoothly and in a timely manner. This situation was not substantially changed until the 2012 amendment of the CPL,[22] which confirmed what the LL provided (Article 37 CPL 2012) and added that, when a defence lawyer files a request for a meeting with a suspect, the detention place shall arrange a meeting in a timely manner, no later than 48 hours after receiving the request. However, the provision then set out several exceptions to the rule. In cases of criminal offences of endangering national security, terrorist activities, and especially serious bribery, a defence lawyer wishing to meet the detained suspect during the investigation phase must obtain permission from the investigating agency. There were heated debates and arguments about the 'extraordinarily significant bribery' cases. In 2012, the investigative power for embezzlement and bribery cases still belonged to the prosecutors. After the promulgation of the 2012 CPL, the SPP formulated the People's Procuratorate Criminal Procedure Rules for Trial Implementation (SPP Rules 2012[23]) Article 45. The SPP interpreted the reference standards for 'extraordinarily significant bribery' to include: (1) suspected bribes amounts to 500,000 yuan or more;[24] (2) significant social impact; and (3) major national interests. After applying this standard for some time in practice, senior prosecutors recognised

[21] Art 33 of the LL, 2017 amendment.

[22] Wu Xuean, 'Criminal Procedure Law and Lawyers Law Should be Seamlessly Connected', www.npc.gov.cn, 26 August 2011.

[23] This 'Rule' was revised in 2020.

[24] Approximately US$76,805 or €63,776 at April 2021 exchange rates.

that there had been a problem with expanded interpretations of '500,000 yuan and aggravating circumstances of the crime', 'significant social impact' and 'major national interests', which had resulted in improper use of the power to ban meetings between suspects and defence lawyers.[25]

Now, both the revised 2018 CPL (Article 39) and the SPP Rules as revised by the SPP in 2020 have deleted the category of 'extraordinarily significant bribery' cases. This means that only in criminal cases of endangering national security and terrorist activities do defence lawyers need to apply to the case handling authorities in advance to meet with suspects.

Article 52 of the newly revised MPS Provisions specifies in detail the processing procedures for public security organs (police) after receiving an application from a defence lawyer. The requirements shall be reported to the person in charge of the public security organ at or above the county level for approval within three days; the permission or disapproval decision should be made; and the defence lawyer should be notified in writing. This provision also puts forward a review principle, that is: 'Except for situations that hinder investigations or may reveal state secrets, a meeting between defendant and counsel shall be permitted'. Specific situations that 'hinder investigations' are listed, and concern:

(1) a risk of destroying or forging evidence, interfering with the witness's testimony or collusion with respect to confessions;
(2) a risk of causing the suspect to commit self-harm, suicide or escape;
(3) a risk of causing an accomplice to evade or hinder the investigation;
(4) where the suspect's family members are involved in the crime.

Another extremely controversial issue pertains to the question of whether the defence lawyer has the right to investigate and collect evidence during the investigation stage. This evidence-related issue addresses two questions: whether the defence lawyer's may conduct his own investigations and whether a lawyer may request investigators to collect evidence. This issue was not clearly addressed in either the 2012 or the 2018 CPL. However, the mainstream view of legal scholars and practitioners is that either from the perspective of protecting the suspect's defence rights, or from the viewpoint of systemic interpretation of the CPL's provisions, defence lawyers should have the right to investigate and search for evidence by themselves or through investigators during the investigation stage. According to the provision of Article 42 CPL, the defender shall inform the public security authority or procuratorate in a timely manner of evidence gathered regarding a suspect's alibi, or the fact that the suspect has not attained the age of criminal liability, or an assessment of a defendant's mental problems which exempt him from criminal liability. It can be inferred from this provision that if defence lawyers did not have the right to investigate and collect evidence during the investigation stage, then they would not be able to inform the public security organs

[25] Sun Qian, SPP Deputy Attorney General, 'Several Thoughts on the Implementation of the Criminal Procedure Law' (2015) 7 *People's Procuratorate*.

or procuratorates of the aforementioned relevant information. Furthermore, Article 41 CPL provides that where a defender believes that any evidence gathered by the public security authority or procuratorate during the period of investigation or examination of the prosecution regarding the innocence of a suspect or defendant or the pettiness of crime has not been submitted, the defender shall have the right to apply to the procuratorate or court for the submission of such evidence. This provision obviously shows that defence lawyers also have the right to request that the prosecutor or judge collect evidence from which their clients may benefit. The subsequent revision of the procedural law (Article 43) widened the defence lawyers' right to investigate and collect evidence by themselves or request the prosecutor or judge to take evidence which may benefit suspects or the accused.

As to a defence lawyer's right to access the case files during the investigation stage, there is still a blank in the current law. The lawyer cannot access the confession or statements made by the suspect during the investigation, nor can he/she access the technical expert evaluation report. In addition, defence lawyers do not have the right to be present at all during interrogations conducted by investigators. The law only provides a right for the lawyer to receive information from the investigative authority about the suspected criminal offence and relevant case information (Article 38 CPL). The Procedures of Public Security, mentioned above, explain the scope of the case that the defence lawyer can learn from the public security organs. This includes the suspect's alleged crimes and the facts of the case that have been ascertained at that time as well as information on coercive measures adopted, and whether the detention period has been extended, etc (Article 50 of the Procedures of Public Security). This information is limited and insufficient for defence lawyers to provide effective legal advice to suspects. In this situation, it would be difficult for lawyers to achieve their task of 'providing legal assistance to suspects' (Article 37 CPL) stipulated by the law.

In the last 40 years, after three amendments to the CPL and two amendments to the LL, the space available for defence lawyers has gradually expanded, but there are still some areas that need further reforms, especially in the investigation stage. The main problems that need to be addressed concern:

(1) during the investigation stage, lawyers do not have the right to attend the interrogation of suspects by investigators. Therefore, if a false or wrongly-obtained confession results from interrogation in the investigation stage, this will affect the subsequent procedures and may even be one of the decisive factors in miscarriage of justice cases;
(2) defence lawyers cannot participate in the compulsory investigation measures taken by investigative agencies, such as search and seizures, or freezing of property. This is not conducive to the supervision of the legality of evidence collection, and it is more likely that the suspect's fundamental and in particular also property rights are violated;
(3) with respect to pre-trial detention decisions, defence lawyers can only make requests for changes to coercive measures on behalf of the suspect, and cannot participate in the decision procedure dealing with these measures.

> Also, neutral judges are not involved in decisions on pre-trial and post-event investigation measures. Therefore, the suspect's right to liberty and the right to be free from illegal and arbitrary detention are greatly at risk of being infringed.[26]

Comparing the rights of defence lawyers at the prosecution stage and the investigation stage, defence lawyers can consult, extract, and duplicate case material after the investigation is concluded (while defenders other than defence lawyers still must obtain the permission of the procuratorate to exercise this right according to CPL Article 40). The law itself does not define the scope of 'case file materials'. In the SPP Rules (2019 revision, Article 47) case file materials are interpreted as 'procedural documents and evidence materials'. To ensure that lawyers can access and read the files in a timely manner, this rule stipulates that when the defender requests this with the procuratorate, the procuratorate shall arrange for the defender to read the files within three days (SPP Rules, Article 49). At present, most procuratorates and courts can provide electronic files.

Since the 2012 revision, the CPL has stipulated that prosecutors 'should' or 'can' listen to the opinions of defence lawyers with respect to three procedural activities:

(1) as mentioned above, in China, pre-trial detention is mainly reviewed and approved by the procuratorate. Before the decision is made, the procuratorate shall hear the opinion of the defence lawyer. If the defence lawyer makes a request, the opinion of the defence lawyer should be heard (Article 88 of the CPL 2018);
(2) if the suspect decides to enter a plea of guilty and also accepts the suggested punishment, the opinion of the defender or the duty lawyer should be heard (Article 173 of the CPL 2018);
(3) the law requires that pre-trial detention measures for juvenile suspects should be strictly limited. If prosecutor or judge consider the detention of a juvenile suspect before trial, the opinion of the defence lawyer shall be heard (Article 280). The right of defence lawyers to submit opinions is based on the special status of Chinese prosecutors in criminal proceedings. The status of prosecutors is different from that of prosecutors operating under the adversarial model and in the common law tradition. Chinese prosecutors have the obligation to pursue the 'truth' and monitor the effective implementation of the law. From this perspective, the right of defence lawyers to make suggestions is of positive significance. However, there is no empirical research to analyse its impact on the course of proceedings. In order to establish a basis for evaluating the effects of defence lawyers' suggestions in the future, opinions should be submitted in written form and become part of the case file.

[26] Chen Ruihua, 'Retrospect and Prospect of Criminal Defense System in the Past Forty Years' (2019) 6 *Political and Law Forum* 3.

ii. The Defender's Role in the Adjudication Stage

Part Three of the CPL in its English translation is entitled 'trial'. However, the term 'trial' is somewhat misleading when it is translated back into Chinese (法庭审理, *fa ting shen li*) (see also Chapter 3 above, which discusses translation issues in some detail). Part Three of the CPL should, rather, be entitled 'adjudication', because it includes not only the 'trial' and 'court hearings' – it also includes the appeal procedure, the proceedings for private prosecution cases, and a special trial procedure for death penalty cases.

The rights of defenders related to court hearings are as follows:

(1) after a court's decision to hold a hearing, the defender and the accused shall receive a copy of the indictment no later than ten days after that decision (Article 187);

(2) before a court hearing, the judge may organise a pre-trial meeting (this is also translated as conference before the trial) to hear opinions on trial-related issues, such as challenging the judge or prosecutor (recusal); the list of witnesses to testify at the trial; and exclusion of illegal obtained evidence. The defender has the right to request the court to hold the meeting and also has the right to participate at the meeting (Article 187). During the meeting the defence lawyer has the right to apply for a supplementary expert's evaluation, or for the expert evaluation to be redone, or apply for additional witnesses to attend the court hearing (Article 24 of 'Provisions of Lawyer's Rights);

(3) after the court has determined the date of the court hearing, the defender has the right to receive a notification of the time and venue of the court hearing three days before the court hearing (Article 187). If a lawyer applies to postpone the date of the court hearing due to a conflict with the date of a court hearing for another case, or any other justified reason, the court shall, under the premise of not invoking limitation, consider the issue and adjust the date (Article 25 of 'Provisions of Lawyer's Rights);

(4) in Chinese trials there is no typical adversarial cross-examination, but the law allows the defender, with the permission of the presiding judge, to question the accused (Article 191 CPL). If a witness, or an expert witness does not attend the trial and give testimony, and if the defender believes that the witness's testimony may have a significant effect on the conviction and sentencing of a case, the defender can ask the court to summon the witness or the expert witness, and the witnesses shall testify before the court. If an expert witness fails to attend after being summoned, his written evaluation shall not be accepted by the court as evidence, and also shall not be used as a basis for deciding the case (Article 192 CPL). If the witnesses or the expert witnesses attend the trial, the defender, with the permission of the presiding judge, can question the witness or the expert witness (Article 195 CPL). During the trial, the defender has a right to request the court to summon a

new witness to testify at the court, or for new physical evidence to be submitted, or a new forensic evaluation to be carried out (Article 197). During a trial, the defender has the right to present an opinion and debate that with the prosecutor (Article 198).

The defender's rights during appeal proceedings still represent a weak area, because most appellate cases will not be held in an open hearing, but will be tried by judges through dossiers. According to a statistic covering the period 2007–2011, in the whole of China's courts, only 15.3 per cent of appellate cases were tried in an open court hearing.[27] The defender of the first instance case has no direct appeal right. If the defender wants to file an appeal, it must be with the consent of the accused (Article 227). The CPL provides very strict conditions for holding open court hearings for second instance cases (Article 234 of CPL). The conditions are:

(1) where a defendant or a private prosecutor or the legal representative has raised any objection to the facts and evidence determined in the trial at first instance, which may affect conviction and sentencing;
(2) where the case is an appellate case and the defendant is sentenced to the death penalty;
(3) where a case is appealed by the prosecutor.

Although the defender's opinion may be heard by the court in those second instance cases where the court decides not to hold an open court hearing, the defender has lost the opportunity to challenge the evidence in a face-to-face debate. This then seriously affects the effectiveness of the defence.

C. The Defender's Role in Death Penalty Cases

The protection of the rights of an accused who is facing the death penalty is of paramount importance. The UN document on 'Safeguards guaranteeing protection of the rights of those facing the death penalty'[28] states that:

> Capital punishment may only be carried out pursuant to a final judgement rendered by a competent court after legal process which gives all possible safeguards to ensure a fair trial, at least equal to those contained in Article 14 of the ICCPR, including the right to anyone suspected of or charged with a crime for which capital punishment maybe imposed to adequate legal assistance at all stages of the proceedings. (Article 5)

Although the right to life is not explicitly provided for in China's Constitution, rules governing the criminal justice area express some recognition that life must be placed under particular legal protection. In the CPL, an accused who is facing

[27] Li Guihong, 'Application of the Second Instance Criminal Trial Mode', www.chinacourt.org, 24 June 2016.

[28] Approved by Economic and Social Council Resolution 1984/50 of 25 May 1984.

the death penalty falls into the category requiring mandatory representation by a defence counsel. Article 35(3) of the CPL provides that:

> where a criminal suspect or defendant who may be sentenced to life imprisonment or death penalty has not retained a defender, the people's court, people's procuratorate, and public security authority shall notify a Legal Aid Agency to designate a lawyer to defend him or her.

It is recognised that this provision does not exclude a defender who is not a professional lawyer from defending an accused who is facing the death penalty. However, the CPL itself does not provide clear rules on whether the accused can reject the lawyer who is designated by the legal aid agencies. In the SPC's Interpretation of the 2012 CPL, Articles 50 and 311 spell out that the accused who falls into the category for legal aid assistance can reject a designated lawyer once. The court can then designate a lawyer a second time to offer assistance, but if the accused rejects the second lawyer, the court shall not permit that application for rejection. This means that for cases falling into the legal aid category, in fact, every accused person has to have a lawyer offering legal assistance.

Another issue concerns the stages at which a legal aid lawyer's assistance must be provided for an accused who is facing the death penalty. According to the principles of the Constitution and the CPL, the accused who is facing the death penalty shall be provided with free legal assistance from the beginning to the end of criminal proceedings. However, both the CPL and the SPC's 'Interpretation' are silent about whether the SPC must designate a legal aid lawyer during the SPC's final review of death penalty cases. There are two steps for reviewing death penalty cases (a detailed discussion will follow in Chapter 9, which discusses remedies). If the accused is sentenced to death after a second instance trial, then the high court shall review the case first, and if the high court upholds the death penalty, then the case shall be transferred to the SPC for final review. However, the SPC's Interpretation specifies only the obligation of the high courts to designate a legal aid lawyer for the accused who has no defender during the review proceedings (Article 47, SPC Interpretation). The silence of the SPC and legislators on this issue has drawn continued criticism from legal scholars and lawyers. In 2007, the SPC, SPP, MPS and MOJ issued their 'Opinions on Strengthening Handling Cases in Strict Accordance with Law and Guaranteeing the Quality of Handling Death Penalty Cases'. Article 40 of these Opinions states that, if the accused's defender requests that his opinions be heard during the review of a death penalty case, the court shall listen to the defender's opinions, make transcripts and attach them to the case file. The defender's written opinions shall also be attached to the case file. It should be noted that such defenders' involvement in the death penalty review only related to an accused who has their own defender. That means, in cases where the convicted person has no defender during the final review proceedings, the SPC is not obligated to designate a legal aid lawyer. In 2008, the SPC and the MOJ issued 'Several Provisions on Sufficiently Guaranteeing Lawyer's Performance of the Defence Duty According to Law to Ensure the Quality of Handling Death Penalty Cases'

(Several Provisions on Defence). In this document, some progress has been made. It allows the lawyer to meet the judge to state his opinion or submit evidence face to face (Article 17, Several Provisions on Defence). This progress was confirmed in the CPL revisions of 2012 and 2018, but the involvement of the defence lawyer is limited to offering opinions (Article 251 CPL). Until now, these important issues still remain without a solution. A 2013 survey carried out on China Judgements Net found 49 SPC review decisions in death penalty cases. Out of these, seven decisions included information on 'receiving lawyer's opinion'. Telephone interviews with judges of the SPC involved in these decisions confirmed that the information extracted from China Judgments Net was accurate. Among those 49 defendants whose death sentences were reviewed in 2013, only 14.3 per cent had a defence counsel during the final review proceedings.[29] In addition, lawyers did not have full defence rights. So, for example, lawyers could not access the case file, and when asking to meet the sentenced defendant in the detention centre, administrative staff would give numerous excuses for not allowing a meeting, although SPC's judges did not openly oppose the lawyers' demands. Further, some difficulties for lawyers in carrying out investigations resulted from failing to include the defence lawyer's name and the name of their law firm in the SPC review decisions. In regular criminal cases, this information should appear on the SPC decisions.[30] The data clearly show that both the law and the SPC have so far failed to endorse a proper status for defence lawyers in final death penalty review proceedings.

D. Legal Aid

Legal aid became operational in China with the enactment of the CPL in 1996. Article 34 of the 1996 CPL provided three conditions for a legal aid lawyer to be designated during the trial stage:

(1) the accused has, due to financial difficulties or other reasons, not retained a defender: in this situation, the court has a discretionary power to decide whether legal aid services should be offered;
(2) the accused is blind, deaf or mute, or a minor: in these cases the appointment of a defender is mandatory. The court 'shall' designate a legal aid lawyer if the accused does not have a defender;
(3) in cases eligible for the death penalty, defence is also mandatory and the court shall designate a legal aid lawyer for the accused.

Before the 1996 CPL came into force on 1 January 1997, the Central Legal Aid Centre and local legal aid agencies had not yet been fully established.[31] For a while,

[29] Chen Xuequan, 'Guarantee of the Right to Defense in the Death Penalty Review Procedure' (2015) 2 *Legal and Commercial Research* 44.
[30] ibid.
[31] The author learned of this situation from an international conference which was held in May 1996, where the author met the Vice minister of the Ministry of Justice, Zhang Geng, who was responsible for

the courts had to find their own ways of designating lawyers in order to implement the CPL's provisions on mandatory defence. The National Legal Aid Centre was set up on 18 December 1996. After this, local legal aid agencies were gradually built up. In 2003, the State Council issued the first Legal Aid Act.[32] The main purpose of this Act is 'ensuring that citizens with economic difficulties obtain necessary legal services' (Article 1 of the Act). With regard to criminal legal aid services, the Act provides a detailed application process for obtaining free legal aid services (Chapter 3 of the Act). This was the first time that victims and private prosecutors were included within the range of legal aid (Article 11(2), (3) of the Act).

With the spread of legal reform, especially the reform of the CPL, people gradually realised that according to the 1996 CPL, the accused can only formally retain a defender or apply for legal aid at the review prosecution stage, while at the investigation stage, only few criminal suspects could retain a lawyer to provide limited legal consulting services instead of full defence. In response to this situation, the MoJ launched a pilot legal aid project for duty lawyers in Henan Province, which was successfully implemented.[33] The success of this project led, in the 2012 CPL amendment, to the expansion of legal aid to criminal suspects at the investigation stage. This revision was followed by the introduction of the criminal expedited procedure (the fast-track procedure) and the guilty plea and leniency policies, which increased the relevance of the investigative stage. Thus, the implementation of these policies is inseparable from the protection of the right to a fair trial of criminal suspects and defendants in criminal proceedings, especially with respect to the balance between prosecution and defence. In the implementation of these reforms, relevant legal institutions issued a number of documents, in which they suggested adopting the duty lawyer system to assist those suspects or accused with issues such as making a decision on guilty plea or the choice of proceedings. Legal institutions also carried out pilot projects. Those projects established legal aid stations in detention centres, procuratorates, and courts, and duty lawyers were sent to these places. In the document 'Guiding Opinions on Leniency System', the goal of 'full coverage of criminal defence' was proposed. The document refers to increasing the number of defenders in criminal cases. In the 2018 CPL amendment, all of these changes were adopted. In practice, progress can be demonstrated by the following promising statistics. In 2018, 473,852 criminal legal aid cases in China were counted, which amounts to 32.6 per cent of the total of legal aid cases.

organising legal aid services. In order to support the establishment of the legal aid system, the author together with Professor Chen Guang Zhong carried out a research project on legal aid. The project was supported by the British Council, which organised a visit to England and Scotland's legal aid-related institutions with the first Director of the National Legal Aid Centre, Gong Xiao Bing. The author wrote a report to introduce the British legal aid system into China: see Yue Liling, 'The British Legal Aid System is Facing Reform' (1997) 8 *China Lawyer* 14. After this visit, the first legal aid clinic was established at the China University of Political Science and Law. The clinic was placed directly under the guidance of the MoJ and was supported by the Ford Foundation of the US for more than eight years.

[32] The Act was adopted at the 15th executive meeting of the State Council on 16 July 2003 and became effective as of 1 September 2003.

[33] Wu Hongyao, 'Development and Prospects of China's Criminal Legal Aid System' (2015) 4 *China Law* 87.

In 412,038 of these cases legal aid was requested by the police, prosecutor or judge. From the total number of criminal legal aid cases, 53,853 were at the investigation stage, 79,993 at the review and prosecution stage, while the bulk (278,192) were associated with the trial stage.[34]

With respect to criminal defence, a number of issues are currently subject to challenge and are being debated. These debates probably signal the direction of future reforms. First, one important question is how to improve the quality of defence when the defence rate is increasing so rapidly. In this respect, the concept of effective defence is discussed, introducing particularly developments and evidence from the US. Lawyers and scholars insist that effective defence should be examined through empirical analysis, emphasising a particular need for the establishment of evidence-based standards for effective defence in death penalty cases. Second, the status of the duty lawyer is questioned. The role of duty lawyers should be restricted to the investigation stage: providing emergency legal assistance within a short period of time when the suspect is arrested. It is then important to ensure that the suspect quickly obtains full professional legal service. Finally, some lawyers and scholars are concerned that in the supervision investigation process, the Supervision Law does not currently stipulate that a person under investigation has the right to obtain assistance from a lawyer. This is of relevance especially when the person is under supervision detention for a maximum of six months,[35] and evidence collected at this stage may be used in subsequent prosecution and trial proceedings. Lawyers here should have the right to intervene to provide legal assistance in order to be able to effectively protect the suspect's rights.

III. Victims of Crime

A. Definition of 'Victim of Crime'

The UN resolution, 'Declaration of Basic Principles of Justice for Victims of Crime and Abuse of Power' defines crime victims as

> persons who individually or collectively, have suffered harm, including physical or mental injury, emotional suffering, economic loss or substantial impairment of their fundamental rights, through acts or omissions that are in violation of criminal laws operative within Member States, including those laws proscribing criminal abuse of power.[36]

[34] Fan Chongyi and Shi Hansheng (eds), *Report on the Development of China's Legal Aid System (2019)* (Beijing, Social Sciences Archives Publishing House, 2019) 36.

[35] Chen Ruihua, 'Retrospect of Criminal Defense System in the Past Forty Years' (2019) 6 *Politics and Law Forum* 3.

[36] General Assembly Resolution 40/34, 29 November 1985, annex.

Meanwhile, in EU Directive 2012/29 'Establishing minimum standards on the rights, support and protection of victims of crime', Article 2 defines the victim of crimes as

> A natural person who has suffered harm, including physical, mental or emotional harm or economic loss which was directly caused by a criminal offence.

Neither the Chinese CPL nor its judicial interpretation explicitly provide for a definition of the victim of crime. Such a definition, however, may be inferred from Article 101 of the CPL, which limits the status of victims to natural persons and excludes legal persons. The article provides that: 'where a victim has suffered any material loss as a result of the defendant's crime he shall have the right to institute a subsidiary civil procedure during criminal proceedings'. It should be noted that the first half of the provision restricts the scope of the victim, from a substantive point of view, because only 'material losses'[37] are mentioned, and intangible harm[38] is missing. The second half of the article limits the scope of persons who have the right to initiate a subsidiary civil procedure in criminal proceedings. This includes the legal representative and close relatives of the victim when the victim is deceased or incapacitated.

It has been argued for some time that the procedure as addressed in Article 101 CPL is 'subsidiary civil procedure', and that accordingly it should follow the rules of civil law. Article 1183 of the Code of Civil Law provides that:

> where the infringement upon a natural person's personal rights and interests causes serious mental suffering, the infringed party shall have the right to claim compensation for mental suffering.

It is the author's view that the principle of statutory consistency requires that the civil and criminal law adopt different concepts of harm that are subject to compensation. Now that the Code of Civil Law has come into force,[39] Article 101 of the CPL should be amended, adding the victim's right to compensation for intangible losses.

B. The Legal Status and Procedural Rights of Victims in Criminal Proceedings

The status of the victim in criminal proceedings has developed through the three revisions of the CPL. In the 1979 CPL (Article 58(4)), the victim was assigned the status of a participant in the criminal procedure, and the victim's statement was listed as an independent source of evidence and kept separate from the witness

[37] The range of 'material loss' will be discussed in the following parts of the book.
[38] In Chinese this is also referred to as 'spiritual loss' (精神损失).
[39] The Civil Code of PRC was adopted at the 3rd session of the 13th NPC on 28 May 2020 and came into force on 1 January 2021.

testimony. However, classification as a participant of criminal procedure comes with technical problems. Under the law, the parties of criminal proceedings include the public prosecutor, the private prosecutor, the defendant, and the plaintiff and the defendant in the subsidiary civil procedure. In practice, in most cases both the private prosecutor and the plaintiffs in subsidiary civil procedures are at the same time victims. Thus, there is an overlap in classification, which has an impact on the procedural rights of the participants. Under the 1979 CPL, the victims play only a marginal role in criminal proceedings, where their main right is to be involved in the subsidiary civil procedure and to apply for compensation from the defendant.

With the 1996 CPL reform, the legal status of the victim was changed. The most significant change was the inclusion of the victim as one of the parties. The legislative purpose of this change in the legal status of the victim was to strengthen the protection of the victim's rights in criminal proceedings. However, in theory and in practice, changing the status of victims from a participant in the proceedings to a party did not result in an improvement in the protection of the victim's rights. First, in China as in other jurisdictions with a Continental law tradition, except for a very small number of private prosecution cases, most cases are prosecuted by prosecutors on behalf of the State. Public prosecution to some extent includes protecting the interests of victims, but when some public prosecution cases are allowed to be converted into private prosecution cases, the rights of victims are not better protected. For example, in order to strengthen the supervision of the victim's right of public prosecution, the 1996 CPL stated that, in the case where a prosecutor made the decision to dismiss the case, the victim had the right to be informed about the decision. If the victim was not satisfied with that decision, the victim had a right to make a complaint to the next level of public prosecution, to review the decision. If the decision of the prosecutor office to dismiss the case was sustained, the victim then had the right to file a lawsuit directly with a court (Article 145 of the 1996 CPL). This provision ignores the fact that for most cases the prosecution's decision to dismiss a case is based on an analysis of the evidence and a comprehensive consideration of the public interest. It is appropriate for the victim to have the right to file an application for review when they have objections. However, when the prosecutor's original non-prosecution decision is upheld by the review, the victim could directly file a private prosecution with the court. The law does not request the procuratorate to transfer the evidence collected in previous investigations to the victim. As a result, the victim's chance of winning the case after switching to private prosecution was very small. Fifteen year of practice showed that the number of cases transferred from public prosecution to private prosecution was very small.[40] A possible solution might be to introduce the German approach and list the victim as a subsidiary prosecutor in cases involving serious criminal offences,[41] strengthening the communication

[40] Chen Huanzhong, 'Survey and Research on Criminal Private Prosecution' (2012) 2 *Applicable Law* 75.
[41] Arts 395–402 German Criminal Procedure Law.

between the victim and the prosecutor, and establishing appeal proceedings in cases of non-prosecution which take the request to continue public prosecution to a court.[42] Effective monitoring of the prosecutor's decision not to prosecute and the victim's complaint about non-prosecution should finally be reviewed and decided by a higher level of court. Second, the victim as a party should enjoy the same rights as the accused in criminal proceedings, especially in a court hearing. The 1996 CPL added more rights for the victim, such as the right to question the witness (Article 156 CPL), to request that a new witness be summoned, new material evidence be obtained, or a new expert evaluation be made (Article 159 of the 1996 CPL), to give comments on evidence and debate the evidence (Article 160 of the 1996 CPL), the right to obtain evidence, etc.

The accused has the right to cross-examine the victim, which means that the victim and the accused will meet face to face at the trial. The law does not provide special protection measures for vulnerable victims. As has been recognised internationally, a cross-examination which results in a confrontation of victim and offender may cause a second traumatisation and 'a second harm' for the victim. Therefore, criminal procedural law should be adjusted, with the aim of protecting victims as far as possible from secondary victimisation.[43] It follows from this that the victim's role should be designed as that of a special participant in the criminal proceedings, and include special protection measures according to the vulnerability characteristics of the individual victims.

The 2012 CPL amendments retained the victim's status as a party, but the procedural rights of the victim and his agent did not increase. However, the SPC'S interpretation of the CPL confirmed that the victim's agent has the right to access the case files in the court. This supplement is meaningful in strengthening the victim's right to obtain information about the case. In addition, the 2012 CPL added a reconciliation procedure for the defendant and the victim in public prosecution cases. The SPC's Interpretation furthermore states that when the victim dies, his or her close relatives can also settle the case with the defendant in the reconciliation procedure (Article 588 of the SPC's Interpretation').

The 2018 CPL amendments introduced the guilty plea and leniency system. The 2018 provisions do not elaborate on how to protect the rights of victims in these procedures. However, after the amendments came into force (on 10 November 2019) the SPC and SPP, MPS, MSS issued 'The Guiding Opinions on Leniency'). In this document three clauses address rights of the victim. The fifth part of the document stipulates the protection of the rights and interests of victims. The first right is about 'listening to the victim'. The public security organ and the procuratorate are obliged to write down and record the hearing of the opinions of the victim into the case file (Article 16 of the Guiding Opinions on Leniency). Second, when the

[42] Arts 172–177 German Criminal Procedure Law.

[43] See for example Council of Europe Recommendation Rec (2006)8 on assistance to crime victims, 14 June 2006.

victim and his *agent ad litem* disagree with a lenient punishment of the defendant, although the disagreement would not result in terminating the proceedings, leniency shall be reduced as appropriate if the defendant fails to restitute illegal gains, pay compensation for losses, or reach a mediation or settlement with the victim (Article 18).

Until now China has not adopted a victim protection law or a law providing judicial aid to victims. Also, no official statistical data on victims of crime are available. A survey published in 2010 found that each year, around three million victims of crime receive no compensation at all,[44] either from the defendant or from the state. This lack of compensation prevents closure of the conflict and may even spark violent retaliation. Scholars have conducted comparative studies and have attempted to promote legislation which would improve compensation for victims of crime. The government has gradually realised the importance of legislation to address this issue. In the National Human Rights Action Plan (2009–2010), legislation was proposed to promote the national aid system for victims of crime. In March 2009, the Central Political and Legal Commission, SPC, SPP and eight other ministries and organisations issued 'Several Opinions on Carrying out Criminal Victim Aid Work'. After several years of implementation, the aforementioned state agencies issued 'Opinions on Establishing and Improving the System of State Judicial Aid (for Trial Implementation)'. These Opinions expand the scope of judicial aid from assistance to criminal victims to also include civil tort cases. In this document, the principle of judicial aid is also established:

> State judicial aid is for the victims of crimes, or the victim of civil tort, parties who cannot obtain effective compensation through litigation.

At the same time, the Opinions also set out the methods, standards and procedures of judicial aid, as well as the collection and management of state aid funds. After this document was issued, both SPC and SPP formulated implementation rules. According to SPC statistics, between 2015 and 2018 courts at all levels handled 166,500 cases of judicial aid applications, and more than 300,000 crime victims received assistance. Judicial aid amounted to approximately 3.747 billion RMB yuan.[45]

[44] Li Guangming and Yi Zhibin, 'Analysis of the Value of China's Criminal Victim Aid System and Legislative Ideas' (2010) 2 *Journal of Central South University* Social Science Edition.

[45] Xu Chao, 'Judicial Aid System with Chinese Characteristics Is Initially Effective' *People's Court Daily* 17 September 2019 this amounts to around €479,466,120 or US$576,663,300 (at April 2021 exchange rates).

6

Pre-Trial Investigation

As some scholars have described, 'the criminal process is, to a large extent, an investigative one, existing to prepare cases for effective trial'.[1] China is not different from other jurisdictions, in that the criminal investigative process plays an essential role in the entirety of criminal proceedings. With the protection of human rights written into the Constitution and the CPL, how to balance the repression of crimes and the protection of human rights in the investigation stage has remained a contentious topic in China. In fact, it has been an eternal topic for scholars and practitioners of criminal procedure law around the world. China's model of criminal procedure is much as Professor Herbert L Packer described in his article half of century ago, featuring 'two models of criminal process',[2] basically belonging to a 'crime control model', which:

> is seen as a screening process in which each successive stage pre-arrest investigation, arrest, post-arrest investigation, preparation for trial, trial or entry of plea, conviction, and disposition involves a series of routine operations whose success is gauged primarily by their tendency to pass the case along to a successful conclusion.[3]

It is important to note that the investigative stage is the initial part of the entire process.

I. Initiation of the Investigation Process

As noted in previous chapters, China signed the ICCPR in 1998, but until now it has not been ratified. There has been much research on the right to a fair trial, but few scholars have paid attention to the issues of what 'criminal charge' means and what is the starting point of a 'criminal charge'.[4] This issue is essential for the protection of the subsequent fair trial rights. From a criminal procedure

[1] Liz Campbell et al, *The Criminal Process*, 5th edn (New York, Oxford University Press, 2019) 83.

[2] Herbert L Packer, 'Two Models of the Criminal Process' (1964) 113(1) *University of Pennsylvania Law Review* 1.

[3] ibid, 11.

[4] William A Schabas, *UN International Covenant on Civil and Political Rights - Nowak's CCPR Commentary*, 3rd edn (Kiel, NP Engel, 2019) 363–64; Ben Emmerson et al, *Human Rights and Criminal Justice*, 3rd edn (London, Sweet & Maxwell, 2012) 210–14; Liling Yue, *Criminal Trial and Human Rights Protection* (Beijing, Law Press, 2010) 24–46.

perspective, the CPL contains an initial procedure before the formal investigation process, known as 'filing a case' (立案, *li an*),[5] which every reported criminal case must go through.

According to the CPL, every citizen and institution has the right, and in some instances also the obligation, to report crimes of which they are aware (Article 110 CPL). However, the law provides for the use of three different terms to distinguish between those who report such crimes: 'reporter' (报案人, *bao an ren*) refers to all reporters, including the victim; 'accuser' (控告人, *kong gao ren*) refers only to the victim whose personal or property rights have been infringed upon by the crime; and 'informant' (举报人, *ju bao ren*) refers to any individual or institutions other than the victim. The purpose of this differentiation is to distinguish the rights of the various categories of reporter. If a decision not to file a case is made, only the victim as the accuser has the right to apply for a review.

With regard to the standards of filing a case, the substantive provision states 'there are any facts of a crime which should be investigated for criminal responsibility' (Article 112 CPL). However, the facts must not only generally establish that a criminal offence has been committed but also that it is a criminal offence 'which is not clearly minor'. The threshold of 'not clearly minor', established in Article 112 of the CPL, reflects a substantive offence element adopted in Article 13 of the Criminal Code whereby, in cases of 'obviously minor circumstances', an act shall not be considered to be a crime. Meanwhile, for the procedural criterion, the public security agency or the procuratorate should have jurisdiction for the reported case.

The decision of the police or prosecutor on whether to file a case and to initiate an investigation is crucial for the parties to the case. In practice, when the public security agency makes a decision not to file a case, it causes conflict between the relevant victims and the public security agencies. Indeed, it has even caused concerns on social media. Since the 1996 revision of the CPL, the CPL has provided three paths by which to monitor and supervise the procedure for deciding to file a case. One path is the prosecutor's supervision. If the prosecutor deems that the public security authority failed to file a case which should otherwise have been investigated, the procuratorate shall require the public security authority to explain the reasons for not filing the case. If the prosecutor assesses the reasons for not filing a case provided by the investigative police of the public security to be unfounded, the prosecutor shall instruct the public security to file the case and initiate the investigation (Article 113 CPL). The second path for monitoring the procedure for filing a case is through the victim. If the accuser is dissatisfied with the decision from the public security authority, the accuser may apply for a review of the decision (Article 112 CPL). The third path is that the victim also has the right to initiate a private prosecution directly in the court (Article 114).

[5] Arts 109–114 of the CPL.

In Chapter 4 above, the relationship between police and prosecutors was discussed. Debates on the effectiveness of procuratorates' supervision have persisted for decades. In the author's view, the police should not be afforded the power to terminate a reported case. Some scholars even suggest that a judicial review procedure should be constructed for filing a case.[6]

The dilemma relating to the suspect's rights and the procedure for filing a case is discussed in Chapter 5. On the one hand, the pre-condition for filing a case is the discovery of facts of a crime or criminal suspects, in accordance with the jurisdiction (Article 109 CPL). On the other hand, without the filing a case procedure, the formal investigation cannot be commenced. To solve this dilemma, in the author's view, the current procedure for filing a case should be reformulated and changed into a simple registration process. After a complaint has been received and entered into the register, the investigator should then conduct a preliminary investigation aimed at finding out whether suspicion of a criminal offence is strong enough to justify a full-blown investigation. During this phase, the investigator should question the victim and witnesses, interrogate the suspect, visit the crime scene, etc. But all of the investigative actions within this model should focus on the question of whether suspicion can be established and the decision as to whether the investigation should be continued or terminated. The infringement of the rights of suspects and other participants must be kept to a minimum.

II. Coercive Measures

Basic concepts of criminal procedure are discussed in Chapter 3. For example, the term 'coercive measures' is not found in common law jurisdictions, and the meaning of the term in China's CPL differs from that in civil law jurisdictions, where it can be defined as:

> those taken by judicial organs in accordance with the law to restrict the personal rights of a citizen or deny him or her of such rights. When a coercive measure is taken against a person, the person's honor, freedom and other rights are bound to be adversely affected.[7]

It should be noted that the Chinese law term 'coercive measures' has a narrower range than such terms in civil law jurisdictions. The phrasing of 'coercive measures' (强制措施, *qiang zhi cuo shi*) in the CPL refers to a collective term which includes all forms of measures to restrict or deprive the suspect or the accused of their liberty during investigation or further proceedings (Chapter Six, Articles 66–100 CPL), but this does not include search and seizure measures and so on. Coercive

[6] Ma Guixiang and Shi Lan, 'On the Construction of Criminal Judicial Review Procedure for Filing a Case' (2018) 5 *Journal of Political Science and Law* 53.
[7] See http://china.org.cn/english/government/93200.htm.

measures follow the apprehension of a person suspected of a crime, either in the form of a 'citizen's arrest' (Article 84 CPL) or in the form of police taking a suspect into custody (Article 82 CPL).

According to the CPL, five measures qualify as 'coercive':

(1) summons for questioning;
(2) release on guarantee;
(3) residential surveillance;
(4) arrest;
(5) pre-trial detention.

A. Summons for Questioning

A summons for questioning (拘传, *ju chuan*), regulated by Article 66 of the CPL, may be translated as 'compelled appearance'. Although Article 66 of the CPL invests the power to issue a summons for questioning equally in the police, the procuratorates and the courts, in practice it is the police who will be the first to be faced the interrogation of suspects. Article 119 of the CPL, moreover, shows that a summons for questioning shall be reserved for those suspects who 'do not need to be taken into custody'. Thus, this measure represents the least intrusive form of coercion.

The Chinese law governing the powers of the police is set out in two pieces of legislation (and parallels, in principle, civil law systems). Both, the People's Police Law (PL) and CPL establish police powers to take individuals into custody. The PL, with several conditions, provides the power 'to interrogate and inspect the person suspected of having violated law or committed a crime'. The normal period of time for the police to hold an interrogated person shall not be more than 24 hours, but in special cases, the interrogation period can be extended to 48 hours.[8] The maximum time for police to hold a person according to this measure is 24 hours longer than the maximum for a measure of 'summons for questioning' which – according to the CPL – may amount to 24 hours (Article 119).

A CPL-based summons for questioning issued to suspects or defendants (Article 66 CPL) includes an order to appear at a designated place in the city or county where the suspect resides. The law also allows the interrogation of a suspect at his/her residence. The CPL does not specify whether the interrogation can be held at a police station, but the MPS Provisions state that the interrogation can be conducted in the place where the police handle the case. The time limit for holding a suspect for interrogation, in a normal case, is up to 12 hours. For serious and complicated cases, the law allows an extension up to 24 hours. But the law prohibits

[8] Art 9 of the Police Law, which was enacted in 1995, and amended in 2012.

successive summonses (Article 119(3) CPL), explicitly stating that this prohibition is intended to prevent the 'covert confinement' of suspects.

B. Release on Guarantee

Release on guarantee (取保候审, *qu bao hou shen*) is sometimes translated as 'bail' because of its similarity to bail or bond in other jurisdictions. Release on guarantee entails two forms of guarantee: (1) supervision of the suspect by a guarantor; and (2) the depositing of bail money. The police, the procuratorate and the courts all have the authority to use this measure and the law provides several conditions under which this measure may be applied (Article 67 CPL).

Release on guarantee may be applied to:

(1) those who may be sentenced to supervised release,[9] or criminal detention,[10] or a supplementary punishment;
(2) those who may be sentenced to fixed-term imprisonment or a heavier penalty but are unlikely to pose a danger to the public if released on guarantee;
(3) those who are suffering from serious illness or cannot take care of themselves, or for those women who are pregnant or breastfeed their own infants, but are unlikely to pose a danger to the public if they are released on guarantee;
(4) those whose cases have not been closed at the end of the detention period, who must be released on guarantee.

A suspect/defendant may be released on guarantee in two forms. The suspect or defendant either may be ordered to deposit bail money in a designated bank account, or the suspect/defendant may choose a guarantor who satisfies the conditions set out in Article 69 of the CPL. A guarantor must not be implicated in the case, must not have been stripped of civil rights, and must have a permanent address as well as regular income. In addition, the guarantor must have the ability to perform the duties of a guarantor and must be willing to comply with the duties listed in Article 70 of the CPL. These duties concern: first, supervision of a suspect released on guarantee to ensure compliance with the obligations established by Article 71 of the CPL; and second, promptly reporting any violation of those obligations to the agency enforcing the measure. Failure to carry out the

[9] The literal translation from Chinese into English results in the word 'control' (管制, *guan zhi*). Control is imposed only for minor offences. Sentenced offenders are not to be detained but placed under the regime of supervised release by the local public security authority.

[10] Criminal detention (拘役, *ju yi*) is also a criminal punishment to be applied for minor offences. It is a custodial punishment which may be imposed for a period of between one month to six months. Normally the sentenced offender serves this sentence in a detention house. According to the Criminal Code, the regime of detention houses allows the offender to go back home for one or two days per month. If a detainee choses to work, he/she should be paid for the work (Arts 42–44 of the Criminal Code).

duties required by Article 70 may result in a fine or, if a criminal offence was established, in criminal prosecution (Article 70(2)).

Release on guarantee in the form of depositing bail money may be arranged after fixing a sum for the bail money which considers the criteria listed in Article 72(1):

(1) the necessity of carrying out legal proceedings without disruptions (in particular in the form of abscondment of suspects);
(2) the risk to society of the person to be released on bail;
(3) the nature and circumstances of the case;
(4) the gravity of the potential punishment; and
(5) the financial situation of the person to be released on guarantee.

The CPL also lists the general obligations of those released on guarantee (Article 71). The suspect or the accused shall:

(1) not leave the place – usually a city or a county where he/she currently resides – without obtaining a permission from the enforcement authority;
(2) notify the enforcement authority of any changes of address, employment and contact details within 24 hours;
(3) promptly appear before the legal authority in a timely manner when summoned;
(4) not interfere in any way with witnesses;
(5) not destroy or forge evidence or collude with others in producing a false confession.

In addition, obligations may be imposed which are tailored to the specific circumstances of the case. These may include orders: not to enter designated venues; not to meet or communicate with particular persons; not to engage in specified activities; to hand in his/her passport or other documents related to entry/exit of the country or a driver's licence to the enforcement authority (Article 71(2) CPL).

If suspects or defendants violate any of the conditions detailed in Article 71 CPL part or all of the bail money will be forfeited. However, violation of conditions will not automatically result in a custodial coercive measure. Article 71(3) of the CPL sets out potential responses to violations as requesting either a letter of excuse, another guarantor or new bail money; or the placing of the person into detention. Such a graded response to violations of conditions placed on alternatives to pre-trial detention corresponds to the principle of proportionality (and underlines the legislator's intention to reduce custodial measures prior to trial).

C. Residential Surveillance

From the 2012 CPL amendment, it can be inferred that the purpose of the legislator's retention of residential surveillance (监视居住, *jian shi ju zhu*) as a coercive measure was to reduce the use of pre-trial detention. This was reflected in Article 73 (Article 74 2018 CPL) which increases the general applicable conditions for residential surveillance. Criminal suspects and defendants who meet the pre-trial conditions and other conditions provided by law can be placed under residential surveillance. The suspected crimes are generally more serious than those for which release on guarantee may be applied. From another angle, the legislator ranks residential surveillance as more restrictive than release on guarantee. Article 76 of the CPL requires the period of residential surveillance to be subtracted from the final sentence. For cases involving a sentence of controlled release, one day shall be subtracted for each day spent under residential surveillance, while in case where the accused is sentenced to detention or imprisonment, each two-day period under surveillance will result in one day being subtracted. Residential surveillance parallels the concepts of 'home detention' or 'house arrest' which are today internationally recognised as promising alternatives to pre-trial detention.

The provision sets out several detailed pre-conditions which will enable a suspect to be placed under residential surveillance:

(1) the suspect or defendant suffers from a serious illness, and cannot take care of themselves;
(2) the suspect or defendant is a pregnant woman or a woman who is breastfeeding her own baby;
(3) the suspect or defendant is the sole supporter of a person who cannot take care of himself/herself.

    These first three elements reflect the spirit of humanitarianism, but a further two conditions are also introduced, either to allow for flexibility or for the purpose of smoothly carrying out the proceedings:

(4) considering the special circumstances of the case or as needed for handling the case;
(5) where the term of custody has expired, but the case has not been closed.

An additional condition has been added by the Article 9 of the MPS Provisions practice code, which is:

> A criminal suspect whose pre-trial detention is not approved by the procuratorate (which needs to continue investigation) and meets the conditions for residential surveillance, may be placed under residential surveillance.

This explanation is obviously contrary to the general conditions mentioned above, required by the law 'to meet the conditions of pre-trial detention'. It seems that this may be considered to be an ultra vires interpretation aimed at allowing flexibility and effective control, which runs counter to the aim of the legislation, ie to reduce the rate of pre-trial detention.

Before the CPL was revised in 2012, residential surveillance was usually carried out at the domicile of the suspect or defendant. However, there was no clear provision for this in the law and in practice. There have been cases involving corruption-related crimes, where in order to use the six-month period of residential surveillance, some criminal suspects or defendants have been placed in dedicated guest houses or other locations, cutting off contact with the outside world, which is actually a form of disguised detention. In the 2012 CPL amendment, this practice was legalised, and the imposition method of designated residential surveillance was added into the law. There are two conditions for using this method: one is that the suspect or defendant does not have a permanent domicile, and the other is that the suspect or defendant's case involves endangering national security, terrorism, or particularly serious bribery, and there are concerns that if the measure was carried out at the suspect's residence, it might obstruct investigations (Article 73 CPL 2012).

The revised draft of the CPL published on 30 August 2011 stated that there were two circumstances which may prevent notification of the family of a suspect or defendant. One was where it was impossible to notify them; the other was where it was thought that notifying them would endanger national security or create a risk of terrorism (Article 73(2) of the draft amendment). This became the most controversial part of the draft amendment, because the 'impossible to notify' provision is very general, carries great discretion, and as a result is difficult to monitor. Further, when a suspect's family are not notified of the surveillance it is difficult to exercise the right to hire a lawyer. In such cases, there is a real risk that the suspect will be legally disappeared, and the period of surveillance may be as long as six months.

The CPL amendment in 2012 deleted the unnotified cases of endangering national security or terrorism, but the more subtle change was that the content of notification to family members was also modified. The original draft required family members to be notified of the 'reasons for residential surveillance and the premises for execution' within 24 hours of the imposition of the measures. In the final amendment, the 'reasons for residential surveillance and the place of execution' were deleted, and the provision only states that family members must be notified. This led to difficulties in protecting the rights of suspects. In the 2018 CPL amendment, the 'serious bribery' pre-condition was deleted.

Empirical research has produced evidence that, in practice, the proportion of such measures used is not high. However, the public security organs have a great deal of discretionary power when using this measure, and as the 'designated residence' is not fixed, there is a risk that this provision could evolve into a disguised detention measure. It is recommended that this measure be deleted in future updates to the CPL, or at least that residential surveillance in designated residences is removed as an option.[11] At the same time, a widening of the scope of Article 119(3) of the CPL could be considered. That article aims to prevent the use of the summons for questioning as a covert confinement, and could perhaps be expanded to cover all alternatives to pre-trial detention.

Article 78 of the CPL authorises the monitoring of suspects who are under residential surveillance, through unscheduled inspections (or visits) and electronic devices. The latter in principle would allow the implementation of what is called

[11] Guo Shuo, 'Residential Surveillance at Designated Residence as "Harsher than Detention"' (2016) 6 *Journal of Wuhan University (Philosophy and Social Sciences Edition)* 119.

electronically monitored house arrest (or other forms of electronically supervised restriction of movement). However, neither the CPL nor the Interpretations provide any detail on electronic monitoring. While electronic monitoring evidently is implemented in China as an element of 'community correction',[12] research on whether and to what extent electronic monitoring is applied to enforce residential surveillance is not available.

D. Arrest

As explained in Chapter 3 on Basic Concepts, the term 'arrest' (拘留, *ju liu*) in common law jurisdictions has been mis-translated into Chinese as '逮捕' (*daibu*). In China, 'arrest' does not mean the police power to hold and detain a suspect for a short period of time in order to carry out interrogation or identification, but instead means the longer and more restrictive coercive measure before the final court decision is made. The police power to hold a suspect is known in Chinese as 拘留 (*ju liu*). A literal translation into English would result simply in 'detention'. In the following text, the author uses 'arrest' in the English sense, to explain the police power to deprive a suspect of his right to liberty, and also try to avoid further confusion surrounding this measure.

Article 82 of the CPL sets out the grounds for arrest. The grounds justifying arrest fall into two distinct groups. A first group of pre-conditions deals with the strength of suspicion. A person may be taken into custody according to Article 82(1)–(3) if:

(1) he is in the process of preparing or committing a crime or is discovered immediately after committing a crime (addressing a situation where an offender is caught 'red-handed');
(2) the victim or an eyewitness on the scene identifies him as the person who committed the crime;
(3) criminal evidence is discovered with him or at his residence.

Article 82(4)–(7) lists further grounds for an arrest where there is a risk of adverse effects on the carrying out of criminal proceedings. A person may be arrested if:

(4) they attempt to commit suicide or to abscond, or if the person is a fugitive after committing the crime;
(5) there is a risk that they will destroy or falsify evidence, or collude with others to produce a false confession;
(6) they do not reveal their true name and residential address, and their identity is unknown;
(7) there is a strong suspicion that they are involved in cross-regional criminal activities, repeat and multiple crimes or gang crime.

[12] Enshen Li, 'The Rhetoric and Practice of Community Corrections in China' (2017) 12 *Asian Criminology* 143.

The permissible length of arrest is not easy to establish from the CPL. This is a major difference between the CPL and the legislation of other jurisdictions, where the time limits for arrest are clearly provided for by the law, usually counted in the exact number of hours before the suspect is to be brought before a judge. According to the provisions in the CPL, police are required to interrogate a detainee within 24 hours of the arrest. If it is found that the detainee should not be arrested, the detainee shall be released immediately (Article 86 CPL). However, one of the characteristics of the coercive measures is that arrest and pre-trial detention are connected with each other. In practice, most arrested suspects will be subjected to pre-trial detention until the time when a final judgment is made;[13] hence, the provisions have added two periods together. According to Article 91 of the CPL, if the police think an arrestee needs to be further detained under pre-trial detention, the police must seek the prosecutor's examination and approval. In a normal situation the time limit for filing the request is three days after arrest. In special circumstances, the time limit for filing such a request may be extended for one to four days. But Article 91 further provides that, if a person is strongly suspected of committing cross-regional crimes, repeat crimes, or gang crime, the time limit for filing the pre-trial detention for examination and approval may be extended in major cases to 30 days. After this, the prosecutor has seven days to provide a decision. If approval for the detention is denied, the police may seek review but must release the detainee. To add these days together, police can detain suspects for up to 37 days.

In recent decades, Chinese legislators and legal scholars have advocated that arrest is an emergency and temporary measure in the investigation.[14] However, judging from the application of the above-mentioned conditions and the period of detention after arrest, as well as the high arrest rate, it can be concluded that arrests have deviated from the original intention of the legislation. At present, arrest has become a routine measure before pre-trial detention. Some scholars have suggested that arrest should be restricted to being a temporary measure in emergency situations, which conforms to the legislative spirit of the Constitution and is beneficial to protecting citizens' right to personal liberty.[15]

One controversial issue is the time limits on arrest. Before the 2012 CPL revision, as the second draft was being debated, the author was asked to provide information about the time limits for police arrests in other jurisdictions, especially the time limits for detention in terrorism cases. The author answered that, on average, police may hold a suspect for around three days or, in some jurisdictions, counted in hours, normally for 48 hours without charge. For terrorist crimes, some

[13] According to the results of empirical research conducted in 2015, in selected basic courts (one each in Eastern, Western, and central China), among the 2,458 defendants, 2,289 were in criminal detention (ie arrest), and the arrest rate was 93%: Sun Changyong and Wu Xiaolin, 'The Basic Situation of the Criminal Detention, Changes and Improvement of the Application, after the Implementation of CPL' (2015) 1 *Gansu Social Science*.

[14] Lang Sheng (ed), *Criminal Procedure Law Amendment and Application* (Beijing, China Legal Publishing House, 2012) 177.

[15] Xie Xiaojian, 'On the Emergency Characteristics of Criminal Detention in China' (2016) 4 *Modern Law* 110.

European countries had extended this period to five days. At that time, according to the UK's law, a detainee could be held for a maximum of 28 days without charge.[16] As highlighted by the above description, China's CPL allows the police to legally hold a suspect for 10–14 days in ordinary cases. If the case is more serious or complicated, as stated in Article 82(7), the time limit for arrest is extended to 37 days. After the 2012 amendment of the CPL came into effect, it was found that, in some regions, this time limit had been extended illegally; the longest period a suspect was held by police was 58 days.[17]

E. Pre-Trial Detention

First, the term '逮捕' (*daibu*) used in the Chinese CPL still causes confusion. This measure is similar to pre-trial detention in other jurisdictions, but the difference is that *daibu* it is not only a measure of continuation after short-term arrest. Pre-trial detention is an independent coercive measure that can deprive the criminal suspect or defendant of their liberty until the court makes a final judgment, and this measure also has particular conditions. However, the problem with the legal formulation is that 逮捕 (*daibu*) is sometimes used as a verb to indicate the act of arresting a criminal suspect (Articles 80, 93) and sometimes as a noun to indicate the state of detention (Article 81). When this term is translated into other languages, it results in misunderstandings.

Amendments to the pre-trial detention provisions have taken place in each of the past three revisions of the CPL. In the 1996 amendment, the evidence criteria for pre-trial detention was changed from the 1979 CPL 'major criminal facts have been verified' to 'there is evidence to support the facts of a crime' (Article 60 CPL 1996). The 2012 amendments detailed the social risk elements of pre-trial detention, ie the necessity elements, and created a system for reviewing the necessity of pre-trial detention. In the 2018 revision, a paragraph was added under the listed conditions for pre-trial detention, emphasising the consideration of social danger. These reforms mainly demonstrated the legislative aim of working towards the effective implementation of pre-trial detention measures.

The CPL stipulates three conditions applicable to pre-trial detention (Article 81 CPL). These are:

(1) there is evidence to prove the facts of a crime;
(2) a criminal suspect or defendant may be sentenced to imprisonment, or a heavier punishment;
(3) if the release on bail is insufficient to prevent dangers to society, the defendant shall be placed in pre-trial detention.

[16] This occurred in 2011, when the UK's legal basis was found in the Terrorism Act 2006. This period has now been reduced to a maximum of 14 days by the Protection of Freedoms Act 2012.

[17] Sun Changyong and Wu Xiaolin, 'The Basic Situation of the Criminal Detention, Changes and Improvement of the Application, after the Implementation of CPL' (2015) 1 *Gansu Social Science* 166.

In the 2012 CPL reform, the law expanded on the detailed circumstances of 'dangers to society'. A relevant danger to society is established through:

— the risk of a repeat crime;
— an imminent risk to national security, public security or social order;
— a risk of the destruction or forging of evidence, interfering with the testimony of a witness, or colluding with witnesses for testimony;
— the risk of retaliation against a victim, informant, or accuser;
— a risk of suicide or absconding.

Although the above-mentioned conditions have been continually refined with each revisions of the law, scholars and legal practitioners still argue about the vagueness and inaccuracy of these conditions.[18] For example, for the first requirement, as to evidence, the law does not specify the degree of proof which must be established. Article 128 of the SPP rules required that 'the evidence to prove the criminal act has been verified'. Such a condition is obviously unrealistic, because when the police apply to the prosecutor for pre-trial detention, it is often in the early stages of the investigation when it is difficult for evidence to reach the level of 'verification'. Thus, this condition is difficult to achieve in practice. Meanwhile, the interpretation of the SPP seemingly requires the confirmation of the suspects' guilt in the earlier stage of criminal proceedings. This criterion may violate the principle of the presumption of innocence, and it may have an impact on further proceedings, such as prosecution and trial. The 'dangers to society' include the risk of repeat crimes. This involves controversial issues, such as, for example, the issue of the legitimacy of the preventative function of pre-trial detention, which has been debated internationally for decades. This condition cannot be justified by the basic rationale of pre-trial detention, ie to ensure that criminal proceedings are properly carried out. In the author's view, based on the principles of the presumption of innocence and of proportionality, preventive detention should be carefully imposed and strictly limited to situations which either indicate a grave risk of obstructing the course of criminal proceedings or imminent grave dangers to individuals or society.

In jurisdictions of continental Europe, such as Germany, criminal procedure law does not provide absolute time limits for pre-trial detention, but introduces limitations and exemptions thereto which reflect a careful balancing of the principle of the presumption of innocence (and the individual's interest in liberty) against the state's interest (and duty) to effectively implement criminal law. In China's CPL, the time limit for pre-trial detention is governed by the time limits of procedural phases provided by the law and, in principle, when compared with the German criminal procedure law offers a far less generous period of pre-trial detention. While German Criminal procedural law (Article 121 of the German Criminal Procedure Law) sets a limit on pre-trial detention (before a first instance

[18] Kong Jun, 'On the Perfection of Pre-trial Detention System' (2012) 1 *Beijing University of Aeronautics and Astronautics Law Review* 291.

judgment) of six months (which may be extended), the CPL states in Article 156 for the investigation phases that:

> the time limits for detaining a suspect for investigation shall not be more than two months after he/she was arrested. But where a case is too complicated to be concluded before the time limit expires, the time limit may be extended for one month with the approval of the procuratorate at the next higher level.

For the review prosecution phase, Article 172 of the CPL states that:

> a procuratorate shall, within one month make a decision on a case transferred by a supervisory authority or by public security authority for prosecution, and in a major or complicated case, the period may be extended by 15 days.

However, the law allows for the prosecutor to send the case back to the police for supplementary investigation, in which case the police shall complete the supplementary investigation within one month. But this kind of supplementary investigation can be conducted twice. However, after the supplementary investigation of a case is completed, and when the case is transferred back the procuratorate, the period of review of the prosecution shall be counted anew by a procuratorate (Article 175(3)). Adding up these various time limits, suspects or the accused could be in custody for investigation without charge (prosecution) from 3–6.5 months.

The following table is an official statistic accounting for pre-trial detention rates from 1979 onwards.

Table 1 Suspects for whom pre-trial detention was decided and approved and public prosecutions filed by procuratorates nationwide (1979–2018)[19]

Years	Number of suspects for whom pre-trial detention was approved	Number of accused for whom public prosecution was filed	Number of cases of pre-trial detention/ Number cases of public prosecution
1979–1982	790,000	800,000	98.8%
1983–1987	2,210,000	2,160,000	102.3%
1988–1992	2,701,009	2,664,848	101.4%
1993–1997	3,037,528	2,989,901	101.6%
1998–2002	3,601,357	3,666,142	98.2%
2003–2007	4,313,595	4,840,570	89.1%
2008–2012	4,688,544	6,018,489	77.9%
2013–2017	4,530,927	7,173,835	63.2%
2018	1,056,616	1,692,846	62.4%
2019	1,088,490	1,818,808	60%
2020	770,561	1,572,971	49%

[19] This statistical table (1979–2017) is partly derived from: Liu Jihua, 'Review of my Country's Pre-trial Detention System' (2019) 5 *The Journal of China Law* 137. The author added the data for 2018, 2019 and 2020. The added data are from SPP Annual reports.

The data set out in Table 1 show a significant decline in the proportion of prosecuted defendants detained prior to trial since the end of the 1990s. While before 1998 virtually all defendants who were prosecuted and went to court had been detained prior to trial, the proportion of detained defendants dropped to less than two thirds in 2018. Tentatively, this drop in the rate of accused detained might be explained by a growing reluctance on the part of police and procuratorates to use pre-trial detention (and successful implementation of the government's policy aimed at reducing pre-trial detention). However, the data show also a significant increase in the number of public prosecutions filed, which could support an interpretation which explains the drop as an increasing pressure on the correctional system and its resources.

F. Citizen's Right to Arrest a Suspect[20]

Article 84 of the CPL authorises citizens under certain circumstances to seize and turn over a suspect to a public security agency, procuratorate, or a court for further handling the case. The CPL does not use the term 'arrest', but the word 扭送 (*niu song*). This term includes two characters, the 扭 (*niu*) can be translated as 'apprehend', which means that this action may carry some degree of force. The 送 (*song*) means 'turn over', so, put together, the meaning is similar to 'seize and turn over' in English. In the following text the term 'citizen's arrest' will be used.

Article 84 lists four groups of individuals who may be arrested lawfully by any citizen:

(1) individuals who are caught 'red-handed' (or immediately after committing a crime);
(2) wanted criminals;
(3) escaped prisoners;
(4) individuals pursued for capture.

The first group addressed in Article 84 is defined essentially by 'committing a crime', or 'caught immediately after committing a crime'. The term 'crime' establishes a rather low threshold which differs for example from English law requiring a reasonable suspicion that a person has committed or is committing an indictable offence in order to make a citizen's arrest lawful.[21] However, other European criminal procedure laws require, as provided in Article 84 CPL, only the suspicion of a criminal offence. However, the concept of the 'citizen's arrest' authorises private force and private force should be subject to effective restrictions. Therefore, criminal procedural law which allows room for the use of private force should be guided by the principle of proportionality and impose restrictions which consider the seriousness of the criminal offence in question and the state's interest in effective

[20] 'The citizen's arrest' is not a term used in the Chinese CPL.
[21] Police and Criminal Evidence Act (PACE) 1984, s 24A.

prosecution of crime. In light of this, it seems reasonable to advise law makers to raise the threshold for citizen's arrests to those crimes that are sufficiently serious (though this might possibly discourage citizens from contributing to law enforcement).

Another much debated issue concerns the question of how much force may be applied when carrying out a citizen's arrest. The CPL is silent on this point and introduces no restraints for the performance of an arrest. As a result of this, in practice, there have been cases where citizens have performed an arrest and it led to the death of the arrested person. In one of these cases, two persons who had seized the wanted person were sentenced to 10 years' imprisonment for the offence of illegal detention.[22] This also raises the issue of substantive criminal law, as a citizen's arrest provides a justification for an otherwise illegal act. Unlike the English law,[23] Chinese criminal law does not stipulate the elements required to make a citizen's arrest lawful. However, also on the basis of the provisions of English law, it is not easy to determine what 'reasonable force' means in practice.

The range of lawful citizen's arrests as provided by Article 84 of the CPL is significantly wider than in most criminal procedural laws, including wanted individuals or escaped prisoners. Future reforms should consider restricting the justification for force just the arrest of those individuals who are caught red-handed.

G. Pre-Trial Detention and International Human Rights Laws

In the past few decades, through amendments to the CPL, the legislature and legal institutions have made great efforts to balance the interests of combating crime and protecting the rights of criminal suspects and defendants exposed to pre-trial detention. For instance, in the 2012 CPL revision, reviewing the necessity for pre-trial detention (Article 95) was added, and the procuratorates also established the mechanism for the review of the necessity for pre-trial detention. However, these provisions are still some way from the principles set out in the various UN provisions that China has agreed to or signed up to. There is, therefore, still room for further reform.

In the past, Chinese legal scholars and practitioners have mainly focused their attention on the lawfulness of the measures that deprive suspects and defendants of their liberty but have neglected, to some degree, the procedural issues of reviewing and monitoring the decisions to arrest or to impose pre-trial detention. The right to a review of the lawfulness of arrest and detention prior to trial is set out in international human rights instruments. For example, Article 9 of the Universal Declaration of Human Rights (UDHR) confirms the principle that arrest or

[22] Wei Xiaona, 'Being brave for righteousness and being sentenced is all trouble caused by seizing and turning over', *Legal Daily*, 23 March 2010.

[23] Section 3 of the Criminal Law Act 1967: 'a person may use such force as is reasonable in the circumstance in the prevention of crime, or in the effecting or assisting in the lawful arrest of offenders or suspected offenders, or of persons unlawfully at large'.

detention must be substantiated, a principle which is also expressed in other UN and regional human rights instruments and in Article 9(1) of the ICCPR: 'everyone has the right to liberty and the security of the person. No one shall be subjected to arbitrary arrest or detention'. It is notable that the UN Committee of Human Rights has emphasised in its implementation of the law that it is not enough for deprivation of liberty to be provided for by the law: the enforcement of the law in a given case must not take place arbitrarily. Arbitrariness is not to be equated with 'against the law', but must be interpreted more broadly to include elements of inappropriateness, injustice, lack of predictability and due process of law.[24] Based on those international human rights instruments, several legislative and practical issues in China are the subject of some debate.

(1) The right of a detainee to be brought before a judge or other judicial officer. As mentioned above, the arrest is approved by the head of public security and pre-trial detention is not approved by courts but is mainly approved by procuratorates, as in some Eastern European countries before transition. Some Chinese scholars have misunderstood the meaning of 'other officer authorised by law to exercise the judicial power' in Article 9(3) of the ICCPR and took it to mean that a prosecutor may also be included in this category. However, from the conclusion of cases handled by Human Rights Committee,[25] it is clear that the phrase means that it must 'be exercised by an authority which is independent, objective and impartial in relation to the issue dealt with'. This, in the author's view, means lay judges in common law jurisdictions. The key point of this requirement is that those judges or judicial officers must be independent and impartial. Impartiality in criminal proceedings requires that judges should be independent of both parties. This issue has been a crucial point for reform in China's judicial system and has been debated now for several years. Although Chinese law requires that the prosecutor should handle cases in an independent and objective manner, this mainly means that it is independent from other institutions, but it could not change the prosecuting role of procuratorates in criminal proceedings. Some scholars deem that the existing model of prosecutors reviewing pre-trial detention lacks a theoretical basis. The prosecutor has the power to supervise the investigation and when reviewing the pre-trial detention this may also involve a review of the legality of investigative activities. But this does not constitute supervision of the investigation. The procuratorate's decision to approve pre-trial detention mainly deals with the issue of the suspect's right to liberty before trial; the nature of this review is not 'supervision'. It can be concluded that

> as the main body of prosecution, the procuratorate is actually depriving the suspect's liberty in the name of false investigation supervision, the essence is that

[24] William A Schabas, *UN International Covenant on Civil and Political Rights – Nowak's CCPR Commentary*, 3rd edn (Kiel, NP Engel, 2019) 248.

[25] No 521 Communication 1992, *Kulomin v Hungary*. See also ibid, 258.

> 'the plaintiff catches the defendant', which constitutes the most serious unfairness and injustice in criminal process.[26]

Some senior scholars think it is difficult to reform the mechanism for the review of pre-trial detention, because the Constitution transfers the supervision power for law enforcement to the procuratorate. They have concluded that before the power to review pre-trial detention can be moved in this way, the Constitution must first be revised.[27] In the author's opinion, there is no conflict between the supervisory powers of the prosecutor and giving courts the authority to review arrest and pre-trial detention, because the prosecutor can supervise police investigation in other ways.[28]

(2) Suspects should be released pending trial. Article 9(3) of the ICCPR and other international human rights documents supply the principle that the pre-trial detention may not become the general rule but should be an exception.[29] However, from the data displayed above, it seems that in China in recent years more than 49 per cent of suspects or accused are detained pending trial. This cannot, therefore, be described as an exceptional measure in China's criminal proceedings; rather, it has become the norm. However, statistics on pre-trial detention in China clearly demonstrate that there is scope for further reducing its use. The significant decrease in the number of defendants detained prior to trial also bears witness to the fact that such scope can be effectively used. Legislators and legal practitioners should recognise that this practice of widespread application of pre-trial detention also violates to some extent the principle of the presumption of innocence. One positive trend is that, since the 2012 CPL reform, alternatives to pre-trial detention are available which might have played a role in reducing the rate of pre-trial detention.

(3) Remedy for unlawful arrest and detention (or right to *habeas corpus*). Article 9(4) of the ICCPR states that:

> anyone who is deprived of his liberty by arrest or detention shall be entitled to take a proceeding before a court, in order for that court to decide without delay on the lawfulness of his detention and order his release if the detention is not lawful.

This is a right to complain against unlawful arrest and detention. In the Chinese CPL, four paths to review the lawfulness of pre-trial detention are provided:

(a) the obligation of the legal institutions: According to Article 94, the relevant legal institutions shall interrogate the suspect within 24 hours of the commencement of pre-trial detention. In the event that they discover that the person should not be detained, they must release the person immediately, and a certificate shall be issued to the person;

[26] Liu Jihua, 'Review of Pre-trial Detention System' (2019) 5 *The Journal of China Law* 137.

[27] Chen Guang Zhong (ed), *ICCPR and Chinese Criminal Procedure* (Beijing, the Commercial Press, 2005) 141–42.

[28] Yue Liling, *ICCPR and Criminal Justice in China* (Beijing, the Law Press, 2007) 64–65.

[29] William A Schabas, *UN International Covenant on Civil and Political Rights – Nowak's CCPR Commentary*, 3rd edn (Kiel, NP Engel, 2019) 260.

(b) the review of the necessity for pre-trial detention: this must be carried out by the procuratorate, after a review by a prosecutor; if he/she thinks that pre-trial detention is not necessary, the prosecutor shall suggest the release of the detainee or modify the coercive measure;
(c) the suspect's or defendant's complaint: Article 97 of the CPL allows suspects, defendants, or their legal representatives, close relatives, or defenders the right to apply for modification of a coercive measure. The law requires the relevant legal institutions to review the application and to make a decision within three days;
(d) the detainee shall be released when the time limits of stages in criminal proceedings are over: Article 98 of the CPL states that when a case in which the criminal suspect or the defendant is detained cannot be concluded within the time limits specified by the law, including the phases of investigation, prosecution, trial at first instance and second instance, the suspect or the defendant shall be released.

It should be noted that none of the above-mentioned review proceedings are dealt with by courts. In this respect, doubts have been raised about whether the detainee's rights can be effectively protected by the procuratorates, as they are not in an impartial position but are the party pursuing prosecution. In further law reforms, concrete proceedings for the right to habeas corpus should be established.

III. Other Investigative Measures

A. Interrogation of the Suspect and the Accused

The CPL has a special section in the investigation chapter setting out the rules for interrogating criminal suspects. Before discussing these rules, a few issues relating to terminology must first be introduced. Similar to English, 'interrogation' and 'interview' are two different terms in Chinese law. In the official English translation of the CPL, 'interrogation' of the suspect has been used. However, in the original, the words for interrogation (讯问) and interview (询问) both contain two Chinese characters. These can be separated, and the second character '问' (*wen*) means 'questioning'. The other characters '讯' and '询' show the hierarchical relationship between the questioner and the questioned person. 'Interrogation' is a question that superiors put forward to subordinates, which usually makes the interrogated person feel in a weaker position and compelled to answer.[30] Meanwhile, questions put forward in an 'interview' do not come with the same nuance of subordination and coercion. Thus, in Chinese law, 'interview' is used when putting questions to witnesses. The author

[30] Peng Junlei, 'On the Protection of the Rights of Criminal Suspects in Investigation and Interrogation' (2018) 4 *Law Forum* 152.

agrees with the view of some international scholars, that 'interview' carries a more friendly and non-inquisitorial connotation than 'interrogation'.[31]

The provision for obtaining a statement or confession is not provided for in the section on interrogation of the suspect but in the chapter on criminal evidence. Article 52 provides that:

> Judges, prosecutors and criminal investigators must under legal procedures, gather various kinds of evidence that can prove the guilt or innocence of a criminal suspect or defendant and the seriousness of the crime. It shall be strictly prohibited to extort confessions by torture, gather evidence by threat, enticement, deceit, or other illegal means, or force anyone to commit self-incrimination.

The SPC lists in Article 123 of its Interpretation three methods of collecting confessions that are illegal and should be excluded. These illegal methods are:

(1) the use of violent methods such as beatings, illegal use of restraints, or harsh methods of disguised corporal punishment, making it difficult for the defendant to bear suffering. A confession made against the will of the defendant and caused by the pain he endured;
(2) using methods of threatening violence or seriously harming the lawful rights and interests of the person and his close relatives, etc, causing the defendant unbearable suffering and making a confession against his will;
(3) the defendant's confession collected by illegal detention and other methods that illegally restrict personal liberty.

However, the SPC's Interpretation does not elaborate in further detail 'threat, enticement, and deceit'. Meanwhile, it should be noted that there are different legal consequences for the exclusion of confessions obtained through various illegal means. Article 56 of the CPL states that confessions of criminal suspects and defendants extorted by torture or by other illegal means should be excluded, but there is no mention of confessions which are extorted by means of threats, enticements, and deceit. Some legal practitioners believe that the provision reflects the complexity of legislation. For example, for some special investigative methods, such as 'controlled delivery' (discussed in more detail later in this chapter), which in principle could also be regarded as a kind of deceit, the law cannot prohibit one kind of 'deceit' in one article of the law but allow it in another article. Several practitioners believe that the provisions of Article 52 of the CPL should be regarded as a kind of declaration from the legislator that on the one hand all evidence obtained by means of torture, threats, enticement, and deceit is illegal and on the other hand, that the legislator wants to leave a space of discretion for the judiciary. In the practice of interrogation around the world, it is very hard to find a clearly defined boundary between proper interrogation strategies or techniques and 'enticement

[31] Marijke Malsch and Meike M de Boer, 'Interviews of Suspects of Crime – Law and Practice in European Countries' in Darryl K Brown et al (eds), *The Oxford Handbook of Criminal Process* (New York, Oxford University Press, 2019) 318.

or deceit'. One lawyer has suggested that when elaborating the exclusionary rules, a list of serious means of threat, enticement and deceit should be established, or typical cases of violation be edited into guiding cases in order to promote the effective implementation of the exclusionary rule.[32]

The detailed procedural requirements or technical rules of interrogation are provided for in the second section, 'interrogation of the criminal suspect'. The first rule is about the interrogation body: the law provides that only the investigator (police or prosecutor) has the authority to conduct the interrogation and during the interrogation there must be two or more investigators present (Article 118(1) CPL).

The second rule is about the venue of interrogation. In the 2012 CPL revision, a paragraph was added to Article 118 which states that: 'after a criminal suspect has been delivered to a detention centre for custody, the investigator shall conduct the interrogation inside the detention centre'. This revision has been regarded as a positive step, as one of the primary purposes for its inclusion is to attempt to prevent torture during interrogation. Before the revision, in practice, the police interrogated the suspects in various venues; sometimes torture had occurred, or suspects withdrew their confession and complained that they had been tortured.[33] For those suspects who have not been arrested or placed under pre-trial detention, the law allows exceptions: the suspect shall be summoned to a designated place in the city or county where the suspect residence for interrogation, but before doing that, the credentials from the procuratorate or public security authority must be produced (Article 119 CPL).

The third rule is about the method of interrogation. Article 120 CPL states that:

> when interrogating a criminal suspect, the investigator first shall ask whether the suspect has engaged in any criminal conduct and let him state the circumstances and the events of his guilt or innocence, and then put forward other questions. A criminal suspect shall truthfully answer the questions raised by an investigator based on facts, but has the right to refuse to answer the questions which are not relevant to the case.

This article is the most controversial one, and it has been debated for many years. This provision was discussed in Chapter 3 above, in the context of the principle of the presumption of innocence. The provision could enable conclusions to be drawn that the suspect has not been afforded the right to silence. The so-called right to refuse to answer questions that are irrelevant to the case has no operability in practice. The key issue here is who is to decide which questions are relevant and which are not. As explained in Chapter 3, it is clear that the police define what is relevant.[34] Furthermore, the author and other scholars agree that this provision also conflicts with the right not to self-incriminate provided for in Article 52 of the CPL, as it requires that the suspect truthfully answer the questions of the

[32] Wang Liangbao, 'Threats, Enticements, and Deceits. The Regulatory Path of Illegally Obtained Evidence' (2017) 10 *Shanghai Lawyer*, www.lawyers.org.cn.

[33] Lang Sheng (ed), *The Revision and the Implementation of Criminal Procedure Law* (Beijing, Xinhua Press, 2012).

[34] Liling Yue, *Criminal Trial and Human Rights Projection* (Beijing, Law Press, 2010) 218–19.

investigators. This sentence also shows that the burden of proof does not rest fully on the state, although the law does not provide legal consequences when a suspect remains silent or where the suspect's confession differs from the version which the investigator believed. These concerns have been raised, and debates among legal scholars and practitioners have lasted for decades. What happens if a suspect is then convicted? Is this an indication that the suspect did not tell 'the truth' and that his or her punishment should therefore be harsher? Issues of this kind have existed in practice for a long time and the author is concerned that their persistence could subvert the principle of privilege against self-incrimination.

The fourth rule is about recording and preserving the procedure and content of the interrogation of criminal suspects. Before the CPL was revised in 2012, the main method of recording the content of interrogations was to make transcripts. In 2012, a new method of recording the processing and content of interrogation was added, and these must now be carried out in the form of audio and video recording (Article 123 CPL). The purpose is to improve the quality of evidence, and also to curb the use of torture to extract confessions and reduce the occurrence of miscarriage of justice cases. However, there are different requirements for cases of different severity. For ordinary criminal cases, audio and video recording can be carried out, and for cases that may result in sentences of life imprisonment or the death penalty, or for other serious crimes, the law specifically stipulates that audio and video recordings should be conducted for the 'whole process' to 'maintain integrality'. The MPS explains in its MPS Provisions what the phrase 'maintain integrality' means: 'No selective recording, editing, or deletion is allowed' (Article 208 of the MPS Provisions). A law enforcer has pointed out that, in practice, some investigators make audio and video recordings only after breaking through the suspect's psychological defences and obtaining confessions, or record only a single interrogation and confession of crime. This results in the undermining of the integrality of the interrogation process. Further the law provides no legal consequences for the failure to make these audio and video recordings available in court, which must bring the admissibility of this new type of evidence into question.[35]

With regard to further interrogation rules, the author, scholars and legal practitioners generally regard there as being two major legislative flaws: first, the law does not clearly stipulate the limits on the duration of interrogation, resulting in excessively long interrogation in practice, and even night interrogation, thereby undermining a criminal suspect's right to rest. The second is the carrying out of interrogations without the presence of a lawyer. As noted in Chapter 5 above, although the law states that criminal suspects have the right to receive assistance from their lawyers during the investigation, especially from duty lawyers, the duty lawyer has very limited rights, and the law does not state that lawyers have the right to be present during the interrogation of suspects. This situation also means

[35] Wang Rui, 'A Study on Procedure Regulations and Procedure Behavior in Criminal Interrogation' (2016) 4 *Journal of Shandong Police College* 135.

that the interrogation is carried out completely without external supervision. The author believes that these issues will become key topics in future revisions of the CPL and the Lawyers Law.

B. Interviewing Victims and Witnesses

China's CPL does not seem to pay adequate attention to the interviewing of victims and witnesses, unlike academic research. The CPL only uses four very brief provisions to stipulate the general rules for interviewing witnesses and victims, such as, before the interview, the investigator shall inform the victim or witness of: legal liability for perjury or concealing criminal evidence (Article 125); the venue of the interview; and the credentials that should be presented during the interview (Article 124) and so on. However, in practice, the testimony obtained through such interviews in the investigative stage plays an important role in the subsequent criminal process. The witness and victim testimonies form an important part of the case file and can have a strong impact on the trial. Moreover, investigators' method of interviewing witnesses and victims is rather controversial. The law does not prohibit investigators from asking witnesses and victims leading questions. There is also no special protection for vulnerable witnesses and victims, such as child witnesses and victims of sexual crimes. The MPS Provisions only stipulate that investigators shall not disclose the facts of the case to witnesses or victims or express their views about the case. It is strictly prohibited to use violence, threats and other illegal means to interview witnesses and victims (Article 221 of MPS Provisions). These weaker parts of legislation and research should be taken seriously in future legal reforms. It may be helpful to learn from the experience of England in formulating the guidelines, such as 'Achieving Best Evidence in Criminal Proceedings' and use it as a guideline to train the investigators.[36]

C. Inspection, Examination and Forensic Evaluation

In accordance with the provisions of the law, investigators have the power to conduct inquests and inspections of crime-related premises, objects, persons, and corpses. The law allows persons with expertise to be assigned or retained under the direction of investigators when necessary to conduct crime scene investigation or examinations (Article 128 CPL). The law also allows investigators not only to examine victims or criminal suspects, but also to take fingerprints, and collect biological samples such as blood and urine for the purpose of determining certain characteristics, condition of injuries, or physiological conditions (Article 132 CPL). The same provision states that if a criminal suspect refuses

[36] Liz Campbell et al, *The Criminal Process*, 5th edn (New York, Oxford University Press, 2019) 83.

to be examined, the investigators can make a compulsory examination when they deem it necessary. It may inferred from the wording of this provision that victims cannot be compulsorily examined in this way. These physical inspections and samples involve an intrusion into the bodies of citizens and also interfere with a citizens' right to privacy. However, unfortunately, these measures are taken without judicial review and control. They are approved by the heads in charge of the investigation agency. When a procuratorate is reviewing a case, if it considers that a re-examination is necessary, the public security agency can request such re-examination.

With regard to the DNA analysis, DNA profiles have been used in criminal investigations since 1987,[37] and the MPS established a DNA database in 2003. Between 2011 and 2014 one study counted 782,000 DNA profiles in criminal cases.[38] DNA analysis is often used in criminal investigations. However, unfortunately, neither the CPL nor the MPS' Regulation to implement the CPL specify rules involving DNA sampling and analysis procedures, the scope of DNA analysis (for example phenotyping) and retention of DNA profiles in the DNA database. From the perspective of criminal procedure, there are still some deficiencies in DNA identification procedures, including:

(1) only investigators can initiate the DNA identification: criminal suspects and victims have no right to apply for the initial DNA identification; they only have the right to apply for supplementary evaluation or reappraisal of the first evaluation results;
(2) lack of review procedures for the qualification of the evaluation subject;
(3) when the conductor of the evaluation has an interest in the case, there is no provision for his appointment to be challenged;
(4) lack of review of the legality of the source of the inspected materials;
(5) lack of review of the extraction, storage, and inspection process of the inspected materials;
(6) the law states that when the public prosecutor, the party or defender or the agent ad litem disagrees with the expert opinion, if the judge believes that the expert must appear in court, the expert should appear in court to testify. However, in practice the attendance rate of experts is relatively low. Taking the courts in Shan Dong Province as an example, the outcome of a survey shows that the attendance rate of expert witnesses is generally low. From 2016 to 2018, a total of 1,255 witnesses and expert witnesses appeared in court to testify, of which 229 were expert witnesses, and the attendance rate of witnesses and expert witnesses was only 0.3 per cent.[39]

[37] The MPS answers netizens' messages about DNA collection, www.gov.cn

[38] Liu Bing, 'A Preliminary Evaluation of DNA Evidence in Criminal Investigation, Based on National DNA Database' (2015) 3 *Forensic Science and Technology* 199.

[39] Shandong High Court Research Group, 'Analysis of the Practice of Appearance of Witnesses and Experts in Criminal Cases' (2019) 3 *Journal of Shandong Judge Training College*.

Debate about DNA identification is still ongoing. Some scholars suggest that several basic principles should be established, for example:

- the purpose of DNA identification should be clarified in legal amendments;
- it should be limited to only the personal identification;
- the sampling objects of the DNA database should be specified. According to the principle of proportionality, the objects of sampling should be limited to criminal suspects of serious violent crimes or sexual crimes;
- determine the sampling time of DNA data and the time of entering the database;
- specify the storage time limit and destruction requirements of DNA samples; and
- a sanction mechanism for illegal use of DNA databases should be established.[40]

D. Search and Seizure

According to the provisions of the Constitution, citizens' residences are inviolable, and illegal searches and intrusions into citizens' residence are prohibited (Article 39 of the 2018 Constitution). The Constitution also stipulates that freedom of communication and the confidentiality of communications of citizens are protected by law. Except for the needs of national security or the prosecution of criminal offences, public security organs or procuratorial organs shall conduct surveillance of communications in accordance with the procedures prescribed by law. Outside of the inspection, no organisation or individual may infringe a citizens' freedom in relation to communication and confidentiality for any reason (Article 40 of the 2018 Constitution).

The right to privacy is not clearly stipulated in the Constitution. Before 2020, the protection of privacy rights was scattered in separate regulations. The Code of Civil Law was officially promulgated and the Code came into force in January 2021. The Code has set up a special chapter and sections to regulate privacy and protect personal information. As noted above, China has not yet established a constitutional judicial review system. The constitutional principles rely on relevant substantive laws and procedural laws to implement it, therefore criminal procedure law plays an important role.

The Constitution takes the protection of citizens' residence and freedom of communication as important principles. Whilst search and seizure are traditional and commonly used investigative measures in practice, the CPL's provisions on search and seizure are unfortunately very sketchy. There are only ten articles, and in the last three major amendments to the CPL, the part on searches has had no substantial amendments except for the addition of three Chinese characters to

[40] Chen Xuequan, 'Forensic Science DNA Database in the Perspective of Criminal Procedure Law' (2007) 6 *Chinese Journal of Criminal Law* 58–61.

Article 137.[41] This reflects a lag in the legislation on the protection of constitutional rights.

Article 136 of the CPL is the major article providing the principles on searches. It states that:

> To collect criminal evidence and capture criminals, the investigators may search a body, or objects, and residence of a criminal suspect or a person who may hide the criminal or conceal criminal evidence, as well as other relevant places.

In addition to the above provision, the law stipulates only a few procedural requirements related to the search, such as: the search warrant must be shown to the searched person (Article 138); the searched person or his family members, neighbours or other witnesses must be present (Article 139) and so on. These provisions demonstrate that as long as the search is carried out for the purpose of 'collecting criminal evidence and finding criminals' as prescribed by law, hardly any further legal restrictions exist. Other jurisdictions, for example the German criminal procedure law, provide requirements for searching a third person,[42] and also special requirements on the time of the search for night searches.[43] Meanwhile, in terms of the scope of the search, the Chinese search warrant does not require the scope of the search to be specified. The status quo of such legislation shows that the principle of proportionality in searches has not yet been established in China, and the appropriateness, necessity, and balance of searches should be studied in depth, because searches are statutory and compulsory measures that impose restrictions on citizens' property rights, infringe their privacy rights, etc; therefore, it is indispensable to establish an appropriate principle of proportionality.

Although the aforementioned Article 136 of the CPL states that the investigator has the power to search, and Article 138 states that the investigator must

[41] Article 137 stipulates that any unit or individual shall have the obligation to hand in physical evidence, documentary evidence, audio-visual materials and other evidence, which may prove the guilt or innocence of a criminal suspect as required by the procuratorate or the public security authority. This 'other evidence' (等证据) was added when the CPL was revised in 2012.

[42] Art 103 of German Criminal Procedure Code: (1) Searches in respect of other persons shall be admissible only for the purpose of apprehending the accused or to follow up the traces of an offence or to seize certain objects and only if certain facts support the conclusion that the person, trace or object sought is located on the premises to be searched. For the purposes of apprehending an accused who is strongly suspected of having committed an offence under section 89a or section 89c (1) to (4) of the Criminal Code or under section 129a, also in conjunction with section 129b (1) of the Criminal Code, or one of the offences designated in such provision, a search of private and other premises shall also be admissible if they are located in a building in which it may be assumed, on the basis of certain facts, that the accused is located. (2) The restrictions of subsection (1) sentence 1 shall not apply to premises where the accused was apprehended or which he entered during the pursuit.

[43] Art 104 of German Criminal Procedure Code: (1) Private premises, business premises and enclosed property may be searched during the night only in pursuit of a person caught in the act, in exigent circumstances or for the purpose of re-apprehending an escaped prisoner. (2) This restriction shall not apply to premises which are accessible at night to anyone or which are known to the police as shelters or gathering places of offenders, as depots of property obtained through offences, or as hiding places for gambling, illegal trafficking in narcotics or weapons, or prostitution. (3) Night-time shall include, in the period from 1 April to 30 September, the hours between 9 pm and 4 am and, in the period from 1 October to 31 March, the hours between 9 pm and 6 am.

show the search warrant to the person being searched when conducting a search, the CPL itself does not set out the procedures for the issuing of a search warrant. Article 222 of the MPS Provisions mentions that the search must be approved by the head of the public security organ at or above county level. Based on this, it is inferred that the search warrant should be issued by the head of a certain level of investigation agency. The second paragraph of the article states that, if there is an emergency during arrest or pre-trial detention, a search without warrant can also be conducted, and five emergency situations are listed in Article 224 of the MPS Provisions. A further problem relates to the lack of judicial control over search powers, which is the same as the power to review and approve arrest and pre-trial detention. This situation reflects the prevalence of the criminal control model in criminal procedure in China, which is also one of the most compelling points for the reform of the criminal procedure law.

In the 2012 CPL amendments, the category of electronic data was added to the evidence section (Article 50(8)). However, the search section provided no specific procedures for searching for or collecting electronic data. On 9 September 2016, SPC, SPP, and MPS jointly promulgated their 'Provisions on Several Issues concerning the Collection, Taking, Examination, and Judgment of Electronic Data in the Handling of Criminal Cases' (Provisions on Electronic Data), which set out the rules for the collection and extraction of electronic data and examination. In practice, the document has become a reference source for search and seizure of electronic data. In Article 1 of the Provisions on Electronic Data, 'electronic data' is defined as:

> data that is formed in the process of occurrence of a case, stored, processed, and transmitted in digital form, and can prove the case facts and several forms of electronic data are listed.

The article then sets out several types of electronic data. The list is non-exhaustive, thus other categories are possible:

(1) information published through such network platforms as web pages, blogs, micro blogs, moments, post bars, and network disks;
(2) communication information in such network application services as SMS, e-mail, instant message, and communication group;
(3) information including user registration information, identity authentication information, electronic trading records, communication records, and logon logs;
(4) electronic documents including documents, pictures, audio and video records, digital certificates, and computer programs.

In subsequent articles, the Provisions on Electronic Data provide several methods for protecting the integrity of the electronic data which may be used as evidence. These methods are as follows:

(1) seizing or sealing up the original storage medium of electronic data;
(2) calculating the integrity check value of electronic data.

(3) preparing and sealing up the backup of electronic data;
(4) freezing electronic data;
(5) keeping video records of the relevant activities of collecting and taking electronic data;
(6) any other method for protecting the integrity of electronic data.

Obviously, with the rapid development of information technology and computer networks, electronic data as evidence will play an increasingly important role in criminal justice activities, but it also involves the protection of citizens' freedom of communication and privacy. With respect to this, China faces the same challenges as other jurisdictions. Legislation on electronic data is still in its infancy and more in-depth research is required.

E. Technical Measures of Criminal Investigations

The use of covert, secret or technical investigative measures does carry significant value for an effective criminal justice system, especially in the face of so-called victimless crime. In specific drug trafficking and other transaction crimes, terrorist violence has fuelled the development of secret and technology-based investigation methods and has contributed to a blurring of the boundaries that separate repression and prevention. These special investigative measures may interfere with the rights guaranteed by international human rights documents, such as the right to privacy, family, home, or correspondence provided for in Article 17 of the ICCPR and the right to respect for private and family life as set out in Article 8 of the ECHR. Balancing privacy and the effective implementation of criminal law as well as the pursuit of security pose challenges for every jurisdiction.

i. Issues of Definition

In the 2012 CPL revision, surprisingly and eventually rules covering so-called 'technical investigative measures' were adopted (Articles 148–152 CPL 2012, section eight Articles 150–154 CPL2018). 'Technical measures' normally refer to the investigative use of technology, which includes various devices, tools, and techniques.[44] Articles 150–154 of the CPL regulate 'technical investigative measures' and include, in Article 153, an investigative technique which is not based on technology but concerns 'undercover policing'. An undercover investigation may be initiated, according to Article 153(1):

> in order to clarify the facts of a case, when necessary, and upon the decision of the person in charge of the public security authority, the relevant personnel may conceal their identities to carry out the investigation.

[44] US Department of Justice, Office of Justice Programs, Special report, www.ojp.usdoj.gov/nij, October 2007.

The law then restricts undercover policing activities insofar as the police are not permitted to induce others to commit a crime. This restriction corresponds to standards requesting that the state refrain from using entrapment. However, a sort of exception is added in Article 153(2) of the CPL, which regulates controlled delivery and states that:

> for criminal activities involving the delivery of drugs and other contraband or property a public security authority may, as needed for criminal investigation, conduct controlled delivery.

Some scholars argue that the special investigative measures mentioned in Articles 150–154 of the CPL should be referred to as 'secret investigative measures', and should focus on the characteristic of being secretly carried out.[45] Secret investigations are the opposite of conventional and open investigative measures, such as search, seizure, and the interrogation of criminal suspects or witnesses. However, the key point is how to define 'secret investigations'. Secret investigations concern the collection of information, where the fact of that collection is hidden from the suspects being investigated. From this point of view, in Chinese legal practice, various investigative measures are carried out secretly by police or prosecutors, and, except for the interrogation, suspects normally do not know what is going on in the investigation, and what evidence the investigators have collected. Therefore, those investigative measures which hide the fact of collecting information from a suspect should be classified as special investigation measures. The Council of Europe provides the following definition, which could usefully be used as a starting point by the Chinese authorities:

> special investigation techniques means techniques applied by the competent authorities in the context of criminal investigations for the purpose of detecting and investigating serious crimes and suspects, aiming at gathering information in such a way as not to alert the target persons.[46]

ii. Categories of Special Investigative Measures

The CPL itself does not specify any type of technical investigation. Nor are details on this type of measure provided in the MPS Provisions. This differs from the regulation of secret and technical measures of investigation as found, for example, in European countries. There, various technical measures are separately dealt with in criminal procedural law, providing normative conditions of application graded according to the depth of intrusion into privacy. The following provisions would

[45] Jia Zhiqiang and Min Chunlei, 'A Comment on Measures of Technical Investigation under New Criminal Procedure Law' (2013) 5 *The Journal of Shan Dong Police Institute* 75.

[46] Council of Europe Committee of Ministers, Recommendation Rec (2005) on 'Special investigation techniques in relation to serious crimes including acts of terrorism', adopted by the Committee of Ministers in April 2005.

benefit from legislation which adopts a carefully and systematically designed normative regime guided by the principle of proportionality:

- the use of listening devices outside and within private premises;
- surveillance of telecommunications content;
- the use of various kinds of telecommunication metadata informing on location or relationships between individuals;
- the infiltration and search of computer systems by spyware or data mining based on comprehensive data collection and joining of datasets, as well as telecommunication metadata retention.

In Articles 1 and 150–154 of the CPL and Article 264 of the MPS Provisions an approach can be observed which can and should be further developed into a sophisticated normative system which considered differences in the extent of interference with privacy carried by the investigative methods mentioned above. Article 264 of the MPS Provisions points out that:

> Technical investigation measures refer to measures such as monitoring of whereabouts, movements, communication implemented by the public security organs of the city level divided into districts and above.

The UN Convention on Transnational Organized Crime Article 20 addresses special investigation techniques, which include electronic or other forms of surveillance and undercover operations, as well as controlled delivery.[47] Since ratification, China has had an obligation to implement this Convention, and all the special measures listed in it are used in China's legal practice. Chinese scholars have called for specific investigative measures to be clearly listed in future legal reforms, which will help formulate corresponding supervision measures and balance the protection of the rights of criminal suspects and defendants against the need to effectively investigate serious crimes.

iii. The Scope of Application of Special Investigative Measures

The CPL stipulates the general scope of applicable technical investigation measures, which correspond to investigations by public security authority and investigations by procuratorial authorities. For investigations by public security authority, the scope is defined as and restricted to 'crimes endangering national security, terrorist activities, organised crimes of an underworld nature, major drug crimes, or other crimes that seriously endanger society' (Article 150 CPL). The MPS Provisions, in addition to the above-mentioned crimes, also specifies a

[47] China signed this Convention on 12 December 2000, and ratified it on 27 August 2003; the Convention came into effect for China on 23 October 2003.

category of 'other crimes that seriously endanger society'. This is divided up into four types of crimes:

(1) serious violent crimes, such as intentional homicide, intentional injury causing serious injury or death, rape, robbery, kidnapping, arson, explosion, and release of dangerous substances;
(2) group, serial, and cross-regional major crime cases;
(3) major crimes committed using telecommunications, computer networks, and mailing channels, as well as major crimes committed against computer networks (cyber crime);
(4) other criminal cases that seriously endanger society and which are punishable with more than seven years' imprisonment.

Some scholars argue against the expansion of 'other crimes that seriously endanger society and may attract long prison sentences' by the public security authorities. Compared with other countries, China has relatively severe punishment patterns. According to judicial statistics in 2018, 155,638 offenders were sentenced to imprisonment for more than five years or the death penalty.[48] According to this statistic, special investigative methods could in principle be permitted in a large number of cases. Therefore, some scholars think that the interpretation of CPL by the public security authority is ultra vires and violates the legislative intent of restricting the application of technical investigation measures.[49]

According to the CPL, for major criminal cases the procuratorate can also use technical investigative measures where any justice functionary takes advantage of his or her functions and seriously infringes a citizen's personal rights (Article 150(2)). In addition, public security authorities and the procuratorates may use technical investigation measures required in the pursuit of fugitive criminal suspects or defendants who are wanted or who have been approved for pre-trial detention (Article 150(3)).

The above description of the scope of special investigative measures highlights another of their characteristics: the target is a case, rather than a specific suspect. Although Article 264(2) of the MPS Provisions states that 'The applicable objects of technical investigation are criminal suspects, defendants, and persons directly associated with criminal activities', in practice and under normal circumstances, a decision to deploy special investigative methods is generally made when a case is still in the filing case stage, and no clear suspect can be identified. In fact, special investigative techniques such as surveillance of telecommunication or investigation of telecommunication metadata and data mining play a prominent role in identifying potential suspects. In light of future reform of China's CPL, criminal suspects of serious crimes should be the exclusive target of special investigative

[48] *Law Year Book of China* (2019, Beijing) 1331.

[49] Wang Chenchen and Zhou Yi, 'Review of the Technical Investigation System' (2014) 2 *Applicable Laws* 43.

methods, and conditions of use should emphasise the principle of proportionality and the goal of strictly limiting surveillance methods to protect privacy.

iv. The Procedures for Applying the Special Investigative Measures

As for the procedures for applying special investigative methods, the principles stipulated by the CPL are very general, though they reflect partially the need for a regulation graded according to proportionality. In a total of five articles in this section of the CPL, the words 'through strict approval procedures according to the needs of criminal investigations' are repeated three times. The specific approval procedures are mentioned briefly in the MPS Provisions, which only state that the approval must be by the person in charge of the public security authority at or above the level of the city (Article 265 MPS Provisions). This indicates the administrative character of the approval procedures.

Special investigative measures call for particular scrutiny of proportionality. With respect to investigative measures, proportionality may be implemented through substantive and procedural criteria. A substantive element has been introduced into the CPL, as outlined above, by restricting special investigative measures to a range of criminal offences, though rather broad, assessed to be serious and calling for effective implementation of the criminal law. The procedural elements of proportionality can be found in Articles 151 and 152 of the CPL. According to Article 151 'the approval decision is effective for three months from the date on which it is signed and issued'. While the period of three months can be extended upon a finding that this is necessary, Article 151 states the general understanding that proportionality must be implemented through establishing strict time limitations. Article 152 then requires that investigators who become aware of state secrets, commercial secrets or private personal information during the course of employing technical investigative measures shall preserve their secrecy. Furthermore, information unrelated to the case that is acquired through the use of technical investigative measures must be promptly destroyed. While Article 152 recognises a general principle that information collected through special investigative measures must be kept secret and eventually destroyed (when not related to the case), the question of whether and to what extent witness and professional privileges should restrict collection and the use of collected information is not addressed. And finally, Article 152 introduces, though in a rudimentary manner, a most important procedural standard which states that 'materials gathered through the use of technical investigative measures can only be used in criminal investigation, prosecution and adjudication, and cannot be used for other purposes'. However, this procedural element should be further expanded to restrict the use of material collected to those criminal cases which would allow the application of special investigative measures according to Article 150 of the CPL.

It is expected that in view of the procedural safeguarding of the principle of proportionality and accordingly restricting infringement of citizens' privacy and other rights, in future reforms, judicial supervision and review of special investigative methods should gradually replace the current system of monitoring. A judicial review which effectively scrutinises the necessity of deploying special investigative measures and other procedural limitations will be most important in ensuring that proportionality is a prime concern. The introduction of investigative judges at the lowest-level basic courts, specifically responsible for reviewing and approving measures that may infringe upon basic rights of citizens in criminal proceedings could, on the one hand, fulfil the need for effective (and rapid) investigation, and on the other satisfy the equally important interest of safeguarding proportionality.

IV. Conclusion of Investigation

When the police conclude an investigation, it can be done in two ways:

(1) if the facts of a crime are clear and the evidence is confirmed and sufficient, then the police may provide a prosecution recommendation, and deliver it along with the case file and evidence to the same level of prosecutor office for review and decision regarding prosecution (Article 162 CPL);

(2) if, during the process of investigation, it is found that the suspect should not bear criminal liability, the case should be dismissed; if the suspect has been arrested or detained, he/she shall be released immediately and be given a certificate of release. The investigative police should inform the prosecutor office who originally issued the warrant for pre-trial detention (Article 163 CPL).

7

Public Prosecution and First Instance Trial

I. Standards of Prosecution

When the procuratorate receives a case, through a file transferred from the public security agency (police) or the supervisory agency, the case must be reviewed and it must be decided whether or not the case should proceed to trial. This is different from other jurisdictions, where the decision on whether to prosecute is made at the end of the investigation, and not in an independent process. For ordinary cases, the procuratorate has a one-month time limit to review and make a decision; for major and complicated cases, the time limit can be extended by 15 days (Article 172 of the CPL)

According to the CPL, a prosecution decision should be made only when the procuratorate deems that the facts of an offence committed by a criminal suspect are clear, the evidence is confirmed and sufficient, and the criminal suspect will be subject to criminal liability according to the law (Article 176 of the CPL). The SPP in its rules for implementing the CPL details the specific circumstances of 'the facts of an offence are clear':

(1) for a single criminal offence case, the facts found are sufficient for conviction and sentencing, or the facts related to conviction and sentencing have been clarified and only facts that do not affect the conviction and sentencing cannot be clarified;
(2) in cases that pertain to several crimes, some of the crimes investigated meet the conditions for prosecution, and other crimes cannot be clarified;
(3) it is impossible to find the tools used for the crime and the whereabouts of the stolen goods, but there is other evidence sufficient to convict and sentence the defendant;
(4) the main content of witness testimony, the criminal suspect's confession and defence, and the victim's statement are consistent with each other; individual circumstances may be inconsistent but they do not affect the conviction.

It should be noted that, in the CPL revisions between 1996 and 2018, the evidence standards for the termination of investigation, prosecution and conviction are basically the same. This issue has been the subject of debate in academic circles for decades. The mainstream view is that, in the circumstances prevailing in China, it is beneficial to unify the standard of evidence at different stages of criminal process.

Under normal circumstances, the prosecutors only interrogate the criminal suspect, or listen to the opinions of the defender, the victim, etc (Article 173) before making a decision to prosecute or not. Prosecutors do not conduct further investigations or evidence collection activities, and, when prosecutors bring a public prosecution to the court, in accordance with the law, the court merely examines whether 'there are clear facts of the alleged crime in the indictment'. If clear facts are recognised, then the court will open the trial (Article 186). Therefore, in such cases the unified standard of prosecution and conviction can improve the quality and efficiency of prosecution, prevent the abuse of prosecutorial powers, save judicial resources, and at the same time protect potentially innocent persons and prevent situations where evidence is inaccurate. In particular, innocent persons do not have to go through lengthy criminal proceedings. However, some scholars are of the opinion that requiring prosecutors to implement evidence standards that meet conviction standards at this earlier intermediate stage of proceedings is not satisfactory. These scholars argue that the court must further confirm facts and evidence through trial procedures, so prosecutors should be bound by a lower standard at the stage of examining prosecution.[1] This standard should require that there exists a high probability of conviction as a condition of a decision to prosecute. However, the author deems that this view is questionable. Although investigators, prosecutors, and judges play different roles in criminal proceedings, they share the common goal of making judgments on the basis of facts. In practice, it is understandable that for various reasons, the evidence collected by investigators is not perfect, and prosecutors will apply a different approach when analysing evidence. But this does not affect the setting of higher prosecution standards which equal the standards applied by courts. All legal institutions and participants to criminal proceedings may explain and implement the standards in their own ways, but subject to the checks and balances method. Finally the neutral judge should make a judgment.

In China several scholars have suggested that the English law-based criteria should be adopted when testing whether evidence is sufficient to justify prosecution. This approach calls for a 'realistic prospect of conviction'.[2] In fact, legal scholars and law practitioners in England are also still discussing the meaning of these criteria.[3] The 2018 version of the Code for Crown Prosecutors stated that: 'prosecutors must be satisfied, on an objective assessment of the evidence, that there are reasonable grounds to suspect that the person to be charged has committed the offence'. The author has discussed this issue with a full-time prosecutor in England, who said that, when evaluating whether the evidence will justify an indictment, the criteria considered are not very different from the criteria used by the judge when adjudicating the case.

[1] Wang Chao and Yao Xiaodong, 'Criminal Prosecution Standard Mode Selection' (2009) 5 *Times Law* 62.

[2] The Code for Crown Prosecutors in 1986.

[3] Liz Campbell et al, *The Criminal Process*, 5th edn (New York, Oxford University Press, 2019) 200–205.

II. Non-Prosecution Policies

The CPL provides for five conditions which authorise a prosecutor to make a decision not to prosecute. In China, this is called 'non-prosecution' (不起诉). With this decision, criminal proceedings are terminated. The conditions concern the following:

- statutory non-prosecution;
- non-prosecution due to insufficient evidence;
- discretionary non-prosecution (petty crime);
- conventional non-prosecution in case of juvenile delinquents;
- special non-prosecution to protect major national interests.

A. Statutory Non-Prosecution

Statutory non-prosecution is also referred to as absolute non-prosecution. Non-prosecution here is because the legal conditions required for continuation of criminal proceedings are lacking. Article 16 of the CPL sets out the following instances:

(1) the circumstances of the alleged conduct clearly exhibit only a minor wrong, not causing serious harm. The alleged conduct therefore is not classified as a crime. China has adopted a doctrine of criminal offending which sets a threshold below which an offence (although displaying all objective offence elements) is not considered a criminal wrong;
(2) the time limit for criminal prosecution has expired;
(3) an exemption from criminal punishment has been granted in a special amnesty decree;
(4) if the alleged crime belongs to the category of private prosecution, which should be handled only upon complaint according to substantive criminal law, and where no complaints are filed or where the complaints have been withdrawn;
(5) the suspect or defendant is deceased;
(6) when other laws provide for exemption from criminal liability.

If any of these circumstances are established at any stage of the criminal procedure, the proceedings must be terminated.

B. Non-Prosecution in Cases with Insufficient Evidence

The legal basis for non-prosecution because of insufficient evidence is found in Article 175(4) of the CPL. The law allows the procuratorate to return the case to the original investigative agency for supplementary investigation. A decision to request supplementary investigation can be issued no more than twice. If, after a second supplementary investigation, the procuratorate still assesses the evidence to be insufficient and not meeting the conditions for prosecution, it should decide not to prosecute. The SPP has issued a further explanation in its SPP Regulation (Article 368) on what 'insufficient evidence' covers:

(1) the essential facts of the crime are not supported by necessary evidence;
(2) the evidence on which the conviction would be based is in doubt and cannot be verified as true;
(3) the contradiction between the evidence on which the conviction is based, or between the evidence and the facts of the case cannot be reasonably excluded;
(4) the conclusions drawn on the basis of evidence are faced with reasonable doubts which cannot be ruled out;
(5) the facts of the case based on evidence do not conform to logic and empirical rules, and the conclusions reached are obviously not in line with common sense.

C. Discretionary Policies of Non-Prosecution of Petty Crime

Article 177(2) of the CPL provides that:

> where the circumstances of a crime are minor and criminal punishment is not necessary or the criminal suspect is exempted from criminal punishment in accordance with Criminal Law, procuratorate may decide not to initiate a public prosecution.

Unlike English law, the Chinese CPL does not use 'the public interest test' as a criterion to guide prosecutor's discretion when deciding on public prosecution. In addition to the discretion-based non-prosecution policy in case of juvenile delinquency,[4] prosecutors have the discretionary power not to prosecute only in cases of petty crimes. However, the concept of petty offences mentioned here is different from the concept of petty offences which is used in the context of statutory non-prosecution under Article 16(1). The statutory non-prosecution category pertains to cases which are minor according to substantive criminal law, and which do not reach the threshold of a criminal wrong. Offences falling below the substantive threshold of a criminal wrong are treated as administrative offences which may result in administrative sanctions. Offences above the substantive threshold of a criminal wrong are nevertheless subject to discretionary non-prosecution. The prosecutor has to weigh the public interest in prosecuting a criminal case on the one hand as well as costs of full trial proceedings or the interest in rehabilitating a juvenile offender on the other hand, before deciding on prosecution or non-prosecution.

[4] Discussed in detail in Chapter 10 on special criminal procedures on juvenile criminal proceedings.

Table 1 Grounds for Non-Prosecution

Year	Number of suspects	Total suspects not prosecuted %	Grounds for Non-Prosecution (Column 3) %		
			Statutory non-prosecution	Insufficient evidence	Discretionary non-prosecution
2014	80,020	5.3	8.6	21.9	69.4
2015	81,087	5.3	7.4	26.0	66.6
2016	90,694	5.9	6.4	24.6	69.0
2017	114,994	6.3	4.9	21.9	72.9
2018	140,650	7.7	4.4	20.7	74.9

Source: Tong Jianming (Deputy General Prosecutor of SPP), 'On the rationality of the power of non-prosecution', www.jx.jcy.gov.cn, 30 September 2019.

As can be seen from the table above, in general, China's non-prosecution rate, especially the rate of discretionary non-prosecution, is relatively low compared to other countries.[5] According to research data covering a large province and the period 2013 to 2016, the rate of discretionary non-prosecution amounts to 3.4 per cent (2013), 3.8 per cent (2014), 3.5 per cent (2015), 3.7 per cent (2016).[6] The prosecutors who conducted this survey believe that the low rate of discretionary non-prosecution demonstrates a failure to effectively divert criminal cases from full trial proceedings, causing a large number of minor cases to flow into the courts and resulting ultimately in a waste of judicial resources. According to prosecution statistics, in the past five years, the average rate of court-imposed lighter non-custodial sentences oscillates around the 50 per cent mark. These cases could be also subject to conditional non-prosecution. The reason for not resorting to diversion policies supposedly lies in a considerable number of prosecutors still being influenced by the statutory prosecution principle (legality principle). Prosecutors believe that as long as the evidence is sufficient, the case should be prosecuted, and that trial and judgment are the responsibility of the judge. A second reason might be the fear of errors in applying the law, because the procuratorate also implements a responsibility system. In order to prevent the abuse of discretionary powers, the law and the prosecutor's internal rules have set up a stringent review procedure. Prosecutors therefore might be afraid of finding themselves in trouble when opting for non-prosecution. In the author's view, it would be helpful to implement something like the English 'public interest test' and set up detailed criteria for discretionary non-prosecution in order to achieve the objective of filtering out the less serious cases and avoiding unnecessary trial proceedings.

[5] Hans-Joerg Albrecht and Chen Guangzhong (eds), *Non-Prosecution Policies: A Sino-German Comparison*, vol I 7 (Freiburg, Interdisziplinäre Untersuchungen aus Strafrecht und Kriminologie des Max-Planck-Instituts für ausländisches und internationales Strafrecht, 2002).

[6] Zhang Shuzhuang et al, 'The Operational Considerations and Improvement Paths of the Discretionary Non-Prosecution System' (2019) 1 *Research on the Rule of Law* 46.

D. Special Non-Prosecution

In the 2018 amendment, a new type of non-prosecution was added to the CPL. Article 182 now states that where a criminal suspect voluntarily and truthfully confesses to the facts of the suspected crime or has earned significant merits, or where a case involves any major national interest, with the approval of the SPP, the public security authority may dismiss the case, and the procuratorate may decide not to initiate prosecution of one or more crimes (if multiple crimes are suspected).

Part of the reasoning behind the creation of this provision is the guilty plea and leniency system. A voluntary and truthful confession establishes the normal condition for a guilty plea and the awarding of leniency. With 'significant merits' and 'major national interests', two additional special conditions have been introduced. Some prosecutors believe that the meaning of 'significant merits' in Article 182 of the CPL is different from the meaning of 'major meritorious service' stipulated in Article 68 of the Criminal Law.[7] Article 68 provides for mitigation of or exemption from criminal punishment if an offender has informed about other crimes and contributed to solving these crimes. In contrast, Article 182 of the CPL should be understood as combining 'major national interests' such as political, foreign affairs or economic interests and crown witness related considerations. This interpretation of Article 182 is underlined by the specific approval procedure established by law requiring approval of this type of non-prosecution by the SPP.

III. The Trial

A. Preparation for Trial

i. Proceedings for Reviewing a Public Prosecution Case

After receiving the indictment and when the case file is transferred by the prosecutor's office, the trial court should, as a first step, briefly review the case. This practice has been transplanted directly from continental law. In the German criminal procedure code (Articles 199–211), a review procedure applies before the opening of the main trial proceedings: after receiving the indictment, the criminal court has to assess whether there are grounds to oppose the opening of a trial (for example, the statute of limitation) and whether probable cause exists. However, the main difference between the German and Chinese criminal procedural law is that the German court's review has a substantive nature, and one result of its review may be to not open main trial proceedings, so there will be no further court hearings. The Chinese court's review is different from those carried out in Germany. In the first 1979 CPL, review proceedings close to the German model had been adopted: the trial court could reject the indictment and return the case to the procuratorate.

[7] Dong Kun, 'Special Non-Prosecution in Guilty Plea and Leniency' (2019) 6 *Legal Research* 172.

But this part of the law was changed in the 2012 CPL amendments. Now, the review proceedings do not pertain to a substantive but a procedural review. According to Article 186 of the CPL, 'After examining a public prosecution, a court shall decide to hold a court hearing if the indictment contains clear allegations of crime'.

ii. Detailed Preparatory Steps before the Court Hearing

Article 221 of the 2021 SPC Interpretations sets out details of the tasks which must be finalised by the court before a hearing begins:

(1) the presiding judge and the members of the bench must first be assigned. In China's trial rules, defendants do not enjoy the right to a pre-determined judge (as required, for example, by the European Convention on Human Rights, Article 6, or German constitutional law).[8] However, in recent years, in practice and in order to prevent interference with the trial, some courts have adopted computerised random assignment procedures;
(2) copies of the indictment shall be delivered to the defendants and their defence counsel 10 days before the beginning of the court hearing. This provision means that the defendant and his counsel have a minimum of 10 days to prepare their defence. While 10 days may be sufficient to prepare a defence in small cases, this time frame is completely insufficient for serious and complicated cases. In practice, the judge in charge of the hearing may negotiate with the prosecutor and the defence counsel on the date of the trial, but the law and the judicial interpretation of the SPC do not clearly guarantee that the defence will have sufficient time to prepare an effective defence. As sufficient time to prepare a defence is necessary to establish equality between prosecution and defence (clearly spelled out in Article 6.3(b) of the European Convention on Human Rights), a more flexible rule on time frames would be advisable;
(3) the parties, their legal representatives, defence counsel, and agent ad litem must be informed and provided with the names of witnesses and experts witnesses, and the list of evidence to be presented at court five days before the court hearing starts; where witnesses, expert witnesses, or a person with special knowledge is to appear at court, their names, sexes, ages, occupations, addresses, and correspondence methods shall also be clearly listed;
(4) the prosecutor must be informed about the time and the venue of the court hearing three days before the court hearing starts;
(5) the trial court shall deliver the subpoenas of parties and the notices requiring the appearance in court of defenders, agents ad litem, legal representatives, witnesses, and expert witnesses, three days before the start of court hearings;
(6) for cases that are to be heard publicly, the name of the accused, the time and venue of the trial shall be published three days before the beginning of the court hearing.

[8] Art 101(1) of the German Constitution (Basic Law).

iii. Pre-Trial Conference

In the 2012 CPL amendment, the legislators carried out an important reform of the preparation of trial proceedings and introduced the procedure for pre-trial meetings. Pre-trial meetings exist in common law countries, as for example in the US criminal procedure. Article 187(2) now stipulates that before a court hearing, the judges can call the prosecutor, parties, defenders, and agents ad litem to gather information and hear opinions on trial-related issues. Such issues concern possible recusal of a judge, court clerk, or prosecutor, updating the list of witnesses to testify in court, and the exclusion of illegally obtained evidence. The main purpose of this reform was to improve the efficiency of court trials and achieve the aim of having trial-centered proceedings. After several years of judicial practice, in 2018 the SPC issued its Rules for Pre-trial Conferences in the Handling of Criminal Cases by People's Courts (for Trial Implementation) (SPC Rules for Pre-trial Conferences). These Rules clarify that the issues dealt with by the pre-trial conference are limited to 'procedural issues that may lead to the interruption of the trial'. The determination of the scope of pre-trial conferences seems to be in line with the original intention of the legislator and limits 'trial-related issues'.

Regarding the scope of the pre-trial conference, in addition to the three situations listed in Article 187(2) above, the SPC Rules for Pre-trial Conference also enumerate other matters that may arise in trial proceedings:

- objections with respect to the jurisdiction of the court;
- the application of rules on non-public hearings;
- discovery disclosure of evidence;
- the application for retrieval of new evidence,
- the application for re-evaluation or inspection, and
- mediation of incidental civil lawsuits.

As regards the mediation of an incidental civil lawsuit, a controversy among legal scholars has occurred. Some scholars argue that this is beyond the scope of the pre-trial conference of 'procedural matters' outlined by the SPC.[9] But in the author's view, the incidental civil lawsuit's nature must follow civil procedure. According to China's civil procedure law, before the trial the judge carries out a mediation and it is in general expected that reconciliation between the parties can be achieved. China's CPL also allows courts to carry out mediation for several categories of cases. Thus, it is satisfactory to enter mediation proceedings before a trial, as all parties may benefit from it, and judicial resources will be saved.

After eight years of practice, empirical research on the effect of introducing 'pre-trial conferences' has been carried out. On the basis of this research it has been concluded that the procedure faces challenges and needs further reform. One

[9] Bu Yangyang, 'A New Analysis of the Criminal Pre-trial Conference on the Context of Trial Centralism' (2018) 7 *Hebei Science of Law* 53.

of the main problems to arise in practice is the lack of efficiency. The original goal of establishing this procedure was to improve the efficiency of court hearings. However, when holding 'pre-trial meetings', it is necessary to coordinate all participants, especially if the defendant is also to participate in the conference, as defendants need to be brought from the detention facility to the court. Further, there is no clear indication in the law or in the SPC Rules about the degree of evidence that must be discovered. The evidence disputes emerging in a 'pre-trial conference' will be repeated in the subsequent court hearings. The conclusion of the research was that pre-trial proceedings do not achieve the goal pursued by legislation, and its potential for solving procedural issues is very limited. In practice, the pre-trial conference has developed into an extended hearing which sidelines the conventional trial hearings. This further weakens the function of a 'court centered trial'. In fact, the move towards pre-trial conferences has resulted in simplifying the actual trial proceedings and reducing their relevance.[10]

B. Trial Phases after Public Prosecution Cases Have Been Brought to Court

The phases of court hearings are spelled out in Articles 190–200 of the CPL. In 2018, the SPC published its Rules for Court Investigation in First-Instance Ordinary Procedure in the Handling of Criminal Cases by People's Courts (for Trial Implementation) (SPC Rules for Court Investigation), which provide details of the main steps in court hearings.

i. Step 1. Opening the Public Hearing

Before the trial formally begins, according to Article 234 of the SPC's Interpretation, the court clerk performs the following tasks in the following order:

(1) ascertain that the prosecutor, the parties, the defender, the agent ad litem, the witnesses and other participants appear before the court;
(2) check whether there are witnesses, expert witness, and people with expertise among the observers;
(3) ask the prosecutor, defender, agent ad litem and other participants to be seated;
(4) read the court rules aloud;
(5) ask the presiding judge and other judges or lay assessors to be seated;
(6) report to the presiding judge after the presiding judge is seated.

[10] Wu Xiaojun, 'Functional Positioning and Practical Reflection of Pre-trial Conference' (2020) 4 *Law Journal* 132.

After announcing that a court session is opened, and summoning the defendant to present himself before the court, the presiding judge will verify the defendant's identity and whether the parties appear in court. The presiding judge will then: specify the criminal offence to be tried; present the members of the collegiate bench and the names of the court clerks, the public prosecutor, the defender and the interpreters; and inform the parties of their procedural rights during the course of the trial. In the 2018 SPC Rules for Court Investigation, the pre-trial conference was added to the list of issues that the judge must introduce:

> For a case in which a pre-trial conference was held, the results of deliberations on procedural issues at the pre-trial conference will be communicated at the step of giving notification of procedural rights in the court trial.

In the 2018 CPL amendment a paragraph was inserted about guilty plea and leniency cases. This rule states that where a defendant admits guilt and accepts punishment, the presiding judge must inform the defendant of his procedural rights and the provisions of the law on the admission of guilt and acceptance of punishment. The judge must ensure that the admission and acceptance were voluntarily obtained, and with due authority and legality (Article 190(2)).

ii. Step 2. Examination at Trial

This phase is also referred to as the court's investigation at trial. After the opening phase, the presiding judge will announce the beginning of the examination phase. This begins with the prosecutor reading out the indictment. Similar to in an adversarial procedural system, the trial begins with a statement by the prosecutor. The purpose of this proceeding is to familiarise all participants of the trial with the nature of the charge. Following the prosecutor's statement, the defendant and the victim may present statements regarding the crime alleged in the indictment, and the prosecutor may then question the defendant. Further, if a subsidiary civil action is brought, the plaintiff or his legal representative may also read out the complaint.

The 2018 SPC Rules for Court Investigation added two paragraphs relating to the issues of the pre-trial conference. These rules state that for a case in which a pre-trial conference was held, the court shall announce the main content of the pre-trial conference report after the public prosecutor has read the indictment. In a case involving multiple crimes, the court may separately announce the relevant content of the pre-trial conference report before the court investigation of the facts of crime commences. The court may confirm any matter agreed upon at the pre-trial conference after obtaining verification from prosecution and defence; and for any matter not agreed upon, the court may summarise the disputed issues at the step in the court trial related to the matter, listen to the opinions of the parties, and proceed in accordance with the law (Article 6 of the SPC Rules for Court Investigation).

iii. Step 3. Statement of the Accused and Victim

Following the statement of the prosecutor, the accused and the victim are given the opportunity to alternately make their statements regarding the criminal facts, which are presented in the indictment. This is designed to give both the accused and the victim an opportunity to outline their version of the case; however, there is no provision in the law to suggest that the accused is to be informed about his right to remain silent.

Following the statements of the accused and the victim and under the supervision of the presiding judge, the accused is cross-examined by the prosecutor and the victim or his legal representative. The defender of the accused, with the permission of the presiding judge, may also ask questions. Although the author uses the term 'cross-examination', a proper translation of the Chinese words would amount to 'prosecutor's interrogation'. Here we can see the significant differences between adversarial and inquisitorial systems. In Chinese criminal proceedings, the accused is still at the centre of the court's investigation. Chinese judges will first of all be interested in a confession of the accused, as a confession is considered a most important source of evidence. In this situation it is very difficult to safeguard the right not to self-incriminate. Under the rules of the old 1979 CPL, it was usually the presiding judge who began questioning the accused. The CPL reforms of 1996, 2012, and 2018 have tried to move criminal proceedings more towards the adversarial system. This move is the reason why the law now puts the presiding judge at the end of the list of persons who may question the accused (Article 191 of CPL). In the SPC Interpretation, the phrase 'when it is necessary' has been added. In fact, the core of the adversarial system is the principle of equality of arms. But when such equality does not exist, the order of questioning is of no great help and does not make much difference.

iv. Step 4. Witness Testimony and Cross-Examination

The CPL creates an obligation for witnesses to testify before the court. It further provides that 'a witness statement may be used as a basis for deciding a case only after the witness has been cross-examined in court by the prosecutor, the victim and the defendant, the defense counsel, and if it has been verified' (Article 62). However, as may be seen from Article 192 of the CPL, the appearance of witnesses to testify seems to be a matter of discretion. Article 192 of the CPL states that where the prosecutor, a party or the defender or an agent ad litem raises any objection against a witness statement which would have a material effect on conviction and sentencing, the witness shall testify before the court if the court deems it necessary. From this provision, it may be deduced that the court decides which witnesses should appear in court and testify. The SPC Rules for Court Investigation 2018 provide a clearer interpretation of Article 192, stating that both the prosecution and the defence can apply to the court to summon witnesses, experts, investigators and persons with expertise to appear in court. From this interpretation it can be concluded that it is the court's task to decide which witnesses will be called to testify. The CPL also stipulates that if the police are required to testify about the crimes they witnessed while performing their duties, the court can call police officers to appear in court. The SPC rules also stipulate that witnesses who cannot appear in court for objective reasons, such as illness, are allowed to testify through a video link. But if they fail to appear in court, without a legally accepted reason, the court may force the witness to appear before the court, unless the witness is next of kin to the defendant (spouse, parent, child) (Article 193(1) CPL). If a witness refuses to testify after appearing before the court without justifiable reasons, he shall be cautioned; if the circumstances are serious, and with the approval of the president of the court, the witness may be detained for not more than 10 days. Such a detainee may appeal against the detention decision to the superior court for reconsideration (Article 193(2)). The law does not clearly indicate the purpose of a judicial order to detain a witness. However, the legislator indicates that the detention is punishment for 'refusal to appear in court and refusal to testify' (and contempt of court).[11] The author argues for a clear distinction in the procedural code between punitive responses to contempt of court on the one hand and coercive measures applied to enforce a judicial decision. Where there are unwilling witnesses, cautioning and detention should be a coercive approach and through that the procedural goal of hearing witness testimony.

The CPL does not require witnesses to make an oath prior to testifying before the court. The law only requires the judges to inform the witness of the obligation to testify truthfully and the legal liability for perjury or concealing criminal evidence (Article 194 CPL). In practice, courts follow the SPC's Rules, by which a judge may ask the witness or an expert witness to sign a statement that the testimony will be truthful (Article 18 SPC's Rules).

The CPL does not specify the order in which witnesses should testify and be questioned. The SPC Rules provide more details and state that, after a witness has presented his testimony to the court, the witness then may be questioned by the party who produced the evidence. After that, the opposing party may also put forward questions. As required for the trial of the case, the mover of the motion to summon the witness may also put questions first (Article 19 SPC Rules). From this provision, it can be seen that the SPC draws on the cross-examination rules of the common law, and the trial judge is not the first to question the witness.

The SPC has also set out rules with respect to the questioning of witnesses:

(1) the content of the questioning shall be relevant to establish the facts of the case;
(2) leading questions are prohibited;
(3) the witness may not be threatened or misled;

[11] Lang Sheng (ed), *Criminal Procedure Law Amendment and Application* (Beijing, China Legal Publishing House, 2012) 237.

(4) the witness may not be treated in a degrading way;
(5) the privacy of the witness must be respected.

However, in practice, witness testimony seems to pose significant problems. Some courts have conducted empirical surveys and analyses on whether witnesses appear and testify in court when summoned. Chengdu City Court, located in Sichuan Province (Chengdu is the capital of Sichuan Province and has a population of 16.33 million in 2019) analysed some 210 criminal cases decided before 31 August 2016. These cases involved 265 witnesses. However, witnesses only appeared in court and gave testimony in 18 of the 210 cases, which amounts to an appearance rate of 8.6 per cent of cases. Out of the total 265 witnesses, only 26 appeared in court, which accounts for 9.8 per cent of witnesses complying with court orders to give testimony.[12] The rate of witness attendance at trials held by a court in a metropolitan area is so low, that it can only be assumed that rates of witness attendance in trials in remote regions will be even lower. In fact, evidence on low witness appearance rates provided by research on criminal proceedings in Chengdu is supported by in-depth studies carried out by the Evidence Institute of the China University for Political Sciences and Law.[13] From research carried out on Chinese criminal proceedings and the particular issue of witness testimony it can be concluded that police, prosecutors and judges still rely heavily on written testimony by witnesses based on questioning during the pre-trial stage of proceedings. Although criminal procedural law reform in China seeks to strengthen adversarial trial elements, until now the trial is evidently still characterised by written rather than by oral testimony (which could be subject to cross-examination). Strong adherence to written statements and the disregarding of oral presentation of evidence has been explained by a mix of cultural and historical factors, as well as by the application of law-related grounds.[14] Among these grounds we find a strong belief on the side of judges that oral testimony of what is already available in writing is redundant and cause delay. Procedural law, furthermore is not clear on that issue, as Article 187 of the CPL requires oral testimony only if the judge believes it to be necessary. The need to subject witness statements to the scrutiny of cross-examination by the parties is not mentioned by the law. Furthermore, witnesses are – as are judges, prosecutors and other criminal justice staff – deeply influenced by cultural values and norms which stress the importance of harmony (和为贵), avoidance of conflict and taking sides (明哲保身) and avoidance of trouble (多一事不如少一事). Such values have a bearing on the willingness of witnesses to appear in court. In addition, there is no clear prohibition of the hearsay rule in

[12] Zhengrong, 'Empirical Research Report on the System of interviewing witnesses in Criminal Trials', 18 January 2017, www.chinacourt.org.

[13] For a summary see Zhuhao Wang, 'Why Chinese Witnesses do not Testify at Trials in Criminal Proceedings', www.bu.edu/ilj/files/2015/03/Zhuhao-WANG_WHY-CHINESE-WITNESSES-DO-NOT-TESTIFY-BEFORE-THE-JUDGE-IN-CRIMINAL-TRIALS.pdf.

[14] Zhuhao Wang and David RA Caruso, 'Is An Oral-Evidence Based Criminal Trial Possible in China?' (2017) 21(1–2) *International Journal of Evidence & Proof* 52.

the CPL. The law, moreover, does not give clear guidance on how the obligation of a witness to appear before the court might be enforced. Detailed rules on witness compensation do not exist. Finally, this reliance on written statements and documents is endorsed also by a system which entrusts an adjudicatory committee with the task of determining the final judgment in cases of difficult or sensitive questions which cannot be resolved by the trial judges.

Thus far, the reality of Chinese criminal proceedings speaks for serious defects in implementing the legislative goal of a 'trial-centered' criminal process.

Following the cross-examination of witnesses, the prosecutor and the defence counsel shall adduce physical evidence. The parties have the right to examine this evidence (Article 195 CPL).

v. Step 5. Parties' Closing Arguments and the Accused's Closing Statement

When the panel of judges deems that all the facts related to the case have been examined and clarified, the presiding judge shall declare that examination of evidence is finished and a debate will begin of all the facts. According to the CPL, the range of this debate pertains to the 'evidence and merits of a case' (Article 198(2)). Article 228 of the SPC Interpretation states that the 'debate covers all the facts, evidence, finding of guilt, sentencing, and other issues related to the case'. In April 2009 the SPC revised and republished its 'Guiding Opinions on Sentencing Procedures of the People's Courts (for Trial Implementation)' (Guiding Opinions on Sentencing). The SPC's Interpretation in 2021 also pointed out that 'during a trial, the facts and evidence related to sentencing should be examined', and added a list of circumstances relevant for sentencing (Article 276).

However, due to the difference between the Chinese trial model and common law jurisdictions, the court hearings on conviction and on sentencing cannot be completely separated. Therefore, in practice, this has caused difficulties for the defence who must also present sentencing arguments when first of all applying for an acquittal. In order to improve the situation, on 6 November 2020, the SPC, SPP, the MPS, and Other Departments issued their 'Opinions on Several Issues Concerning the Regulation of Sentencing Procedures' (OSP). The OSP suggests that, 'where a defendant pleads not guilty or the defender introduces a defence of innocence, court investigation of guilt and innocence and court debates on sentencing shall be conducted separately'. The OSP provides detailed procedural suggestions on the separation of the conviction and sentencing processes. It further holds that at the stage of the court's investigation, relevant sentencing facts shall be also ascertained. The defendant and the defence counsel may produce evidence proving the innocence of the defendant or the pettiness of crime, and express their cross-examination opinions in court. Then at the stage of the court debate, a judge shall urge the prosecution and the defence to debate conviction issues first. Once the debate on conviction issues is completed, the judge must inform the prosecution and the defence that their debate may now pertain to sentencing issues and that they may offer sentencing recommendations or opinions, and give their reasons and basis therefor. The participation of the defendant and the defence in the investigation of sentencing issues does not affect arguments supporting innocence (Article 15 OSP). However, although the efforts of legal institutions could be recognised in the OSP, the author argues that unless conviction and sentencing processes are completely separated, problems of defence will never completely disappear.

The CPL gives the right of a closing statement to the accused (Article 198). In practice, the accused usually makes an apology for the crime that he has committed; sometimes defendants repeat the arguments of their defence counsel. If the accused brings up new facts or evidence in the final statement, the presiding judge with other collegiate bench members may reopen the examination phase of the trial if they deem it necessary (Article 288 SPC's Interpretation).

vi. Step 6. Deliberation after Trial

After the accused has made the closing statement, the presiding judge will announce an adjournment. The members of the panel must then deliberate in private. The Chinese system is similar to that of continental law jurisdictions, eg the German system, in which the professional judges and lay assessors make decisions on guilt and – if the defendant is found guilty – on sentencing in one session. The deliberation will be presided over by the presiding judge. According to the CPL, the decision will be the result of a majority vote, but the opinion of the minority shall be entered in the transcript of the deliberations (Article 184 CPL). If a collegial panel deems it too difficult to arrive at a decision – on a difficult, complicated or significant case – the panel of judges may request the president of the court to submit the case to the judicial committee for further discussion and decision-making (Article 185 CPL). As noted in Chapter 4 above on agencies of criminal justice, this system has been widely criticised by legal scholars because it violates procedural rules, whereby the adjudicator should have the authority to make decisions according to the facts and law. Furthermore, as has been outlined earlier the judicial committee element can be considered to be in conflict with the goal of a trial centered criminal process as it undermines the effective implementation of the principle of oral presentation of evidence and cross-examination.

The CPL lists the possible results of the decision:

(1) a finding of guilt, when the facts of the case are clear, the evidence has been verified and carries guilt (a guilty verdict);
(2) a finding of not guilty when clear evidence demonstrates the innocence of the defendant (a not guilty verdict);
(3) when the defendant cannot be found guilty because there is insufficient evidence to prove the crimes being charged, the panel of judges shall render a not guilty verdict adding that the charges are denied because of insufficient evidence.

With respect to the third kind of verdict, and as discussed further in Chapter 3 above on Basic Concepts, the author believes that this is contrary to logic, as a defendant can only be judged to be guilty or not guilty (a third possibility simply does not exist) and ultimately contradicts the principle of the presumption of innocence. A 'second class' type of acquittal, furthermore, contributes to a possibly lasting stigma. It is also in opposition to the ultimate goal of criminal proceedings, which is final closure of a conflict and the maintenance of social peace.

In the 2018 CPL amendment, a provision relating to the guilty plea and leniency policy was added. This provision states that in a case where the defendant admits guilt and accepts punishment, the court shall, when issuing a judgment in according with the law, generally adopt the charges filed by and the sentencing recommendation from the procuratorate. Exceptions to this are where:

(1) the conduct of the defendant does not establish a criminal offence, or the defendant is not held to be criminally liable;
(2) the defendant has admitted guilt and accepted punishment against his will;
(3) the defendant denies the facts of the crime with which he is charged;
(4) the charges filed are inconsistent with those determined at the trial;
(5) trial fairness has been otherwise affected.

The law suggests that where, after trial, the court holds that the sentencing recommendation is evidently inappropriate, or the defendant or defender raises any objection to the sentencing recommendation, the procuratorate may amend the sentencing recommendation. If the procuratorate fails to do that, or the sentencing recommendation is still evidently inappropriate after the amendment, the court shall render a judgment in accordance with the law (Article 201 CPL).

vii. Step 7. Pronouncement of Judgment

When the judge or the collegiate bench has reached a verdict, the judgment must be pronounced in public according to Article 202 of the CPL.

According to the law, the trial and the pronouncement of judgment can be separated. This means that the judgment may be pronounced immediately after the trial, usually in cases that are relatively simple. The judgment may also be pronounced at a subsequently announced date, usually in cases that are more complicated. The CPL requires that when the judgment is pronounced immediately after the trial, the written judgment must be delivered within five days to the prosecutor and defendant. If the judgment is pronounced on a fixed date, the written judgment must be delivered immediately.

IV. The Subsidiary Civil Action

China's CPL follows the continental law system. The CPL is similar to the German model. When the first CPL was enacted in 1979, a special procedure called 'subsidiary civil action' (附带民事诉讼) was introduced in Chapter Seven, Part One. The chapter contains only four articles (Articles 101–104) which deal with these issues. In the SPC's Interpretation another 27 articles (Articles 175–201) provide more detailed rules. This procedure allows a civil claim to be dealt with as part of criminal proceedings and by the same trial court. The victim joins the proceeding as a party and enjoys the rights that other parties have. Although this procedure raises a number of issues for debate, it does have its advantages. The core function of the procedure is to protect the legitimate rights and interests of the victim. In comparison with a separate action in civil courts, it saves the time of civil courts and makes proceedings easier, faster and cheaper for the victim or his legal representatives or relatives. In addition, this procedure also allows for greater consistency and serves the victims' interests. For the court, this procedure avoids repeated criminal and civil trials, improves the efficiency of litigation and saves judicial resources.

The subsidiary civil claim must flow from the accused's offence. The right to bring a subsidiary civil claim in a criminal trial is accorded to the victim who has suffered any material loss as a result of the defendant's crime. In the 2012 CPL reform, another two conditions have been added. If the victim has passed away, or if the victim has lost legal capacity, then his/her legal representative or close relatives has the right to initiate the proceedings (Article 101 of the CPL).

The most controversial issue in the subsidiary civil lawsuit is the scope of compensation for the victim's loss. In the aforementioned legal provisions on the prerequisites for filing a subsidiary civil lawsuit, reference is made to 'material loss as a result of the defendant's crime'. This obviously excludes damages for pain and suffering. This has been confirmed by the SPC's Interpretation, which states that: 'The court shall not accept any civil lawsuit or subsidiary civil lawsuit that demand compensation for pain and suffering caused by a criminal act' (Article 175 of SPC's Interpretation). As the author mentioned in Chapter 6 on the rights of victims, the provisions of the CPL are inconsistent with the civil law, especially with respect to civil liability. The criminal infringement suffered by the victim represents serious tort. Civil law stipulates compensation for pain and suffering. Therefore, the criminal subsidiary civil lawsuit should also allow compensation for pain and suffering. As a consequence, the SPC uses judicial interpretation to limit the scope of civil liability and even prevents the victim from filing a civil lawsuit, which is inappropriate.

The CPL does not provide a clear definition of the scope of 'material loss'. The SPC's Interpretation emphasises that the term refers to 'material loss suffered by the victim due to criminal infringement of personal rights or financial destruction by criminals' (Article 175(1) SPC Interpretation). In a further explanation, the SPC rules out losses caused by a defendant's illegal possession and disposal of the victim's property, because the SPC assumes that such material losses should be collected or ordered to be refunded in accordance with Article 64 of the Criminal Law. So, this loss is also excluded from the scope of subsidiary civil litigation (Article 176 SPC Interpretation). Finally, the specific scope of material losses is further spelled out in Article 192 of the SPC Interpretation, which includes medical expenses, nursing expenses and other reasonable expenses for treatment and rehabilitation, as well as reduced income due to absence from work. If the crime is the cause of the victim's disability, compensation shall also be paid for expenses such as the cost of equipment to assist the disabled victim's daily living; if the death of the victim was caused, expenses for the funeral shall be compensated. The SPC's explanation of limiting the scope of compensation is as follows:

> In practice, the compensation standards controlled by various courts are inconsistent, and the amount of compensation awarded is too high, resulting in a widespread phenomenon: judgments cannot be enforced (known as 'empty judgment'). This has caused many complaints. It affects the resolution of social contradictions and undermines the authority of the law and the unity of justice.[15]

In the author's view, subsidiary civil litigation should not limit the scope of civil liability. In order to obtain effective compensation for the victim, it is necessary to formulate a national compensation law and a corresponding system of implementing compensation. After the victim has exhausted all legal channels or other remedies, and if he has still not received reasonable compensation, he should be entitled to receive state compensation.

V. Private Prosecution Cases

In addition to public prosecution cases, China's CPL allows a small number of cases to be classified as private prosecution cases. Article 210 of the CPL divides private prosecution cases into three categories:

(1) cases to be handled only upon complaint by the victim. The specific crimes falling in this category are listed in the criminal law. These include:
   (a) insult and defamation (Article 246 of the Criminal Law, but with the exception of cases involving serious endangerment of social order and national interest);
   (b) forcibly interfering with another person's freedom of marriage (Article 257 § 1 of the Criminal Law);
   (c) maltreatment of a family member (Article 260 § 1 of the Criminal Law);
   (d) unlawful possession of property (Article 270 of the Criminal Law).

   The legislator classifies such cases as private prosecution cases because the legal interests affected by these offences are considered mostly personal interests, only rarely reaching the threshold of public interests;

[15] Jiang Bixin and Hu Yunteng, *Understanding and Application of the Interpretation of the Supreme People's Court on the Application of Criminal Procedure Law* (Beijing, China Legal Publishing House, 2003) 147.

(2) minor criminal cases where the victim has evidence to prove the offence and where no public prosecution is brought by the prosecutor:
   (a) cases of intentionally inflicting bodily injury (Article 234(1) of the Criminal Law);
   (b) cases of trespassing (Article 245 of the Criminal Law);
   (c) obstructing freedom of communication (Article 252 of the Criminal Law);
   (d) bigamy (Article 258 of the Criminal Law);
   (e) abandonment (Article 261 of the Criminal Law);
   (f) producing and distributing fake and shoddy goods (Part Two Specific Provisions, Chapter Three, Section 1 Criminal Code, except those instances which seriously damage social order and the national interest);
   (g) minor cases where defendants may be sentenced to fixed-term imprisonment of not more than three years according to the provisions in Chapters Four and Five of the Specific Provisions of the Criminal Law;
(3) when a victim has evidence to prove that an offender has infringed upon his or her personal or property rights which could result in criminal liability according to the law, but a public security authority or a procuratorate decides not to prosecute.

The application to initiate a private prosecution case requires the court to review it. For cases where the facts are clear and sufficient evidence is available, the court must open a trial. For cases lacking evidence, and if the private prosecutor cannot provide supplementary evidence, the private prosecutor should be persuaded to withdraw the private prosecution or the application should be rejected (Article 211 CPL). For private prosecution cases accepted by the court, the law allows mediation and also allows the private prosecutor to reach a reconciliation with the defendant or withdraw the private prosecution before the judgment is announced. In practice, the number of private prosecution cases is very small, especially for the third type of cases stipulated by the law. The reason for the rare commencement of private prosecution may be found in the victim's problems in collecting sufficient evidence. If the police and prosecutors have begun investigations and collected evidence, but the proceedings have been terminated due to various reasons, the evidence they collected will not be passed on to victims. It is very difficult for private prosecutors to collect evidence on their own, so there is little chance of bringing a successful lawsuit and winning the case.

VI. Summary and Expedited Proceedings[16]

One of the main goals of the 2018 CPL revision was to encourage the use of the guilty plea and leniency system. Expedited procedures have been introduced to

[16] It has been also translated as 'fast-track sentencing procedure'.

handle this kind of case. Under the current CPL, there are three types of trial proceedings to adjudicate criminal cases. These trial proceedings concern: ordinary procedures; summary procedures; and expedited procedures.

Compared with the ordinary trial procedures, the latter two are simplified procedures. The process is simplified in some respects. However, it is argued that there are no significant differences between summary procedure and expedited procedure.

In terms of the conditions restricting the application of these two procedures, neither of them can be applied to blind, deaf, or mentally handicapped defendants (ie mentally ill offenders who have not completely lost the capacity to recognise the wrongness of their behaviour or the ability to control their actions).

In criminal cases involving several defendants expedited procedures require that all defendants accept the alleged crime facts, charges, and sentencing recommendations and do not have objections with respect to the expedited procedure. Similarly, in summary procedures all defendants must agree with the summary procedure and plead guilty. Neither procedure may apply if a case may have a major social impact. The expedited procedure rules clearly stipulate that this procedure is not applicable for trials of juvenile delinquency cases (Article 223(2)), which is certainly in line with the primary goal of rehabilitating and educating juvenile offenders. But the summary procedure can, in principle, apply to juvenile cases, as juvenile offenders are specifically excluded either in the law or in the judicial interpretation. In the SPC's Interpretation, a special rule states that when the defender makes a plea of innocence, or the defendant pleads guilty, but the reviewing judge believes that a criminal offence may not be established during the review process, the summary procedure cannot be applied (Article 360(5) SPC Interpretation). An expedited procedure cannot be applied if the defendant and the victim or legal representative have not reached a mediation or agreed on settling matters such as a subsidiary civil litigation compensation.

The main difference between these two procedures in terms of court trial proceedings concerns the following. For the expedited procedure, Article 224 of the CPL states that:

> in general, court investigations and deliberations are not conducted, and only the defender's opinions and the defendant's final statement are required to be heard before the judgment is announced.

Under summary procedures, the law stipulates that with the permission of the judges, the defendant and his/her defender can debate with the public prosecutor or private prosecutor and their litigation representatives (Article 218 CPL), but the case shall not be subject to the provisions which are related to the proceedings of an ordinary trial, such as questioning the defendant, witnesses, expert witnesses or adducing evidence. However, the defendant's final statement should also be heard before the judgment is announced.

As regards the time limits set for the trial in these two procedures, for the summary trial, the court shall conclude the case within 20 days after the case was accepted for summary proceedings. But, if the defendant may be sentenced to more than three years imprisonment, the duration of the trial can be extended to one and a half months. For cases that are tried by the expedited procedure, the law requires that the trial shall be concluded within 10 days after acceptance, and if the defendant may be sentenced to imprisonment of more than one year, the duration of the trial can be extended to 15 days.

According to empirical research, in practice the application rate for summary procedures is declining year by year.[17] Two reasons for the decline can be identified. First, it is argued that the design of the simplified procedure compared with ordinary trial proceedings does not result in a truly simplifying effect. Second, when the expedited procedure was introduced in 2014, the number of summary procedures carried out decreased. The author believes that these two different procedures should be merged into one by the legislator.

[17] Gong Shanan and Wang Lusheng, 'The Practical Dilemma of Criminal Summary Procedure under the Conflict of Internal and External Positioning and Its Reform' (2020) 3 *Journal of Shandong University (Philosophy and Social Sciences Edition)* 22–32.

8

Criminal Evidence

I. Introduction

China, like most countries with a civil law tradition, does not have a general evidence law. The rules on evidence are found separately in criminal, civil and administrative procedure laws. The rules dealing with criminal evidence are to be found in the CPL's General Provisions, Part One, Chapter 5 (Articles 50–65). The mode of criminal evidence is inextricably linked to the mode of criminal procedure. The introduction to China's developments in criminal procedure law in the previous chapters has shown that China's model of criminal procedure is slowly moving towards a mixed model. China's rules on criminal evidence do not, therefore, reflect the 'sports match' model of the adversarial tradition, where the 'parties' dominate proceedings. The Chinese model is closer to the 'judge-dominated' 'drill model' which prevails in inquisitorial systems of criminal procedure. But the Chinese approach does not share completely the typical characteristics of the inquisitorial model, where the judge follows the principle of free evaluation of evidence.[1] However, Chinese criminal procedure law is bound by standards common to the procedural laws of other jurisdictions: it is geared towards the same goal and it corresponds to a 'fact-finding enterprise which requires a decision to be reached'.[2] The standard most important to be observed certainly concerns the fair trial principle that is grounded in international human rights laws. In addition, China is currently strengthening its fight against corruption and terrorism by means of criminal law. The effective combating of corruption and terrorism depends, in the context of globalisation, on international judicial assistance and cooperation. As one of the core issues of international judicial assistance, besides extradition, concerns the exchange of evidence, comparative studies are needed in order to identify differences in the law.[3]

[1] John D Jackson and Sarah J Summers, *Internationalization of Criminal Evidence* (Cambridge, Cambridge University Press, 2012).

[2] ibid.

[3] Elodie Sellier and Anne Weyemberg, *Criminal Procedural Laws across the European Union – A Comparative Analysis of Selected Main Differences and the Impact they Have over the Development of EU Legislation* (Brussels, Directorate General for Internal Policies of the Union, 2018) 52–61.

Since the principles related to criminal suspects and defendants' rights – such as the presumption of innocence, the privilege against self-incrimination, the standard of proof, and the burden of proof – have been introduced in previous chapters, this chapter focuses on the specific forms (means, or sources) of evidence and the main rules of evidence, in particular the exclusion of illegally obtained evidence.

II. Definition of Criminal Evidence

China is one of only a few countries to provide for a statutory definition of evidence and lists in the CPL the forms of criminal evidence. In the 2012 CPL amendment, the definition of evidence which had been adopted in the 1996 CPL ('all facts that prove the true circumstances of a case shall be evidence') was revised. The current definition of evidence now declares that 'all materials that may be used to prove the facts of the case are evidence' (Article 50 CPL). Although this definition may be considered an improvement over the 1996 CPL version, it still has shortcomings. First of all, Article 50 uses the word 'material'. 'Material' serves as a kind of carrier, also mentioned in Anglo-American law.[4] However, the Chinese definition does not really distinguish the 'material' carrying evidence from ordinary material. 'Material' shall be 'objects of sensory perception' and of a 'rational' character relevant for the case. 'Material' should rather be changed to a 'fact' demonstrating evidence (which could be further split up into direct and circumstantial evidence).[5] Second, this definition does not establish a link between evidence and criminal procedure. 'Material' and 'information' are to be presented to legal institutions, especially the trial court, and the evidence should be given orally and directly. Finally, this definition does not distinguish between criminal evidence and evidence in civil and administrative litigation: criminal evidence is presented to prove (or disprove) facts establishing a criminal offence.

III. The Forms of Criminal Evidence

The CPL, after giving a definition of evidence, lists eight forms of evidence (Article 50(2)):

(1) real (physical) evidence;
(2) documentary evidence;
(3) testimony of witnesses;
(4) statement of victims;
(5) statements and explanations by criminal suspects or defendants;

[4] Evidence in Criminal Investigations, 6 July 2020.
[5] Hock Lai Ho, 'The Legal Concept of Evidence', https://plato.stanford.edu/archives/win2015.

(6) conclusion of expert evaluators;
(7) transcripts of examination, inspection, identification, or investigative experiments; and
(8) audio-visual materials and electronic data.

China's CPL provides an exhaustive list of forms of evidence and thus adopts the internationally recognised principle of strict rules of proof which apply with respect to questions of criminal responsibility and punishment. Countries with a common law tradition usually divide evidence into three categories: oral or testimonial evidence (testimony given in court by witnesses); documentary evidence (documents produced for inspection by the court or to be read during trial); and 'real' or physical evidence.[6] Civil law countries such as Germany, for example, do not deal with evidence in a special chapter of the criminal procedural code, but display decentralised rules for the collection and evaluation of types of evidence which address testimonial evidence, expert evidence, documentary evidence, (visual) inspection of (physical) evidence and statements made by the defendant. Chinese scholars, however, question the legislative approach of restricting the legal forms of evidence, believing that such restrictions are unnecessary and 'may stifle the flexibility and vitality of the evidence system'.[7] The CPL's restrictions on the form of evidence correspond to international standards, and, moreover, provide for a separate category of audio-visual materials and electronic data.[8] In fact, the rise of electronic communication and the growing relevance of digital data in the investigation and prosecution of crime call for attention and further development of legislation on this type of criminal evidence.

A. Physical Evidence

Physical evidence covers a rather wide category. Physical or 'real' evidence consists of objects that judges, jurors and other participants of the trial can inspect. Physical evidence pertains to fingerprints, DNA-profiles or instruments and weapons used to commit a crime. The common law perspective emphasises the object character of physical evidence (material objects), while the continental law approach, expressed for example in the German or Austrian criminal procedural law, accentuates cognition by introducing the concept of 'evidence by inspection':

> an inspection involves nothing more than a direct appreciation of the qualities of an object (including persons), an event, or a process, or certain conduct or behaviour, through use of the five senses of sight, hearing, taste, smell and touch, as long as it is not otherwise regulated under the provisions for witness, expert or documentary evidence.[9]

[6] ibid.
[7] Chen Ruihua, 'The Concept and Statutory Types of Evidence' (2012) 1 *Application of Law* 24.
[8] Fan Yang and Jiao Feng, 'Rules of Electronic Data in Criminal Cases in China' (2021) 64 *International Journal of Law, Crime and Justice* 100453, doi.org/10.1016/j.ijlcj.2020.100453.
[9] Michael Bohlander, *Principles of German Criminal Procedure*, 2nd edn (Oxford, Hart Publishing, 2021).

Thus, the definition of civil law countries is more extensive, including evidence formed by the perception of the five sense organs, including also situations like a crime scene (which cannot be physically held). There is no definition of physical evidence in China's CPL, but the statutory classification of evidence in Article 50 of the CPL and the SPC's judicial interpretation separate the investigation of the crime scene and results of inspection of the human body (DNA profiles) from physical evidence. Thus, the scope of physical evidence in Chinese procedural law is narrower than the 'evidence by inspection' concept and is closer to the common law approach.

Before the 2012 CPL revision, physical and documentary evidence were part of the same category. Since the 2012 revision, these two types of evidences have been separated. However, the CPL does not provide detailed rules on collecting and evaluating physical evidence before the court. Only the MPS Provisions and the SPC's Interpretation contain rules in this respect. These require that physical evidence shall, as a rule, be produced as the original items. Only if the original items cannot be moved, or if they are undurable, or if they need to be returned to the victim, may real evidence be allowed to be presented before the court by a photograph or video, which sufficiently reflects the shapes or contents of the original real evidence (Article 64 MPS Provisions, Articles 82–86 SPC's Interpretation).

B. Documentary Evidence

The collection and evaluation of documentary evidence are subject to rules similar to those that govern physical evidence. The MPS Provisions require that documentary evidence collected and retrieved should be original. Only when it is very difficult to obtain the original may a copy or reproduction be used. Copies and reproductions of documentary evidence can only be used as evidence when verified as legitimate copies of the original document. If the documentary evidence has been altered and signs of alteration cannot be reasonably explained, or if the copy or reproduction does not reflect the original document and its contents, it shall not be used as evidence (Articles 65, 71 MPS Provisions).

One area of significant progress in the 2012 CPL amendment concerns the exclusionary rule. The exclusionary rule has been broadened to include physical and documentary evidence that has been illegally obtained, and finally the exclusionary rule has been written into the CPL. As regards physical and documentary evidence, Article 56 of the CPL now stipulates that:

> Physical or documentary evidence collected in violation of legal procedures which may seriously affect judicial fairness shall be supplemented and corrected or reasonably explained. Evidence that cannot be supplemented and corrected or reasonably explained shall be excluded.

Article 56 of the CPL divides illegally obtained evidence into two categories: confession and witness testimony on the one hand; and documents and physical evidence on the other. According to the CPL, different standards apply to these two kinds of evidence. Confessions extracted through the use of torture or other illegal methods, or statements of victims or witnesses which have been obtained by illegal methods such as violence or threats 'shall be excluded'. This is considered by the legislator to be an 'absolute exclusion' (which is discussed in the following text). However, as explained above, illegally obtained physical and documentary evidence is subject to the principle of 'relative exclusion'. Sometimes referred to as the 'discretionary exclusion rule', the threshold of exclusion is set by ultimately assessing the impact that a breach of procedural law during the collection of evidence will have on judicial fairness. The CPL itself does not elaborate on specific circumstances for the exclusion of illegally obtained physical and documentary evidence. The 'Provisions on Several Issues Concerning the Examination and Judgment of Evidence in Death Penalty Cases' (2010) (Provisions on Evidence for Death Penalty Cases) listed four situations in which the collection of physical and documentary evidence did not comply with procedures in Article 9 of the Provisions. It was in these Provisions that 'flawed evidence' was mentioned for the first time. The relationship between 'flawed evidence' and 'illegally obtained evidence' resulted in extended discussions in academic law circles.[10] Article 14 of the 'Provisions on Several Issues Concerning the Exclusion of Illegal Evidence in Criminal Cases' (2017) then supplied an explanation of the meaning of 'seriously affecting judicial fairness'. According to this explanation, exclusion of evidence seriously affecting judicial fairness aims at safeguarding substantive justice. This emphasises the fact that legislators and legal practitioners, when developing and substantiating exclusionary rules, seek to establish the 'substantive truth' in criminal proceedings. This is different from the goals designed by other legal jurisdictions to exclude evidence. So, for example, in the US, the original purpose of exclusionary rules was to deter police misconduct and pursue judicial integrity, while German procedural law and jurisprudence dealing with the exclusion of illegally obtained evidence are based on the balancing of basic and procedural rights of suspects and accused on the one hand with the effective implementation of criminal law on the other.[11] In fact, the goals pursued by exclusionary rules play a decisive role in determining the doctrines that guide the application of these rules and in particular the range of illegally obtained evidence eligible for exclusion.[12] However, this topic has received but insignificant attention from legal scholars and practitioners in China.

[10] Li Xuejun and Liu Jing, 'The Application of Flawed Evidence and Its Remedial Rules' (2020) 5 *Tsinghua Law Science* 103.

[11] Liling Yue, 'Comparing German and American Exclusionary Rules' (2003) 3 *The Journal of China University of Political Science and Law* 178.

[12] Liling Yue, 'Thoughts about Floyd Feeney: An Excellent Scholar and a Good Friend' (2020) 53(4) *UC Davis Law Review* 1781.

C. Witnesses and the Testimony of Witnesses

The CPL does not provide a comprehensive definition of a witness. Article 62 refers to a witness as 'any one with knowledge of facts of the case'. The article then adds that a witness has a duty to testify. This provision follows an approach adopted in some countries (Austria or Switzerland) of defining what a witness is in criminal procedural law, though others (Germany, Scandinavian countries) abstain from a formal definition, assuming evidently that the term 'witness' alone carries a meaning which will allow reasonable interpretation and uniform practice. However, Article 62 exhibits flaws. First, the scope of 'any one with knowledge of facts of the case' is too broad and does not exclude from the definition suspects/defendants or victims and experts, who will also have, to some extent, 'knowledge of facts of the case', but who are discrete from ordinary witnesses and fall into separate evidential categories. Second, in the meaning of the law, the witness should not only have knowledge of certain facts in the case through their own perceptions, but should, at the same time, be the person who provides testimony to the legal institutions. Furthermore, the CPL, unlike other common law countries, for example, does not differentiate between witnesses who have knowledge obtained through their own senses, such as eye witnesses, and hearsay witnesses, who have obtained information about the case from other sources.

The second paragraph of Article 62 CPL excludes persons from testifying as witnesses who are physically or mentally handicapped or who are minors, who are deemed to be unable to distinguish between right and wrong or unable to express themselves fully. Article 62 was criticised for its vagueness, so the SPC, in its Interpretations has further elaborated on the conditions under which a witness must be considered as not competent to testify. The SPC Interpretations explain that disabled persons or minors are not generally regarded as lacking capacity to give testimony as a witness. However, an individual evaluation shall address the question whether 'the inability to distinguish right from wrong and the inability to correctly express oneself' affects testimony. Article 87(2) of the SPC Interpretations states that the witness's testimony, age, cognitive and intellectual capacity, capacity to memorise and the ability of expression as well as physical and mental state at the time of testimony shall be examined in order to find out whether these conditions will influence testimony. However, in practice, uniform standards and evaluation methods, or binding procedures for reviewing the witness's cognitive and intellectual development, and assessing the mental state of the witness are not available. Since the 2012 CPL amendment, Article 88 of the SPC Interpretation has added another rule to be taken into account when deciding on the admission of evidence:

> Testimony provided by witnesses who were clearly drunk, intoxicated, or drugged, and were unable to perceive normally, or accurately express themselves, must not be used as evidence.

In order to implement 'trial-centred' criminal procedural law reform and increase the rate of witnesses appearing and testifying before a court, the 2012 CPL amendment strengthened witness protection provisions, and introduced compulsory measures for those who refuse to testify without a legally recognised reason. Measures to guarantee the safety of witnesses correspond to international standards. The CPL now imposes on courts, the procuratorate and public security organs an obligation to guarantee the safety of witnesses and their close relatives (Article 63(1)). The law also requires that intimidation, insults, assault or retaliation against witnesses or their close relatives which establish a criminal offence shall be investigated and prosecuted in accordance with the law, and those situations that do not reach the threshold of a criminal offence shall be punished according to the provisions of administrative penalties for public security violations (Article 63(2)).

The CPL then has adopted protective measures for selected vulnerable witnesses. Legislation in this field implements the UN Convention against Transnational Organized Crime (Articles 24, 25) which was ratified by China in 2003. In cases of crime endangering national security, terrorism, organised crime of a mafia nature, or drug crime, where testifying before a court will expose witnesses, victims, expert witnesses or close relatives of these to risks of personal safety, Article 64 lists the protective measures to be implemented by courts, procuratorates or public security agencies. Protection can be sought through:

(1) keeping confidential the personal information of witnesses such as name, address and employer;
(2) voice distortion and facial disguise when testifying in court;
(3) prohibiting others from contacting witnesses, expert witness, victims and their close relatives;
(4) special protection measures for persons and residence.

The CPL has not yet introduced protective measures for other vulnerable witnesses and victims. Thus, there is room for reform, which should focus in particular on child victims and victims of sexual violence.

Reimbursement of witnesses is covered by Article 65(1) of the CPL. Expenses for transportation, accommodation, and meals when testifying at a court trial shall be borne by judicial authorities' budget, and guaranteed by the government at the same level.

The CPL does not clearly spell out the obligations of witnesses. Article 62(1) states that 'Anyone with knowledge of facts of the case has the obligation to testify'. However, this provision does not specify the form of witness testimony, whether testimony can be given in writing (through the protocol of an interrogation) or through appearing and testifying before the court. While Article 61 of the CPL declares that:

> The witness testimony must be cross-examined by the prosecutor, the victim, the defendant, and the defender in court and to be verified for its truthfulness before it can be used as the basis for a verdict,

Article 195 accepts that 'the testimony of witnesses who have not appeared in court, the expert's evaluation, examination transcripts and other documents shall be read out in court'.

After reading out protocols, documents etc, judges shall listen to the opinions of the public prosecutor, parties, defenders, and agents ad litem. This provision apparently contradicts Article 61, and it might be inferred that witnesses have a choice whether or not to appear in court (after having testified before trial proceedings) and that the judge has discretion whether to read out written testimony or to hear a witness in person. Judicial discretion for the way in which testimony is presented in court is also supported by Article 192 of the CPL, which states:

> Where prosecutors, parties, defenders or agents ad litem object to a witness's testimony that has a major bearing on the case verdict or sentencing and the people's courts find that it is necessary for them to testify in court, the witness shall appear in court to testify.

In addition, police officers who are eye-witnesses to a crime and expert witnesses must appear in person before the court and testify only if the court finds that that is necessary (Article 192(2) CPL). However, the consequences of not complying when a court finds that it is necessary to hear a witness, expert or police officer in person vary depending on who is providing the evidence. While the law is quiet about the position when a police officer does not appear in court to give testimony, Article 192(3) of the CPL states provides that an expert evaluation may not be used as a basis for deciding the case if the expert refuses to appear. Ordinary witnesses may be compelled to appear before the court.

Article 193 of the CPL provides compulsory measures and sanctions for witnesses who refuse to testify before a court without a legitimate reason. The court may compel the appearance and testimony of a witness, but the law does not define the 'legitimate reasons' for refusal. Article 253 of the SPC's Interpretation lists four circumstances which result in permission not to comply with the summons.

(1) a witness is suffering from serious illness or his mobility is significantly impaired at the time of the trial;
(2) the domicile of the witness is located far away from the court and reasonable transportation is not available;
(3) a witness is abroad and is not able to return to China in the near future; or
(4) other comprehensible reasons prevent appearance before the court.

Failure to appear before the court without legitimate reasons or failure to testify may result in sanctions imposed by the court (Article 193 CPL). The sanctions are graded according to less serious and more serious violations of the duty to appear. For less serious violations the witness may be cautioned by the court admonitions. If the circumstances are serious, detention of up to ten days may be imposed with the approval of the president of the court. If a detention order is issued, the witness may apply for a review by the court of the next level (Article 193(2)).

The 2012 CPL amendment introduced, for the first time in the era of modern Chinese law, a privilege for the defendant's spouse, parents, and children, which protects against compelled appearances before a court and to give testimony (Article 193 of CPL). Here, the Chinese legislator has started to balance the interests of crime control with the interest in maintaining and respecting trust within the family. However, future reforms of criminal procedural law should consider providing for a systematic and comprehensive regulation of witness privileges in conjunction with the general rules on witness evidence (Articles 61–65 CPL).

While a lawyer-client privilege, though with exceptions, is provided by Article 48 of the CPL, giving lawyers the right 'to preserve the confidentiality of their client's information and relevant circumstances that they learn during the course of performing their professional activities',[13] other trust-related professional privileges (medical doctors, psychiatrists, priests) are not covered by the CPL.

D. Statements of Victims

Unlike other criminal procedural codes, the CPL separates the victim's statement from ordinary witness testimony. A distinct treatment of victim testimony is reasonable in principle, because of the involvement of the victim in the case. Victimisation carries physical or psychological suffering to varying degrees, and other adverse impacts which may affect the objectivity or credibility of the victim's testimony. Therefore, in the examination and evaluation of victim statements particular scrutiny is advisable. The special characteristics of the criminal offence in question and its impact on the victim, as well as the relationship between victim and suspect/defendant, all have to be considered. However, in addition, victims who testify in court will sometimes encounter difficulties and problems which are different from those of ordinary witnesses. They may meet and face the defendant during cross-examination, which may cause the victim to suffer secondary harm. Beyond that, the privacy of victims may be affected when obliged to testify in a public trial. As outlined above, the CPL and the SPC's Interpretation do not provide responses to such problems. International documents and recognised standards call for the effective protection of vulnerable victims who need to testify in court. In future, Chinese criminal procedural reform should systematically develop rules geared towards minimising any harm that may possibly result from exposure in a public trial and confrontation with a defendant, especially in cases of sexual violence and involving child victims. Possible steps forward, in addition to *in camera* proceedings for the victim's testimony or the removal of a defendant from the courtroom during the victim's questioning, could include the introduction of testimony via live CCTV links or the presentation of evidence through taped interrogations.[14]

[13] Changyong Sun and Suhao Chen, 'Attorney-Client Privilege in Mainland China's Criminal Proceedings' in Lorena Bachmaier et al (eds), *The Right to Counsel and the Protection of Attorney-Client Privilege in Criminal Proceedings. A Comparative View* (Springer International, 2020) 75.

[14] Wang Xiaoguang and Li Qin, 'Empirical Analysis and System Construction of Victims to Testify in Court', www.iolaw.org.cn.

E. Confessions and Exculpations by the Criminal Suspects or the Accused

The attitude of Chinese legislation towards defendants' confession is different from that of other jurisdictions. The defendant's confession is regarded in the law as a particular type of evidence. As mentioned in Chapter 3 on basic concepts, not only does the law not provide criminal suspects and defendants with the right to remain silent, it actually requires that suspects 'shall truthfully answer the questions of investigator'. Suspects and defendants thus move into the role of witnesses who are also obliged to tell the truth. However, the provision obliging suspects/defendants to tell the truth (ie Article 120 CPL) seems to be in conflict with Article 52 of the CPL. The latter adopts (partially) the internationally recognised principle of the privilege against self-incrimination, which is set out in Article 52 as 'no person shall be compelled to prove his own guilt'.

Chinese legislation regards the defendant's confession as a particularly important type of statutory evidence, which in practice still plays a leading role in criminal proceedings. Investigators, prosecutors and judges consider obtaining a defendant's confession as a core task in criminal investigations. The particular relevance attributed to confession sometimes misleads investigators into the use of illegal methods (torture and threats), practices which have been recognised by Chinese legislators as a main source of miscarriage of justice cases. This in turn has triggered reforms aimed at preventing the use of illegal methods in the interrogation of suspects/defendants and making inadmissible evidence tainted by illegal methods.

F. The Exclusionary Rules Addressing Verbal Evidence

In the 2012 CPL amendment, a basic rule for excluding illegally obtained evidence was introduced. On 20 June 2017, SPC, SPP, MPS, and other departments issued the 'Provisions on Several Issues concerning the Strict Exclusion of Illegally Collected Evidence in the Handling of Criminal Cases' (Provisions on Exclusion of Illegal Evidence. These Provisions supply detailed rules for the implementation of the statutory exclusionary rules. Subsequently, on 1 January 2018, the SPC also created 'Rules for the People's Courts Handling Criminal Cases to Exclude Illegally Obtained Evidence (Trial)' (SPC Rules for Exclusion of Illegal Evidence). Articles 52 and 56 of the CPL are generally considered the statutory basis for defining illegally obtained testimony in the form of witness statements and confessions and setting out how to deal with it. Article 52 strictly prohibits the extraction of confessions by torture and collecting evidence by threat, enticement, trickery, or other illegal methods. Article 52 imposes an obligation to abstain from collecting evidence, including witness and victim statements, through illegal methods, naming three concrete illegal means and enlarging the scope of the norm through the banning also of 'other illegal means'.

Article 1 of the SPC Rules provides an interpretation of the statutory prohibition on extracting confessions through torture in Article 52 of the CPL. According to these rules prohibited methods to obtain confessions include:

(1) use of force such as beatings, illegal use of restraints, or harsh methods of covert physical torture, causing unbearable suffering to the suspect/defendant resulting in a statement against his will;
(2) use of threats of violence or serious damage to the lawful rights and interests of the suspect/defendant and his close relatives, causing unbearable suffering and resulting in a statement against his will;
(3) use of illegal detention and other methods that illegally restrict personal liberty.

The SPC Rules may be also seen as implementing the UN Convention against Torture and Other Cruel, Inhuman or Degrading Treatment or Punishment 1984 with requiring a certain threshold (unbearable suffering) for establishing torture but extending prohibited treatment to include threats and illegal detention and other illegal restrictions on personal freedom.

The SPC Rules also require the exclusion of subsequent repeated confessions after initially confessing due to the use of torture or other illegal treatment. Thus, the SPC Rules adopt an internationally recognised standard which explicitly finds that where a confession has been extracted through torture, a second, voluntary, confession made after such torture must also be excluded. However, the SPC also provides two exceptions to this general rule:

(1) if investigation of the crime results in evidence confirming the confession extracted through torture and investigators other than those involved in the tainted confession interrogate a suspect/defendant again after informing about his rights and the legal consequences of a confession obtain a voluntary confession, then the confession may be admitted as evidence;
(2) if during the period of review of pre-trial detention, review of prosecution, and trial, prosecutors and judges have informed the defendant about his procedural rights and the legal consequences of a confession, and the defendant then voluntarily confesses, the confession may be admitted as evidence.

In the past, Chinese legislators and law practitioners have made serious attempts to define precisely the illegal means of obtaining evidence, in order to provide a comprehensible and feasible approach to the exclusion of illegal evidence. However, actual practice in Chinese criminal proceedings demonstrates that it is extremely difficult to draft a conclusive and comprehensive list of illegal methods of evidence collection. Illegal methods explicitly listed in procedural law, such as deception and deceit, are difficult to distinguish from legitimate interrogation strategies in practice. Not least, controversial debates on the use of entrapment, for example, show internationally that large and varying margins of appreciation exist which may be also a consequence of a particularly great import attached to certain crimes (organised crime, drug trafficking or terrorist violence). Although, the problem of developing a conclusive system of procedural rules to guide the gathering and admissibility of evidence seems to plague many countries,[15] a thorough discussion among Chinese legislators, academics and legal practitioners in this field has yet to develop. Chinese judges do not have principled guidance when making decisions on the question whether evidence has been collected illegally and whether illegally obtained evidence should be admitted or excluded.

Ultimately, consistent and conclusive rules should aim at establishing a fact-finding process which is as reliable as possible, while providing justice in individual cases and implementing an overall fair procedure. The rules on exceptions from the general exclusion of illegally obtained evidence mentioned above show that Chinese judges pay more attention to the reliability of evidence and the purpose of finding the truth, and sideline somewhat the role of exclusionary rules in protecting procedural and human rights and maintaining judicial integrity. From a comparative legal perspective, common law countries, especially the US, emphasise the role of exclusionary rules in deterring police misconduct in investigations and the pursuit of judicial integrity. Placing an emphasis on these aims does not require the exclusion of evidence when police do not engage in illegal acts. In civil law countries, such as Germany, for example, less importance is attached to the role that exclusion of evidence may play in punishing the police for illegal behaviour but (outside the scope of strictly (and statutorily) prohibited forms of collecting and admission of evidence) more weight is attached to the balancing of individual justice, effective implementation of criminal law, the impact of illegalities on basic rights and procedural fairness. This approach allows for the inclusion of all relevant aims, but in the absence of statutory law the judiciary is tasked with finding a proper balance. China's exclusionary rules should be moved towards a concept which establishes absolutely prohibited methods of collecting evidence followed by inadmissibility without exceptions on the one hand, and restrictions on collection and admissibility of evidence which balance procedural fairness, individual justice, human rights and effective application of criminal law on the other.

The CPL and the SPC Rules also regulate some procedural issues related to the exclusion of illegally obtained evidence. First of all, the court, on finding that evidence may have been collected in violation of Article 56 of the CPL, must carry out a courtroom investigation of the possible illegal collection of evidence. Then, the defendant, the defender, and agent ad litem have the right to apply to the court for exclusion of evidence collected by illegal methods. But the CPL requires that the applicant should provide 'relevant clues or materials' when making an application (Article 58(2)). When a courtroom investigation is carried out the prosecutor is obliged to prove that the evidence was collected legally (Article 59). The SPC's Rules also clearly state that the procuratorate bears the burden of proof

[15] See, for example, Grosse Strafrechtskommission des Deutschen Richterbundes, *Gutachten zum Thema: Beweisverbote im Strafverfahren* (Berlin, Bundesministerium der Justiz, 2015) 21–45.

for the legality of evidence. When the procuratorate cannot show proof, or when the evidence provided does not prove legality, the evidence should be excluded (Article 6 SPC Rules). While the CPL does not account for the consequences of the 'exclusion' of illegally obtained evidence, Article 4 of the SPC's Rules elaborates that:

> Illegally obtained evidence excluded in accordance with the law shall not be read out in court, cross-examined during the trial, and shall not be used as the basis for a verdict.

Since the CPL established the exclusionary rule in 2012, implementation of this rule is slowly being advanced. According to an analysis of decisions published in the China Judgment Online,[16] between 2013 and 2015, in 486 cases the question of exclusion of illegally obtained evidence was raised. Out of these, 53 cases were officially initiated by the court, and in eight cases eventually illegally obtained evidence was excluded. Between 1 November 2017 and 31 October 2019, 565 applications involving illegally obtained evidence have been noted. Finally, in 59 cases evidence was judged to have been illegally obtained. This rate amounts to the 6.5 times the number observed from 2013 to 2015.[17] On the basis of these findings, it can be concluded that the rate of exclusion of evidence suspected to be illegal is rather low. However, the rate seems to be on the increase and demonstrates increasing judicial efforts to probe situations of suspicion of illegally obtained evidence.

G. Expert Opinion

When looking at expert opinion from the perspective of terminology, the CPL does not really use an equivalent to the term 'expert'. If the Chinese term '鉴定意见' is literally translated into English, the result would be 'Opinion on identification and evaluation'. This expression can only be construed by reference to other provisions of the CPL. The so-called 'identification and evaluation' refers to Article 146 of the CPL, which states that

> in order to ascertain the facts of the case and when it is necessary to solve certain special fact-related issues, a person with specialised knowledge should be assigned to conduct identification or evaluation.

It can be concluded from the wording of Article 146 of the CPL that 'the evaluator' corresponds to the 'experts' in other jurisdictions. Article 146 also clearly states that an expert has to be called when the court lacks the knowledge and expertise to establish or evaluate facts.

Chinese legislation separates 'expert opinions' from witness testimony and classifies it as a special type of statutory evidence. This separation and the provision of

[16] http://wenshu.court.gov.cn.

[17] Guo Pengfei, 'Scope of Exclusion of Illegal Obtained Evidence' (2020) 10 *People's Justice (Application)* 88.

specific rules for expert evidence are well-founded. Although experts share some of the characteristics of other witnesses, in that they must attend the court hearing and accept cross-examination when summoned by the court, they nevertheless also display differences compared to ordinary witnesses. Experts give special opinions on special issues of the case based on their professional expertise. Witnesses testify based on their personal cognition and experiences. Thus, witnesses are irreplaceable, while experts can be chosen by the prosecutor or the court, which may of course raise questions about how this choice is made. Therefore, the rules for evaluation and admissibility provided by the law for witness evidence and expert evidence are also different.

At present, the main types of 'identification and evaluation' in China's criminal justice practice include: forensic medicine (including DNA); forensic psychiatry; handwriting expertise; determining the value of stolen goods, food, medicine; and drug identification. Here, the identification and assessment of mental illness (and its possible impact on criminal responsibility) certainly pose the most complicated and difficult problems. Not only does this include the development of psychiatry itself; it also raises issues such as the extent of social and political attention paid to public mental health; attitudes on mental health problems; and perceptions of the relationship between mental health problems and crime.

The CPL does not stipulate any qualifications for experts as evaluators. In 2005, the Standing Committee of the NPC issued its 'Decision on the Administration of Forensic Identification and Evaluation' (Decision), which was amended in 2015. Article 2 of this Decision defines three categories of authenticator and authentication which must be entered into a register:

(1) medico-legal authentication;
(2) authentication of expertise for physical evidence;
(3) authentication of expertise for audio and visual materials.

Three qualification criteria were introduced:

(1) a senior professional technology title related to the judicial authentication for which an expert applies;
(2) professional practice qualifications related to the judicial authentication for which an expert applies or a university diploma related to the relevant special area, and pertinent working experience of at least five years;
(3) at least 10 years' working experience related to the judicial authentication for which an expert applies as well as strong professional skills.

The Decision also provides a rule on exclusion criteria. This rule states that anyone who has a record of criminal punishment for an intentional crime or a duty-related criminal offence, has ever been sanctioned by being dismissed from a government organ, or is a deregistered authenticator, must not engage in judicial authentication.

When the CPL was first promulgated in 1979, expert identification was organised by public security agencies, procuratorates, and courts. In the early years, in-house professional expertise prevailed and only when the public security agencies, procuratorates and courts could not supply expertise were external experts hired. With advancements of judicial reforms, strengthening the neutrality and independence of experts' identification and evaluation became more important, and identification institutions that were once established within the procuratorates and the courts were separated from the legal institutions and became independent. Currently only public security organs still retain identification experts and specialised departments. At present, approximately 80 per cent of expert opinions voiced in criminal proceedings come from specialised departments in public security agencies.[18] These changes have also brought new problems. Under the former system, prosecutors or judges who disagreed with the investigative agency's expert opinions could ask their own internal experts to review the opinion. After the abolition of internal expert departments in procuratorates and courts, this facility for supervision and control was lost. Now, if suspects/defendants or defenders disagree with an expert opinion, according to the law, the only redress is an application for supplementary or new identification or evaluation to the investigative agency (Article 148 CPL). It would, in principle, be possible to mandate a different expert, though this would be rather difficult for the defendant or defender. Most suspects/defendants are detained pending trial, and therefore are not in any position to hire experts on their own. Moreover, most of the materials required for preparing an expert opinion are in the hands of the investigators, and it is difficult for defenders to obtain access to relevant material. Even if a privately hired expert conducted an evaluation for the defendant, under the CPL framework before 2012, it was difficult to cross-examine professional issues introduced by the expert of the prosecutor.[19] This situation caused an imbalance in the powers of prosecution and defence to introduce expert opinions, and in practice this imbalance has resulted in a number of miscarriage of justice cases.

In the 2012 CPL amendment, the legislator added a paragraph on the cross-examination of witnesses in court trials, stating that 'the public prosecutor, parties, defenders, and agents ad litem may apply to the court to notify a person with expertise to appear in court, and re-assess an expert opinion' (Article 197(2)). Here, a new participant in the process has appeared at the trial stage, namely a 'person with expertise', who is currently referred to as an 'auxiliary expert' in legal circles. Since the promulgation of the law, academic discussion on such procedural participants has not ceased. In particular, scholars questioned the legal status and role of this type of person with expertise, because this person obviously is neither an evaluation expert nor an ordinary witness as required by the law. The CPL only requires that the responsibility of 'persons with expertise' is to 'provide opinions on the opinion presented by the identification and evaluation expert'.

[18] Wu Hongqi, 'The Reform and Optimization of the Expert System in Criminal Procedure' (2018) 5 *Chinese Journal of Criminal Law* 73.

[19] Zhang Jun et al, *New Conversation among Prosecutor, Defender, and Judge* (Beijing, Peking University Press, 2014) 254.

According to the legislator's interpretation of this provision, the purpose of allowing 'persons with expertise' to appear in court is to provide support for judges in reviewing and evaluating the expert opinion through cross-examination, to avoid repeated identifications and save judicial resources. From the perspective of comparative law, 'persons with expertise' are similar to privately-retained experts or witnesses with expert knowledge, as stipulated for example in German criminal procedure law.[20] The 'person with expertise' in the Chinese CPL is essentially the same as the identification expert. The difference is that persons with expertise have not been registered and reviewed in accordance with the law. Some scholars suggest that 'persons with expertise' should be included in the register of professional identification experts. The author disagrees with this suggestion. It does not conform to the actual situation in China. Currently, in China the vast majority of registered identification experts are practising professionals, but the 'persons with expertise' are mostly university professors or researchers who cannot register as identification experts. The author believes that in future reforms, legislators should more clearly stipulate the attributes and roles of such persons in criminal proceedings, and include them as special witnesses. This would mean that, in addition to having the rights and duties of ordinary witnesses, they would also have specific rights and duties.

H. Transcripts of Inspection, Examination, Identification, and Investigative Experiment

Article 50(7) of the CPL classifies the evidence presented in court in the form of transcripts as an independent type of evidence, and lists the four following types: inspection; examination; identification; and investigative experiments. In addition, the MPS Provisions (2020) also list records of searches, seizures, and seals.[21] This classification is different from that found in jurisdictions with a common law tradition. There, transcripts are not treated as a separate type of evidence, but are classified as physical evidence, documentary evidence or other evidence and are treated as indirect evidence. Only countries with a civil law tradition, such as Germany, for example, regard inspection as an independent type of evidence that identifies objects, persons, events, processes, or certain conduct or behaviour accessible through a person's five senses. This type of evidence is separated from other types of evidence that are regulated under the provisions for witness, expert, or documentary evidence.[22] Related to this type of evidence are also scholarly

[20] Michael Bohlander, *Principles of German Criminal Procedure*, 2nd edn (Oxford, Hart Publishing, 2021).

[21] Art 59(7) of the Regulation of MPS.

[22] Michael Bohlander, *Principles of German Criminal Procedure*, 2nd edn (Oxford, Hart Publishing, 2021).

discussions in China, especially discussions about how to distinguish this type of evidence from documentary evidence.[23]

The common characteristics of documentary evidence include the following. First of all, most of the objects that the documents refer to cannot be presented in court (for example crime scenes, corpses, persons, events, etc). In fact, documentary evidence might be termed special evidence, whose main function is to verify other evidence. Anglo-American evidence scholars refer to this type of evidence, which records facts that can only last for a short period of time or deteriorate over time, as transient evidence. Hence, this type of evidence is different from ordinary documentary evidence. Under China's CPL, the main function of this type of evidence should be to record statutory procedural activities.

Second, it is usually the investigator, who exercises the power of investigation, who produces this kind of evidence. Therefore, an important function of this kind of evidence is to prove the legality of the investigation or collection of evidence. Third, this type of evidence is different from witness testimony or documentary evidence, as the witness or the document are unique and cannot be replaced. The documented evidence, however, under certain conditions can be reproduced or produced by other persons.

At present, the role of evidence in the form of transcripts is occupying much space in discussions of theory and practice. Most of this type of evidence is produced by investigators in a closed environment, and except for the statutory requirement for an eyewitness to provide a signature, there is no external supervision. In most cases, when this kind of evidence is presented to the trial court, in accordance with the regulations of the CPL, it is presented in the form of reading (Article 195 CPL). The CPL itself does not require the person who prepared the transcript to appear in court. When there is a dispute over the records about investigative activities such as search, seizure, freezing, inspection, examination, identification, investigation experiment, etc, the SPP Rules require investigators and eyewitnesses of these activities to appear in court to confirm the relevant situation. The public prosecutor may suggest that the collegial panel should ask a person involved in preparing such transcripts to appear in court (Article 413 SPP Rules). There is no provision in the law or judicial interpretations to suggest that the defender can file a corresponding application. Hence, the methods for checking the evidence are very limited.

With respect to the exclusionary rule for this kind of evidence, Article 103 of the SPC's Interpretations states that where:

> the transcripts of examination and inspection have been prepared in obvious violation of laws or other relevant regulations, and if a reasonable explanation cannot be made, transcripts shall not be used as the basis for deciding a case.

This is not a typical exclusionary rule, but rather a measure to respond to flawed evidence. Due to the flaws in legislation and the lack of supervision over

[23] Wang Jinglong, 'On the Function of Documented Evidence' (2018) 2 *Jurists* 161.

implementation of the law, several serious miscarriage of justice cases have occurred in practice. Under the existing legal framework in China, the task of supervising the production of evidence in the form of transcripts should be assigned to the procuratorate. In the initial stage of investigation, the main investigation activities should be attended and supervised by prosecutors. Criminal suspects and their defence lawyers should have the right to participate in the preparation of transcripts. Both prosecution and defence should then have the right to apply for the producer of the transcript to appear in court in order to have the possibility of cross-examining the evidence. Illegally obtained transcript evidence should also be listed within the scope of the exclusionary rule, and the corresponding exclusion procedure should be applied.

I. Audio-Visual Evidence and Digital Evidence

In the 1996 CPL revision, audio-visual materials were included as a separate statutory evidence category. The 2012 CPL revision also added electronic data. Most English versions of the CPL have translated '电子数据' (*dian zi shu ju*) as 'electronic data'. However, it would be more appropriate to translate it as 'electronic evidence'. This term has been internationally recognised and in fact 'electronic data' is different from 'electronic evidence'. In academia, there is some debate about whether these two types of evidence should be classified as the same category. Some scholars believe that the two forms of evidence are of the same type.[24] The author agrees with this, and common law scholars also consider digital videos or audio files as one form of electronic evidence.[25]

Neither the CPL nor the SPC Interpretations provide a definition or scope for audiovisual materials and electronic data. In October 2016, SPC, SPP, and MPS issued their 'Provisions on Several Issues concerning the Collection, Taking, Examination, and Judgment of Electronic Data in the Handling of Criminal Cases'. In these Provisions on Electronic Data, 'electronic data' is defined as 'data that is formed in the process of occurrence of a case, stored, processed, and transmitted in digital form, and which can prove the case facts'. The main forms of electronic data are listed, though the Provisions on Electronic Data point out that the list is not exhaustive. The list is set out in Chapter 6.

(1) information published through such network platforms as web pages, blogs, micro blogs, moments, post bars, and network disks;
(2) communication information in such network application services as SMS, e-mail, instant message, and communication group;

[24] Zhao Yiyu, 'The Use of Audiovisual Materials, Electronic Data, and Electronic Evidence is Chaotic and Deciphered – Analysis from the Perspective of Information and Electronic Technology' (2020) 2 *Journal of South China University of Technology (Social Science Edition)* 102.

[25] Stephen Mason and Daniel Seng (eds), *Electronic Evidence* Observing Law-IALS Open Book Service for Law, 4th edn (University of London School of Advanced Study, 2017) 17.

(3) information including user registration information, identity authentication information, electronic trading records, communication records, and logon logs;
(4) electronic documents including documents, pictures, audio and video records, digital certificates, and computer programs.

The Provisions on Electronic Data specifically note that the testimony of witnesses, statements of victims, confession and arguments of criminal suspects or defendants recorded in digital form and other evidence are not included in electronic data. The Provisions further indicate that 'where it is really necessary, these provisions may apply, mutatis mutandis, to the collection, taking, transfer, and examination of relevant evidence'. However, the Provisions do not explain how 'where it is really necessary' should be interpreted. But, it would be optimistic to predict that in cases where the legality of evidence collection in practice is challenged, this provision could provide the possibility for the court to extract electronic data.

Since 2012, when electronic data was added to the CPL as independent evidence, public security organs, procuratorates and courts have separately or jointly promulgated rules for the collection and review of electronic data, but the focus of these rules is to ensure the authenticity and relevance of the date. The rules do not focus on the legality of electronic data, and this results in a lack of due process review. Similar to other investigative measures mentioned above, the collection and freezing of electronic data are approved by the head of the investigative agency or the chief prosecutor. There is no need for a judicial warrant.

Furthermore, Article 28 of the 2016 Provisions on Electronic Data states that three types of electronic data must not be used as the basis for deciding a case:

(1) electronic data that is tampered with or forged or the authenticity of which cannot be determined;
(2) electronic data that is added, deleted, or modified, and which affects the authenticity of these data;
(3) any other circumstance which results in failure to prove the authenticity of electronic data.

In these three situations, the elimination of illegal electronic data from criminal proceedings is mainly the result of emphasising the authenticity of evidence. According to a survey, some illegally obtained electronic data are not excluded in the search, seizure, and storage procedures.[26] This may violate certain rights, such as freedom of communication and privacy, and property rights, and thus should be a cause for concern to be addressed in future legal reforms.

[26] Hu Ming, 'The Positioning and Evaluation Rules of Electronic Data in the Criminal Evidence System' (2019) 2 *Legal Research* 187.

9

Remedies

I. Introduction

Remedies in criminal procedure law internationally are classified into four categories:

(1) the first type of remedies concerns appeals against decisions issued within criminal proceedings, for example remedies against a decision to impose pre-trial detention;
(2) the second category pertains to what can be called ordinary appeals against judgments;
(3) the third category then includes extraordinary appeals, which are made available with an opportunity to bring a case before a constitutional court (or in Europe before the European Court of Human Rights);
(4) finally, remedies may be found in procedural law which offers the possibility to reopen a criminal case after a judgment has become final.[1]

As mentioned above, in China, there is no principle of *habeas corpus*. There is no formal remedy procedure for pre-trial detention: a suspect or defendant can only make a complaint about possible illegal detention. For death penalty cases, there is a special remedy procedure, known as death penalty review. This chapter sets out details of ordinary appeals; the reopening of criminal proceedings; and the death penalty review procedure.

II. Ordinary Remedy: Appeal

UN human rights conventions guarantee the right of convicted and sentenced offenders to have their cases reviewed by a higher tribunal. Article 14(5) of the ICCPR states that everyone convicted of a crime shall have the right to have his conviction and sentence reviewed by a higher tribunal according to law. Although the ICCPR uses 'the right to be reviewed' in Article 14(5), from the drafting process

[1] Monika Becker and Jörg Kinzig, *Rechtsmittel im Strafrecht. Eine international vergleichende Untersuchung zur Rechtswirklichkeit und Effizienz von Rechtsmitteln*, vols 1 and 2 (Freiburg, Max-Planck-Institute for Foreign and International Criminal Law, 2000).

we may conclude that this clause and its content refer to the right to appeal against a first-instance judgment (displayed in the criminal procedural laws of states which have ratified the ICCPR). The Article 14(5) provision is relatively general and does not elaborate on a detailed system of remedies. The delegate of the country that made the proposal emphasised the importance of a right of appeal and assumed that the specific system of appeal should be determined by the domestic law of the contracting state.[2] China has not yet ratified the ICCPR, and the Chinese Constitution does not explicitly provide for a right to appeal. However, Article 41 of the Chinese Constitution introduces the right to make a complaint (申诉, *shensu*), which in principle could be understood as a general basic right to challenge state actions.[3] Apart from Article 41 of the Constitution, remedies against criminal convictions and sentences flow solely from the CPL.

A. The Purpose of the Appeal Process and Setting the Appeal Level

In the CPL's section on guiding principles, Article 10 states that a two-instance trial proceeding is adopted to conclude a criminal case (ie an initial decision followed by a single level of appeal). Article 233 of the CPL also requires the court of second instance to conduct a comprehensive review of the first instance judgment both in terms of the facts and the application of law without being limited by the scope of the issues appealed. For cases where the death penalty is imposed, the CPL has set up an additional special review procedure in the fourth chapter of the trial section (Articles 246–251). This special review procedure does not present a third-instance procedure; it is regarded as a special review procedure within the ordinary trial procedure. The main reason that the two-instance trial system has not been modified since the CPL was first was adopted in 1979 is because a significant number of legislators, judges and scholars support the concept. They believe that the establishment of an adjudication and appeal system should take into account the actual situation in China: China is characterised by a vast territory and sometimes long distances between first instance and appeal courts. In rural areas, transportation is subject to restrictions, which would affect the timely conclusion of cases if the appeal system were to be widened. Widening appeal possibilities, according to these considerations, would increase the litigation burden for the parties and consume the resources of the judicial system.[4] These concerns ultimately triggered

[2] William A Schabas, *UN International Covenant on Civil and Political Rights – Nowak's CCPR Commentary*, 3rd edn (Kiel, NP Engel, 2019) 415.

[3] Benjamin L Liebman, 'Article 41 and the Right to Appeal' (2014) *Columbia Public Law Research Paper* No 14-407.

[4] Xu Deheng (Acting Director of the Legislative Affairs Commission of the Central People's Government), Explanation of the 'Interim Organizational Regulations of the People's Courts of the People's Republic of China', *People's Daily*, 5 September 1951, 4th edition; and Ren Jianxin (then President of SPC) Speech at the Conference of Chief Justices of the Asia-Pacific Region in Manila, Philippines on 28 November 1989.

the establishment of the two-instance adjudication system. Thus, improving the efficiency of the criminal process is at the heart of the two-instance trial system. Chinese scholars have commented that this reasoning favours a utilitarian approach in establishing the legitimacy of the two-instance trial system, and that this approach may neglect the principle of a fair trial and fail to protect a defendant's right to a fair trial.[5] Other scholars also argue that the economic situation in China, especially as regards public transportation, on which legislators and judges based their decisions decades ago has greatly improved. In addition, the number of judicial personnel and judicial budgets have increased. Therefore, it could be concluded that the two-instance system, which pursues only procedural efficiency, should be challenged, and procedural fairness should be considered the core value when designing an appeal system.[6] However, comparative research shows that in Europe two-instance appeal systems can also be observed.[7]

From the author's point of view, the grounds for establishing an appeal system are closely connected to the purpose of the appeal process. The main purpose of China's appeal system is to achieve fairness and justice in individual cases by correcting errors in fact finding, errors in the application of the law or disproportional sentencing, and error correction will prevent miscarriages of justice. However, some differences are noticeable when looking at the core values of other jurisdictions. In particular in common law systems a core value of the appeal process is found in the development and the clarification of the law.[8] Judges in common law jurisdictions pursue the function of making law through judgments, while judges in civil law systems mainly interpret statutory laws. However, with respect to the fundamental goals of criminal appeals, today some convergence may be noted.[9] Despite differences located in the law-making functions of higher courts, in continental legal systems it is also accepted that the appeal process serves the function of interpreting the law in a consistent way, a function which includes, to a certain extent, also the development of law through the interpretation of statutory law. Equal and uniform application of the criminal law is of particular importance in a large country like China, with a vast territory and various levels of social and economic development. Equal and consistent application of the law is also a fundamental right of individual defendants.

In the author's view, the goal of consistent and uniform application of the criminal law is a convincing argument which should result in China establishing a third-instance appeal. The second appeal stage should focus on errors in the

[5] Chen Ruihua, 'Reflections on the Two-Instance Trial System' (1999) 12 *Law Science* 20.

[6] Zhu Liheng and Li Hui, 'Theoretical Reflection on China's Two-Instance Trial System' (2008) 4 *Journal of East China University of Political Science and Law* 86.

[7] Jörg Kinzig, 'Rechtsvergleichender Querschnitt' in Monika Becker and Jörg Kinzig (eds), *Rechtsmittel im Strafrecht. Eine international vergleichende Untersuchung zur Rechtswirklichkeit und Effizienz von Rechtsmitteln*, vol 1 (Freiburg, Max Planck Institute for Foreign and International Criminal Law, 2000) 553, 565–69.

[8] Liz Campbell et al, *The Criminal Process*, 5th edn (New York, Oxford University Press, 2019) 383.

[9] Peter D Marshall, 'A Comparative Analysis of the Right to Appeal' (2011) 22 *Duke Journal of Comparative and International Law* 1.

application of procedural and substantive criminal law, and this function should be borne by high courts and especially the SPC, depending on where the first instance trial started. China's basic courts (the lowest level), handle the majority of first instance criminal cases, and the intermediate courts have the task of dealing with appellate cases from the basic courts as well as first instance felony cases. In cases originating at the basic court level, the intermediate court should continue to hold full appeal trials dealing with facts and the application of law, while a further remedy would take a case to a high court for a review of errors in the application of law. A corresponding system should then apply to felony cases originating at the intermediate courts. Full appeal would here be available at the high court level, while the SPC would deal with appeals on the basis of errors of application of law.[10] Designing the appeal system in this way will strengthen the role of higher courts and in particular the role of the SPC in providing for consistency and uniformity in the application of criminal law.

As mentioned earlier, the SPC's attempts to achieve consistency in the application of criminal law by issuing guiding cases or judicial interpretations have so far been restricted to just a few guidelines. Whether that has, in practice, resulted in improved consistency is still debated. Furthermore, after hearing cases lower level courts must report to superior courts in accordance with administrative methods of reviewing and confirming the results. This further weakens the function of appeals. It is hoped that this phenomenon can be eliminated by establishing appeals which focus on errors in the application of law.

The jurisdiction part of the CPL stipulates that the SPC enjoys the jurisdiction of first instance in criminal cases which are of national importance (Article 23 CPL). As mentioned in Chapter 4 above, since 1979 – a period of over 40 years – the SPC has only heard one first instance trial of national importance, in 1980–1981. This case involved the defendants Lin Biao and Jiang Qing (Mao Zedong's wife) and a counter-revolutionary group (the 'Gang of Four'). Jiang Qing then was sentenced to death sentence with a two-year suspension and this was later commuted to life imprisonment. As to the question of whether the highest court of a country can act as a court of first and only instance, resulting in the absence of any possibility of review by a higher tribunal, the UN Commission on Human Rights has held that this is a violation of Article 12(5) of the ICCPR in a number of cases, unless states made a reservation.[11] In future law reforms, China should completely abolish the jurisdiction of the SPC in first instance cases. Cases that seriously endanger national security or terrorism cases can then be assigned to the high courts for first instance hearings. The SPC will, in case of appeal, make the final judgment.[12]

[10] Liling Yue, *Criminal Trial and Human Rights Protection* (Beijing, Law Press China, 2010) 242.

[11] *Gelazauskas v Lithuania* No 836/1998, see William A Schabas, *UN International Covenant on Civil and Political Rights – Nowak's CCPR Commentary*, 3rd edn (Kiel, NP Engel, 2019) 418; Human Rights Committee, General Comment No 32, Article 14: Right to equality before courts and tribunals and to a fair trial, CCPR/C/GC/32, 23 August 2007, No 47.

[12] Liling Yue, *Criminal Trial and Human Rights Protection* (Beijing, Law Press China, 2010) 241–42.

B. Who Has the Right to Appeal?

According to Article 227 of the CPL, three categories of participants have the right to appeal:

(1) the defendant (which should be translated as convicted and sentenced person) or a private prosecutor, or his legal representatives. The defender of the accused or his/her close relatives may also file an appeal on his behalf, but they must have the consent of the accused;
(2) private prosecutors or his legal representatives;
(3) when the case involves subsidiary civil litigation, the parties and their legal representatives may appeal the part of the judgment or ruling pertaining to the subsidiary civil litigation (Article 227(2)).

Under the CPL, the prosecution may also appeal the judgment, but the law uses a different term in order to distinguish it from the defendant's appeal. This term can be translated as 'protest' (抗诉, *kang su*). However, the CPL restricts the prosecution's appeal. Based on a finding that the ruling or judgment of a people's court is truly in error, the prosecutor shall raise a prosecutorial counter-appeal (Article 228 CPL). Under the 'finding of truth' principle, the prosecution's appeal can be either to the detriment of an acquitted or to the benefit of a convicted defendant.

An international debate still persists on the question of whether the public prosecutor should have the right to appeal an acquittal.[13] However, an asymmetric design of appeal systems is mainly found in common law countries where prosecutors are barred from appealing an acquittal (following a jury verdict).[14] An asymmetric design of appeal is sometimes justified with the prohibition of 'double jeopardy'.[15] Article 14(5) of the ICCPR does not explicitly mention that a prosecutor has the right to appeal but states that 'everyone convicted of a crime shall have the right to his conviction and sentence being reviewed by a higher tribunal according to law'. Article 2(2) Protocol 7 of the ECHR also recognises limitations of the right to appeal which may refer to cases where the 'person was convicted following an appeal against acquittal' or to 'cases of minor character'.[16] In 2007, the Italian Constitutional Court held that the prohibition of appeals of acquittals violates the constitutional principle of equality of arms, by placing the prosecutor in a position inferior to the defence, thus making the collective members of

[13] Pieter G Du Toit, 'A Critical Evaluation of the Prohibition on the South African Prosecuting Authority to Appeal against Decisions on Questions of Fact' (2019) 30 *Criminal Law Forum* 451.

[14] Forrest G Alogna, 'Double Jeopardy, Acquittal Appeals, and the Law-Fact Distinction' (2001) 86 *Cornell Law Review* 1131.

[15] Jörg Kinzig, 'Rechtsvergleichender Querschnitt' in Monika Becker and Jörg Kinzig (eds), *Rechtsmittel im Strafrecht. Eine international vergleichende Untersuchung zur Rechtswirklichkeit und Effizienz von Rechtsmitteln*, vol 1 (Freiburg, Max Planck Institute for Foreign and International Criminal Law, 2000) 553, 632.

[16] William A Schabas, *UN International Covenant on Civil and Political Rights – Nowak's CCPR Commentary*, 3rd edn (Kiel, NP Engel, 2019) 420–21.

the public unable to defend their rights through its representative.[17] In civil law systems a symmetric design of appeal systems prevails.

The Chinese appeal system also adopts a symmetric design. As noted above, the China's procuratorates have the constitutional and legal obligation to ensure the proper enforcement of the law. Therefore, an appeal may be filed in favour or to the detriment of the defendant. But, an appeal may only be filed when the judgment is deemed to be 'incorrect' according to the law. However, the author argues that, based on the principle of a fair trial, the prosecutor's appeal may not result in an aggravated sentence. The standard of *reformatio in peius*[18] should apply also where the prosecutor appeals. Furthermore, in case of a first instance acquittal, appeal by the prosecutor should be limited to cases where conclusive new evidence shows that the defendant who was acquitted is guilty, especially if there is evidence to prove that the defendant deliberately concealed or forged criminal evidence. In such cases an appeal should be an allowed exception. The basis for this recommendation is that in the entire criminal process, the state has strong power to prosecute the defendant, and the defendant is in a weak position. If the state's power is strengthened in the remedy process, it will be more difficult for the prosecution and the defence to achieve a balance.[19]

The victim of a crime may not directly appeal a judgment. However, according to Article 229 of the CPL a crime victim has the right to request that the prosecutor appeals the judgment. However, the prosecutor is only obliged to answer the request within five days.

C. The Grounds of Appeal

According to the law, the defendant's right of appeal can be regarded as an absolute right. The CPL stipulates that if the defendant is dissatisfied with the judgment or ruling at first instance, he has the right to appeal (Article 227 CPL). Here, 'dissatisfaction' can refer to the confirmed facts, or the evidence relied on, and can also pertain to the law applied in the judgment and the penalty imposed by the court of first instance. The law is silent on whether an application for appeal must explicitly set out the grounds for appeal. But, as the requirements for the form of appeal are also relaxed, it can be in written or oral form, an elaboration of the grounds of appeal is not necessary. This is in line with some European systems of appeal.[20]

[17] Stephen C Thaman, 'Appeal and Cassation in Continental European Criminal Justice Systems' in Darryl K Brown et al (eds), *The Oxford Handbook of Criminal Process* (New York, Oxford University Press, 2019) 944.

[18] The meaning is literally 'change for the worse': this occurs when, as a result of the appeal, the appellant is put in a worse position after the appeal than if they had not appealed at all. For example, an appellant in a criminal case might receive a more severe sentence on appeal than in the original trial.

[19] Liling Yue, *Criminal Trial and Human Rights Protection* (Beijing, Law Press China, 2010) 243–44.

[20] Jörg Kinzig, 'Rechtsvergleichender Querschnitt' in Monika Becker and Jörg Kinzig (eds), *Rechtsmittel im Strafrecht. Eine international vergleichende Untersuchung zur Rechtswirklichkeit und Effizienz von Rechtsmitteln*, vol 1 (Freiburg, Max Planck Institute for Foreign and International Criminal Law, 2000) 553, 602.

In the Chinese CPL, leave for appeal is not required. In the author's view, a facilitated access to appeal in China is necessary, because in the first instance trial, witnesses only rarely attend and give testimony. Cross-examination, therefore, is not implemented properly. Furthermore, there is also a low rate of defence lawyers' attendance at trial. In addition, the caseload of lower courts is heavy, the quality of judgments cannot be guaranteed, and there is no appeal on point of law. Thus, if appeals were to be strictly limited, there would be no check on the quality of judgments from the lower courts and more appeals would go through the procedure for an extraordinary remedy.

As mentioned above, procuratorates in China are entrusted with supervision of the implementation of the law. The CPL stipulates stricter conditions for the prosecution to appeal judgments or rulings from first instance trials. Article 228 of the CPL states that an appeal by a procuratorate may be filed only if 'there is actually a true error in a judgment or ruling of the first instance'. The CPL does not explicitly provide the range of 'errors' covered by this article. The SPP Regulations, however, list specific circumstances which allow a prosecutorial appeal:

(1) the facts ascertained are wrong or the evidence on which conviction and sentence are based is unreliable or insufficient;
(2) there is definite and sufficient evidence to prove guilt but the defendant has been acquitted, or a defendant has been convicted and sentenced despite insufficient evidence;
(3) a lenient sentence was imposed for a serious crime, or harsh punishment was imposed for a misdemeanor, and the sentence therefore was evidently improper;
(4) the offence statute applied was incorrect; one offence has been split into multiple offences; multiple offences have been combined to one offence, and these errors have affected sentencing or caused a serious social impact;
(5) there have been mistakes with respect to exemptions from criminal punishment or the application of suspended punishment, prohibition order, restriction on commutation, etc.
(6) the court seriously violated procedural rules during the trial.

From the last item in this list, we can see that the SPP takes the violation of procedural rules as an independent ground for appeal. This can be considered a breakthrough in the development of criminal procedure law, because in the three amendments to the CPL, the violation of procedural rules was not regarded as an independent ground of appeal. The disregarding of such violations of procedural rules might be rooted in China's legal tradition of emphasising substantive law issues and neglecting procedural issues in legislation and practice. Furthermore, there is little research on this issue in academia. In future reforms, an appeal on the point of law should be established, to include abuse of procedural rules. However, the author assumes that even if the legislator provides for an independent ground for appeal located in the violation of procedural rules, controversial debates on the remedies for such 'procedural violations' will persist in China. Adoption of the German approach to determine the relevance of violations of procedural rules might be more promising. In the German criminal procedure law, an appeal on the ground of a violation of law in principle must be substantiated by establishing a causal link between the violation and the judgment (Article 337§1 of the German criminal procedure law). Such a link does not have to be established where there are 'absolute grounds for appeals on the point of law' (listed in Article 338 of the German criminal procedure law). These absolute grounds (or violations of procedural rules) are considered so serious that they always and without substantiation result in the conclusion that a judgment rests on them. In the author's view, this is a reasonable way of grading grounds for the appeal on the point of law and corresponding demands on substantiating such appeals.

D. The Form of the Appellate Hearing

The mode of the appeal hearing has undergone two revisions in the legislative history of the CPL. In the 1979 CPL, the appeal trial was not held as an open and public hearing. The appeal hearing took place in camera and on the basis of the files. In 1996, the CPL was revised and a form of the appeal trial was adopted which gave priority to a review of an appeal case through investigating the case files and assigned an auxiliary role to the court hearing. In the 2012 revision of the CPL, a reversal took place, the court hearing became the principal mode, and a review on the basis of case files turned into the auxiliary role. This situation has continued to the present.

Article 234 of the CPL provides two forms of appeal hearings: one is an oral and public hearing; the second is mainly a review of case files and taking account of the parties' opinion in a proceeding that is closed to the public. Since the CPL was revised in 2012, the scope of hearing an appeal case in public has been restricted. Article 234 lists four kinds of statutory situations which will result in an oral and public hearing:

(1) an appellate case where a defendant, or private prosecutor, or the legal representative has raised objections to the facts and evidence determined in the trial at first instance, which may affect conviction and sentencing;
(2) an appellate case where the defendant was sentenced to the death penalty;
(3) a case appealed by the prosecutor;
(4) any other case which should be heard in a court session (this case category is rather vague).

An analysis of data from the *China Law Yearbook* from 1988 to 2017 shows the following results. During these three decades, 13.1 per cent of first instance judgments were appealed, and 14.1 per cent of the appeal judgments resulted in modifications of the first instance judgment.[21] A survey carried out in three Chinese

[21] Zhan Xiaoping, 'An Empirical Study of Criminal Second Instance Hearing' (2020) 5 *Journal of Sichuan Normal University (Social Science Edition)* 4.

cities studied 2,229 second instance appeal cases. Here, it was found that an average of 11.2 per cent of appeal cases were carried out in the form of a public and open hearing. In 38 per cent of the appeal cases held as a public hearing the first instance judgment was modified, while only in 12.8 per cent of the cases reviewed through case files were modifications observed.[22] From these data it can be concluded that the rate of second-instance hearings which are held in public is rather low, and these cases are concentrated in the category of appeals against the facts determined by the first instance court and on the ground of insufficient evidence.

With respect to the direction of future reforms, scholars voice different opinions. Some scholars suggest that in order to improve the quality of the appeal process, all second instance appeals should be heard in public and on the basis of orally presented evidence (with the exception of legal restrictions), while others assume that under the current reality in China (limited judicial resources, a lengthy appeal process, and public transportation problems) the public and oral trial model is not suitable for all appeal cases. The author shares the latter opinion.

E. Court Decisions in Appeal Cases

The CPL allows for three outcomes of an appeal case:

(1) if the determination of the facts and the application of the law in the original judgment are found to be correct and the punishment appropriate, the court of second instance shall render a ruling dismissing the appeal and sustaining the first instance judgment;
(2) if the determination of facts in the original judgment is found to be correct, but the application of law is considered incorrect, or the punishment inappropriate, the first instance judgment shall be modified accordingly;
(3) if the facts in the original judgment are unclear or the evidence is insufficient, there are two decisions possible: amendment of the original judgment after clarifying the facts; or revocation of the original judgment and remanding the case back to the original court for a retrial (Article 225 CCP).

Article 237 of the CPL sets out the principle of protecting the defendant from receiving a graver penalty (*reformation in peius*). This principle was drawn from European continental law when the CPL was drafted and enacted in 1979. However, in the ECHR this principle is not explicitly stipulated in the fair trial clause. Before the 2012 CPL amendment, the law did not set too many restrictions on the cases appealed by the procuratorate. Once remanded for retrial, the first instance court could aggravate the punishment. This situation in practice undermined the implementation of the principle of *reformation in peius*. In the 2012 CPL amendment, a restriction was added, stipulating that in a case remanded by

[22] Zhang Dan, 'An Empirical Study on the Scope of Second Instance Trial for Criminal Cases' (2018) 1 *China Case Law Review* 1.

the court of second instance to the original trial court for retrial, the original trial court must not aggravate the defendant's penalty unless there are new criminal facts and supplementary prosecution by the procuratorate. At present, in practice, the meaning of so-called 'new crime facts' is still being debated. However, the principle of the prohibition on increasing punishment has basically been established.

III. Extraordinary Remedy: Reopening Criminal Proceedings

In China's CPL, the extraordinary legal remedy of reopening criminal proceedings is named 'procedure for supervising adjudication' (审判监督程序). Although this remedy is addressed as an extraordinary remedy procedure for judgments that have become final and therefore may be enforced, the rules governing the procedure are included in Part 3 of the CPL (on trial or adjudication).

This procedure was adopted from continental law countries, and displays some similarities with the German and Austrian models. However, some differences exist, as the purpose of the procedure is not only to provide a last resort for victims of wrongful convictions. The Chinese version of reopening criminal cases aims at mainly correcting errors of law. The main reason for the design of this procedure may be found in China's appeal system and the lack of an appeal on the point of law, which in some European countries is called 'cassation'. The SPC annual report for 2021 revealed that in 2020, 1,818 final criminal judgments in China were modified after proceedings were reopened. Among these cases, we find that 656 defendants in public prosecutions and 384 defendants in private prosecution were acquitted. The courts handled 18,000 state compensation cases.[23] This category includes cases where wrongful decisions have been made to the disadvantage of a defendant during criminal proceedings (for example wrongful pre-trial detention). Although China is a country with a huge population, this number is still proportionally larger than the number of cases reopened and resulting in acquittals in continental law systems. The data also show that this procedure does not play the role of an extraordinary and rarely applied remedy. From a human rights perspective, the data also show that the principle of '*ne bis in idem*' (the prohibition of double jeopardy) and the principle of finality are not given adequate respect in the law and in practice.

A. The Initiation of Reopening Criminal Proceedings

A most controversial issue concerns the conditions under which criminal proceedings may be reopened. Comparative research on criminal procedure law shows

[23] The Annual Report of SPC for 2021, www.gov.cn.

that there are restrictive conditions on applications to reopen criminal proceedings. These conditions are less restrictive if an application is filed for reopening to the advantage of a convicted person. However, they are very strict if filed by the prosecutor to the disadvantage of an acquitted defendant (if this is allowed at all).[24] Under China's CPL, the parties and their legal representatives, or close relatives may file an application to reopen criminal proceedings, called a 'petition' (申诉, Article 252). But, in addition the president of the courts at any level for the judgments made by his court, the SPC for the judgments made by the lower level courts, the SPP for all level of courts and the upper level prosecutor office for lower level courts, can all file an application to reopen criminal proceedings if they find that there are definite errors in the determination of facts or in the application of laws in the judgments or rulings that have become final (Article 254 CPL). It is acceptable and understandable that under the current China's legal system, the procuratorates have the power to monitor implementation of laws. However, the debatable issue is that the courts have an independent authority to initiate the reopening of proceedings without an application from the parties. Some scholars argue that entrusting power to reopen criminal proceeding to courts is in violation of the principle that courts should play a neutral and impartial role in the proceedings.[25] The origins of this legislation and the philosophy behind it may be traced back to the former Soviet Union, where the presidents of courts had the power to file a petition regarding the final judgment. However, Russian criminal procedure law has moved on since then, and has modified that.[26] As mentioned above, the nature and function of the China's procuratorates are different from the prosecution systems in common and civil law systems. The procuratorate has supervision powers with respect to the implementation of laws. Therefore, prosecutors can file an application to reopen criminal proceedings, both for the benefit and to the detriment of a convicted person. The debated issue in the current law is the conditions which allow the reopening of criminal proceedings. These must be considered to be too wide, whereas in fact they should be strictly limited. In future reforms, the power of the courts to independently initiate the reopening of criminal proceedings should be abolished completely, and the power of the procuratorate to reopen finalised criminal proceedings should be placed under restrictions (while distinguishing between reopening to the advantage and disadvantage of defendants).

[24] Jörg Kinzig, 'Rechtsvergleichender Querschnitt' in Monika Becker and Jörg Kinzig (eds), *Rechtsmittel im Strafrecht. Eine international vergleichende Untersuchung zur Rechtswirklichkeit und Effizienz von Rechtsmitteln*, vol 1 (Freiburg, Max Planck Institute for Foreign and International Criminal Law, 2000) 553, 572–76.

[25] Ma Guixiang and Xu Jiaxiang, 'Analysis of the Legitimization of the Criminal Retrial Procedure' (2017) 4 *Journal of Political Science and Law* 5.

[26] Art 402 of Russian Criminal Procedure Code (2012 amendment).

B. The Grounds for Reopening Criminal Proceedings

In the 1979 CPL, the grounds for allowing criminal proceedings to be reopened were not narrowly defined. The law only stipulated that final judgments and rulings may result in reopening, if errors in the determination of facts or the application of law were found. In fact, this amounted to a rather unrestricted power to reopen criminal proceedings. Uniform standards were not elaborated, and court practice in different regions displayed differences. Therefore, the 1996 CPL amendment introduced four grounds, to define the conditions under which reopening could be applied for. In the 2012 revision of the CPL, restrictions were added. In addition, a new condition addressing anti-judicial corruption was introduced. In the 2018 CPL amendment, these parts of procedural law remained unchanged. Article 253(1)–(5) of the CPL now sets out the five grounds that allow finalised criminal proceedings to be reopened:

(1) where there is new evidence proving that the facts were erroneously determined in the original judgment or ruling and that these errors may affect conviction and sentencing. However, the law does not define clearly the scope of new evidence. In practice, two kinds of situations are discussed: one situation refers to evidence not available at the time of trial, where the unavailability was not wholly or partially attributable to the party applying for reopening, or evidence might have been introduced and considered at the trial, and would have had a bearing on conviction and sentencing, but subsequently the evidence has been found to be false, forged or falsified. This situation shall not fall under 'new evidence'. Evidence thus qualifies as new if it was not known at the time of the second-instance trial, or at the time of review of a death sentence;[27]

(2) where the evidence on which conviction and sentencing are based is not credible, insufficient, inconsistent or should have been excluded. In introducing this ground as a condition for reopening criminal proceedings Chinese criminal procedural law goes far beyond what is accepted internationally as a legitimate ground for interfering with a final criminal verdict. This ground in fact addresses questions of assessing evidence which in principle should be resolved in ordinary appeal stages of criminal proceedings. This rather speaks in favour of introducing a second appeal in Chinese procedural law – as outlined above – to deal with questions of errors in law;

(3) the application of law in the final judgment or ruling was incorrect (truly in error). This ground also falls short of what is accepted internationally as a legitimate condition for breaching finality of a criminal judgment. In general, the reopening of finalised criminal proceedings will be restricted to cases where a constitutional court (or a supra-national human rights court

[27] Lang Sheng (ed), *Criminal Procedure Law Amendment and Application* (Beijing, China Legal Publishing House, 2012) 422.

(for example the European Court of Human Rights) declares unconstitutional a law upon which a criminal verdict is based. Thus, Article 79 of the German Law on the Federal Constitutional Court states that when a final criminal judgment rests upon a criminal statute which has been declared to be unconstitutional, criminal proceedings may be reopened. European countries furthermore should follow Council of Europe Recommendation R(2000)2, which requires that:

> national legal systems should be examined with a view to ensuring that there exist adequate possibilities of re-examination of a case, including reopening of proceedings, in instances where the Court has found a violation of the European Convention on Human Rights.[28]

Article 253(3) of the CPL widens again the scope of reopening criminal proceedings. The rule addresses cases which should be dealt with in ordinary appeal proceedings. As a second appeal on points of law is not provided in the Chinese CPL, the rules on reopening criminal proceedings perform the function of appeal proceedings on points of law. While the 2018 reform of CPL did not touch this issue, future reforms should reconsider the introduction of a second appeal stage and narrow down the scope for reopening criminal proceedings;

(4) Article 253(4) of the CPL allows for the reopening of criminal proceedings where there have been violations of statutory procedural rules which may affect trial fairness. On the one hand, this condition demonstrates that the Chinese legislator has recognised the importance of due process issues. But on the other hand, violations of procedural rules affecting trial fairness fall into the category of errors in the application of law already covered by Article 253(3). It again follows the need for a second appeal on issues of points of law;

(5) Article 253(5) was added in the 2012 CPL revision and allows for the reopening of criminal proceedings if, during the trial, judges or lay assessors engaged in corruption or prejudicial or arbitrary conduct. This provision thus addresses, as well as corruption, other acts resulting in perverting the course of justice. Article 253(5) is in line with international standards. Acts which obstruct (or pervert) the course of justice when committed by judges are legitimate grounds to reopen criminal proceedings. The law, however, should clearly spell out whether the threshold should be a final criminal judgment on corrupt or otherwise obstructive conduct of judges.

Summarising the CPL rules on reopening criminal proceedings, it can be concluded that these rules provide broad scope for interference with final criminal verdicts.[29]

[28] Recommendation No R (2000) 2 on the re-examination or reopening of certain cases at domestic level following judgments of the European Court of Human Rights, 19 January 2000; for a summary of procedural law of European countries in this respect see also the ECtHR case *Moreira Ferreira v Portugal (No 2)*, Application No 19867/12, Judgment, 11 July 2017, 34–39.

[29] Zhang Jun et al, 'China's Theory and Practice on Ne Bis in Idem' (2002/3) 73 *Revue internationale de droit pénal* 865.

These wide margins emphasise individual justice and sideline the principle of legal certainty. However, rules on reopening finalised criminal proceedings have to provide a balance, and carefully weigh legal certainty on the one hand and justice in individual cases on the other. In general, international standards – though displaying large variation[30] – evidently emphasise legal certainty (and the principle of *ne bis in idem*) and assign to reopening rules the function of exceptionally correcting grave injustice on the basis of narrowly defined conditions. Therefore, in future CPL reforms, Chinese legislators should consider rebalancing legal certainty and individual justice, giving more weight to legal certainty. In particular, Chinese criminal procedural law should adopt a distinction between reopening criminal cases to the advantage and to the disadvantage of defendants. Reopening criminal cases to the advantage of defendants may be designed to give more room to the accommodation of individual justice (and the goal of correcting wrongful judgments) while grounds for reopening to the disadvantage of defendants should be restricted to cases where trust in the finality of judgments would clearly would be misplaced.

IV. Death Penalty Review Procedure

A. Introduction

In 2021, there are still 54 countries which retain and use the death penalty.[31] China is one of these countries, and it is assumed that the number of executions is still high, though declining due to various amendments to the Criminal Code.[32] During recent decades, China's law makers and practitioners made significant efforts to reduce their use of the death penalty. The death penalty has been removed from various criminal offence statutes,[33] and procedural amendments have been made which seek to restrict the application of death penalty by adding procedural safeguards. With respect to the latter, the SPC plays today a most important role, as every death penalty sentence has to be reviewed by the SPC.[34]

The death penalty review procedure is an extraordinary procedure, with its own particularities. But, the rules governing this review are not part of the CPL

[30] Jörg Kinzig, 'Rechtsvergleichender Querschnitt' in Monika Becker and Jörg Kinzig (eds), *Rechtsmittel im Strafrecht. Eine international vergleichende Untersuchung zur Rechtswirklichkeit und Effizienz von Rechtsmitteln*, vol 1 (Freiburg, Max Planck Institute for Foreign and International Criminal Law, 2000) 553, 572–74.

[31] https://deathpenaltyinfo.org/policy-issues/international/abolitionist-and-retentionist-countries.

[32] Data on the death penalty in China is not available; it still remains a state secret.

[33] Liling Yue, 'Contemporary Death Penalty Issues in China' in R Haferkamp et al (eds), *Unterwegs in Kriminologie und Strafrecht – Exploring the World of Crime and Criminology. Festschrift für Hans-Jörg Albrecht* (Berlin, Duncker & Humblot, 2021).

[34] Xuanguo Xiong, 'Death Penalty System Reform in China' (2008) *The China Legal Development Yearbook, vol 3, On the Development of Rule of Law in China* 83.

chapter on 'Special Procedures'. They are found in Chapter 4 of the part on trial rules in the CPL (Articles 246–251). However, this procedure is different from ordinary remedies. The procedure does not amount to a further (or second) appeal, but it is a mandatory review which every death penalty case, including cases which have been retried on appeal, must undergo. No judgment imposing the death penalty may be enforced without being reviewed by the SPC. The review may not be waived by the defendant.

The nature of this procedure is a controversial issue among practitioners and academics. Some hold the view that the death penalty review procedure has an administrative character, because the review is not carried out in open court and because the review is based on court files, rather than a hearing of the parties. Furthermore, the review is automatically initiated by courts, which is not in line with the principle of 'no trial without complaint'.[35] In the author's view, the death penalty review procedure has an adjudicative nature. In the CPL, the provisions on review of death penalty cases are to be found in Part Three 'Adjudication'; the review power belongs to the SPC. When the justices of the SPC review a death penalty case, they are required by law to interrogate the convicted defendant and the defence lawyer's opinion shall be heard. In practice, the justices of the SPC travel to the place where the convicted defendants are detained, to interrogate them as circuit judges move to different towns in common law jurisdictions. The SPC conducts a complete review in terms of reviewing facts, evidence and application of law.

At present, heavy caseloads mean that it is not feasible to hold open trials for every death penalty review case. But in the future, if facts and evidence of a case are argued, the trial should be held in a local court and the Justice should travel to it from the SPC. If sentencing issues are concerned, the SPC can review the case in camera, and, if necessary, alter the sentence directly.

B. Authority of the Review Procedure

The provisions of the CPL from 1979 to 2018 have always stipulated that the SPC holds the power to review and approve death penalty cases. However, as noted above, during the 'Strike Hard' campaign in 1983, the Standing Committee of the NPC revised the 'Organic Law of Courts' (OLC). The amendments transferred the power to review and approve the death penalty for five serious violent criminal offences (homicide, rape, robbery, bomb attacks, and other violence carrying threats to public security and social order) to the high courts. Following this authorisation, in 1991 and 1997, the SPC widened the power of the high courts of six provinces to approve death sentences for drug crimes.

One reason for this granting of review and approval power to the higher courts might have been that there was too much pressure on the SPC, with a heavy

[35] Chen Guang Zhong and Tang Lulu, 'On Improvement of the Death Penalty Review Procedure' (2020) 2 *The Journal of Legal Science* 1.

caseload of death penalty cases resulting from the 'Strike Hard' campaign. Another reason might be to speed up proceedings, and to thus increase the deterrent effects of the death penalty in order to reduce violent crime. These reasons display the orientation of Chinese crime control policies at that time. However, the revision also created problems for the implementation of the criminal law. The SPC lost control over consistent and uniform application of the death penalty in China. Disparity in imposing the death penalty also infringes upon defendants' rights to equality before the law and the courts. Moreover, in practice, some provinces have joined the procedures for a second instance appeal and the death penalty review into one proceeding. This has resulted in the loss of the function of review procedures, as well as losing the added benefit of having death penalty cases reviewed by a higher tribunal. These developments drew criticism from legal scholars and legal practitioners. In December 2006, the Standing Committee of the NPC passed a resolution to amend the OLC. The resolution stipulated that 'death penalty cases shall be submitted to the SPC for review and approval, except for those cases in which the death penalty has been imposed by the SPC' (Article 12 OLC). The resolution was known as 'retrieval of the authority to review the death penalty', and took effect on 1 January 2007. One year after the SPC reclaimed the death sentence review power, statistics published by the SPC showed that 15 per cent of death penalty cases had not been approved. For the first time the number of cases with two-year suspended death sentences exceeded the number of death sentences with immediate execution.[36] The data show that the implementation of the review procedure by the SPC resulted effectively in a restriction and reduction of the application of the death.

Under Article 48 of the Criminal Law, two forms of death sentences are provided. A death sentence may be imposed as 'immediate execution', which means that after the exhaustion of all remedies and if the death sentence is confirmed, the sentenced offender will be executed. Another form of the death sentence is imposed with a 'two-year suspension of execution'. This form of execution is not a separate penalty, it is just a different way of executing the penalty. The SPC's final review power extends only to death sentences followed by immediate execution. If the death sentence is suspended for two years, it will be reviewed by the higher courts instead.

C. Review Procedures

According to the CPL, the review procedure must be initiated under the following conditions:

(1) where a defendant is sentenced to the death penalty by an intermediate court which tried the case as a first instance court and does not appeal, then the case

[36] The former spokesman of the SPC, Ni Shouming, answered questions at a media conference at NPC, 21 March 2008, www.legaldaily.com.cn.

shall first be reviewed by the high court. If the high court does not agree with imposing the death sentence, either the sentence can be altered directly or the case can be sent back to the intermediate court for a retrial (Article 247(1) CPL);

(2) where a defendant is sentenced to death by a high court acting as a first instance court and does not appeal, or when a defendant is sentenced to death by a high court acting as an appeal court, cases shall be submitted to the SPC for review and approval (Article 247(2));

(3) where a defendant is sentenced to death with a two-year suspension by an intermediate court, the case shall be reviewed by a high court (Article 248).

With respect to the review procedure, the CPL only provides that when death penalty cases are reviewed by the SPC or a high court, a collegiate panel shall be formed which consists of three professional judges. After the OLC was revised in 2007, the SPC, the SPP, the MPS and the MOJ jointly issued their 'Opinions on Strengthening the Handling of Cases in Strict Accordance with Law and Guaranteeing the Quality of Handling Death Penalty Cases' (Opinion on Death Penalty Cases), which contains detailed requirements for handing death penalty cases. In this Opinion three articles are related to the procedure of reviewing a death sentence. The first refers to the defence lawyer's role in final review proceedings. The Opinion on Death Penalty Cases requires that if the defendant's counsel requests that his opinion shall be heard, the opinion shall be forwarded as transcript and attached to the case file. This requirement was later introduced into the 2012 and 2018 CPL amendments (Article 251 CPL). However, the most controversial issues, relating to the role of the defence lawyer during the final review proceedings, have not been solved. Where a defendant has no defence lawyer during the review period, the CPL is silent as to which court should designate a legal aid lawyer for the defendant. The second issue pertains to the methods of reviewing a case. The Opinion on Death Penalty Cases suggested three methods of reviewing a case. One consists of reading the case file – this is most probably the main method of reviewing death penalty cases in practice currently, although the CPL does not mention it. The second method includes the interrogation of the defendant, which is mandatory. For interrogation the Justice of the SPC shall travel to the place where the defendant is detained. The third method concerns how evidence of the case is reviewed. The CPL does not mention how such investigation of evidence should be carried out by the SPC. In practice, and if the Justice deems the evidence to be doubtful, the case may be returned to the lower level court for retrial. The Opinion on Death Penalty Cases suggests that in cases of doubtful evidence the Justice of the SPC must investigate and check the evidence, or make an on-site investigation when necessary. In 2015, the SPC issued another document on defence counsel in death penalty cases.[37] Article 4 of that document allows defence lawyers to consult, extract, or duplicate case files at the office of the SPC.

[37] 'Measures of the SPC for Listening to Opinions of Defense Lawyers in the Handling of Death Penalty Review Cases', issued on 29 December 2014, and effected on 1 February 2015.

It also provides limitations. Materials that are not allowed to be disclosed according to law shall not be consulted, extracted, or duplicated.

D. Decisions of the Final Review

The 2012 CPL reform added a new article, relating to the decision on the death penalty review. Article 250 of the CPL states that:

> The SPC reviewing a death sentence shall make a ruling to approve or disapprove a death sentence. If the death sentence is disapproved, the SPC may remand the case for retrial or render a new sentence.

In practice, a considerable number of death penalty cases are sent back to the original trial court for retrial after a SPC review. Some scholars believe that this may be because the SPC attempts to impose more lenient penalties than the original courts, and are not swayed by public opinion and pressure from victims and families for the most severe penalties. However, this takes more judicial resources and delays the process.[38]

E. Suggestions for Possible Reform

In recent decades, the legislator, legal practitioners and legal scholars have made significant efforts and contributions aimed at reducing the use of the death penalty in China. The trend, both in legislation and in practice, is in the right direction. However, from a criminal procedure perspective, there is space and scope for further reform. The first important issue concerns assignment of a defence lawyer for the entire proceedings in all cases where defendants are facing the death penalty, especially also in the last phase of review before the SPC. A judicial interpretation issued by the SPC, which took effect on 1 September 2019, states that when delivering the judgment documents to the defendants, higher people's courts should notify the defendants of their rights to be represented by a lawyer when the SPC is reviewing their death sentences. The defence lawyer is obligated to submit relevant evidence materials and documents to the SPC within 10 days after the acceptance or designation to be the defence lawyer, and present the statement of defence within 45 days, the interpretation says.

If the case is not sent back to the original trial court and the defendant who was sentenced to death penalty has no lawyer, the SPC should require assistance through the legal aid center in Beijing; if the case has been sent back to local courts, the SPC should, via the local court, inform the local legal aid centre and request legal assistance.

[38] Chen Guang Zhong and Tang Lulu, 'On Improvement of the Death Penalty Review Procedure' (2020) 2 *The Journal of Legal Science* 1.

The SPC should maintain the trial nature of review proceedings and reduce the administrative element of the process. When the Justices of the SPC travel to local courts to handle cases, it may be helpful to consider establishing a circuit judge system, similar to those was adopted in common law jurisdictions. Where case reviews raise doubts with respect to evidence and facts, the review proceedings should be open to the public. This would make the process more transparent, and strengthen its role as a trial. On the basis of such changes the defence lawyer could play a more effective role in protecting defendants' rights.

The last issue addresses international human rights instruments. These require that everyone who faces the death penalty shall have the right to seek a pardon or commutation of the sentence. The Chinese Constitution provides for the issuing of a pardon. However, the CPL contains no detailed procedures on this. Calls for explicit and clear procedural rules in this field have been voiced for many years. These calls should be answered in future reforms.

10

Special Procedures

In the 2012 CPL revision, the legislator added the fifth Part on 'Special Procedures' to the law. This Part included four chapters:

(1) procedures for juvenile criminal cases;
(2) procedures for reconciliation between parties in public prosecution cases;
(3) procedures for confiscating the ill-gotten gains of fugitive or dead criminal suspects or defendants; and
(4) compulsory medical procedures for mentally ill persons who are exempted from criminal liability according to the law.

In the 2018 revision, a procedure for trial in absentia was also added.

I. Juvenile Criminal Proceedings

A. A Graded System of Criminal Responsibility: Juvenile Criminal Justice

China ratified the UN Convention on the Rights of the Child on 29 August 1990, indicating that China is willing to implement this Convention in a positive and effective manner and accepting that the best interests of a child should be also of relevance when devising special rules for processing, adjudicating and sentencing child offenders. However, in terms of legislation, an independent juvenile justice law for dealing with juvenile delinquency has not been adopted in China. The legal provisions for processing juvenile offenders are still included in the framework of the Criminal Law and CPL that deals with adult criminal cases.

In China, the age at which a person assumes full criminal responsibility and may have criminal law applied to him is set at 18. While Article 17(1) of the Criminal Code states that a person who has reached the age of 16 and commits a criminal offence bears criminal responsibility, Article 17(2) extends criminal responsibility to 14- and 15-year-olds in cases of intentional homicide, assault with serious injuries, as well as a selection of serious offences (including rape, robbery, drug trafficking and arson). However, Article 17(3) exempts all juveniles (14–17 years old) from the maximum criminal penalties carried by offence statutes, and prescribes mitigated or lighter punishment (which also prevents the applicability of the death penalty to juvenile offenders).

In December 2020, the Standing Committee of the NPC lowered the age of criminal responsibility to 12 years in case of intentional homicide, intentionally hurting another person so as to cause death of the person, or by resorting to especially cruel means, causing severe injury to the person, reducing the person to complete disability. This amendment was triggered by some particularly grave homicides committed by children under the age of 14,[1] which received significant media coverage and which were followed by controversial debates on lowering the age of criminal liability.[2] The prosecution of such crimes, committed by children aged 12 or 13 years' old, is subject to prior examination and approval by the SPP. The amendment came into force on 1 March 2021.

While debates on lowering the age of criminal responsibility and corresponding legislative moves can be found internationally, juvenile justice reform should not be motivated by extreme cases of juvenile violence and pressure from media reports. Legislators and judicial officials should be guided by the general principles of dealing with juvenile delinquency also called for by the UN Convention on the Rights of the Child. The best interests of the child are congruent with the long-term interests of society in raising children as law-abiding adults. A response to juvenile offenders which pursues education and prevention while restraining criminal punishment will be better suited to preventing minors from embarking on a criminal career. Some scholars have raised the issue of the ultimate outcome if a 12-year-old minor were sentenced to a fixed-term imprisonment for homicide. Assuming that the sentence was not commuted, the juvenile will be aged about 30–40 when released from prison. At that point, the offender would have been isolated from society for nearly half his life. Release would certainly be associated with a high risk of recidivism and living at the margins of society. This result is not what Chinese legislators and society would want.

In recent decades, China has gradually introduced a bifurcated system of juvenile justice, now providing a separate chapter on juvenile criminal proceedings in the CPL, while children displaying behavioural problems which do not establish criminal offences (and which reflect status offences in the North American tradition, such as alcohol abuse, running away from home etc) or committing criminal offences below the age of criminal responsibility are dealt with under the Law on the Prevention of Juvenile Delinquency, amended 26 December 2020 and the Law on Protection of Minors, amended 17 October 2020, which will be effective as of 1 June 2021. Both these laws emphasise the importance of education and rehabilitation implemented by specialised departments and staff when responding

[1] In October 2019, in the city of Dalian, a 13-year-old boy killed a 10-year-old girl. In December 2018, in Hunan Province, a 12-year-old boy killed his mother.

[2] Su Mingyue, 'The details of the rule of law, besides lowering the age of criminal liability, is there any other way?', https://www.thepaper.cn/newsDetail_forward_9635750, 20 October 2020.

to juvenile behavioural problems (including juvenile crime). In fact, the Law on Protection of Minors furthermore includes Article 101, which states that:

> public security organs, people's procuratorates, people's courts and judicial administrative departments shall designate specialised bodies or appoint specialised personnel to be responsible for handling cases involving minors.

B. Juvenile Crime: Trends and Current Situation

Juvenile crime had been on the rise in China after rapid economic and social change in the 1980s. However, in the new millennium juvenile crime has decreased significantly[3] and seems now, according to SPP statistics, to be remaining stable (2014–2019). In particular, serious violent crimes such as murder, and drug crimes, but also campus bullying cases have declined. However, a slight increase in the total of juvenile crime was observed in 2018 and 2019. The data show that the number of juvenile criminal suspects reviewed and prosecuted by the procuratorates between 2014 and 2019 amounted to 77,405, 67,737, 59,077, 59,593, 58,307, and 61,295 respectively.[4] By European and North American standards, therefore, China still can be considered a low crime country with respect to juvenile delinquency and juvenile participation in crime at large.

C. Special Proceedings for Juvenile Delinquency

In the 2012 revision of the CPL, the legislator collected together the provisions dealing with juvenile suspects and defendants that had previously been scattered through various chapters and placed them into one chapter, which was inserted into the part on special procedures. Eleven articles now address the particulars of juvenile criminal proceedings. However, rules relevant for juvenile criminal proceedings can be also found in the law on Prevention of Juvenile Delinquency and the law on Protection of Minors.

i. The Principles for Handling Juvenile Delinquency Cases

The guiding principle of juvenile criminal proceedings is outlined at the beginning of this chapter. This principle follows the UN Convention on the Rights of the Child in stating: 'for juvenile delinquents, a policy of education, reform, and rehabilitation should be applied'. Article 277(1) of the CPL goes on to say that

[3] Zhitong Liu, 'Current Situation and Prevention of Crime among Youth Aged 18–25 in China' (2018) 300 *Advances in Social Science, Education and Humanities Research* 799–802.

[4] SPP, 'White Paper on Juvenile Prosecution Work 2014–2019', www.legaldaily.com.cn, 1 June 2020.

the goal of the juvenile justice should 'primarily' be accomplished by 'applying educational measures and regarding punitive sanctions as ancillary means'. The realisation of this principle mainly relies on the design of substantive criminal law and the system of sanctions and calls for more alternatives to imprisonment. Under the current legal framework, however, and due to the absence of a special juvenile justice law and a separate system of juvenile sanctions, regular criminal penalties carried by offence statutes of the criminal code (except the death penalty and life imprisonment) apply. Hence, the principle of giving priority to education and restricting punishment to a supplement will be difficult to implement fully. From the viewpoint of the alternatives provided by criminal procedure law, the only provision to be strengthened is that for diverting juvenile cases, which now includes an option for conditional non-prosecution. However, statistical data on the processing of juvenile criminal cases show that there is still much room to expand diversion practices. The Law on the Protection of Minors does, though, make further steps towards criminal proceedings that are adjusted to the needs of young offenders. As noted above, Article 101 requires police, prosecution services and courts to provide staff specially trained to deal with juveniles.[5] Furthermore, Article 102 calls on public security organs, people's procuratorates and people's courts to consider the special needs arising from the physical and psychological characteristics of juveniles, and to use language that is appropriate and comprehensible to minors.

ii. The Juvenile Offender's Rights at the Investigation Stage of Criminal Proceedings

The investigation stage of criminal proceedings is of particular importance in juvenile crime cases, as the scope of information collected will determine how the goal of education can be implemented and whether prosecutors will be fully informed before making decisions on diversion as well as pre-trial detention. First of all, however, Article 277(2) of the CPL reiterates the obligation on police, procuratorates and courts, voiced by Article 102 of the Law on Protection of Minors, to have staff trained to deal with the specific needs and characteristics of juvenile offenders. Article 279 of the CPL states that investigations should cover the social and educational background of juveniles. Future reform should make a full social inquiry report mandatory. This is also recommended by the UN Standard Minimum Rules for the Administration of Juvenile Justice (The Beijing Rules).

The 2012 CPL revision moved the right of juvenile suspects to retain a lawyer to the investigation stage of proceedings. Article 278 of the CPL states that where

[5] See Tian Yu, 'Zhongguo Shaonian Fating Goujian Shiying Wei Chengnian Ren Tedian Shenpan Zhidu' [China Juvenile Tribunals Forming Judicial Systems Adapted to the Minors Characteristics], *China Court Net* (1 June 2007).

juvenile criminal suspects and defendants have not retained a defence counsel, the legal authorities handling the case are obliged to notify the legal aid agency to assign a lawyer. In practice, the proportion of juvenile defendants who have legal assistance from lawyers has increased year on year.[6] However, the law does not provide a right for juvenile suspects to have defence counsel present during interrogation. When interrogating juvenile suspects, the law requires only the legal representative to be notified to be present. If the notification is impossible, or where the legal representative is unable to be present, or the legal representative is an accomplice, any other adult relative of the juvenile suspect or defendant, or a representative of his school, or employer, a basic organisation at the place of his residence, or a juvenile protection organisation may be notified to be present, and the representative may exercise the procedural rights of the juvenile suspect or defendant on his behalf (Article 281 CPL). While the right of the legal representative to be present during the interrogation of a juvenile offender corresponds to international standards, future legal reform in China should introduce the right of defence lawyers to attend the interrogation of juvenile suspects during the pre-trial stage.

The CPL, following the Beijing Rules, imposes restrictions on the use of pre-trial detention of juvenile suspect. Article 280 of the CPL says that detention prior to trial shall be strictly limited. After the 2012 CPL revision, the SPP in 2013 updated its 'Procuratorate Regulations on Handling Juvenile Criminal Cases' (SPP Regulations on Juvenile Cases), originally issued in 2007. In these Regulations, the SPP elaborates on the question of how to proceed when deciding on the pre-trial detention of juvenile suspects. Under the general rule of strictly limiting pre-trial detention, non-custodial measures have priority when they will also achieve the goal of carrying out proper criminal proceedings. According to Article 13 of the SPP Regulations on Juvenile Cases, criteria to be considered include:

— the degree of viciousness exhibited by the juvenile offender;
— available social assistance;
— education conditions; and
— risks of further participating in crime.

Following these principles and criteria, specific guidelines are provided, defining two major categories. For minor offences, the presence of effective guardianship conditions or social assistance and proper education measures and the absence of social risks, and risks of obstruction of a normal criminal process, pre-trial detention should not be applied to juvenile offenders. For felony offences not carried with particular viciousness, manifestation of repentance and effective guardianship

[6] Jiang Zhiru, 'The Game of Power and Rights in the Procedure of Juvenile Delinquent Cases – Based on Empirical Analysis of Juvenile Delinquent Cases in M City, S Province' (2019) 5 *Journal of Sichuan Police College* 92. In that article, the author shows that in 2009, the rate of lawyers assisting juvenile criminal suspects in the investigation stage amounted to 47%. In 2012 and after the revision of the CPL the rate increased to 79.9%.

conditions or social assistance and education measures should result in pre-trial detention not being imposed if a juvenile offender meets one of seven conditions listed in the SPP Regulations on Juvenile Cases:

(1) the alleged crime is a first or negligent offence;
(2) the alleged crime has not been completed;
(3) the juvenile offender has surrendered or performed meritorious services;
(4) the juvenile offender truthfully confesses the crime, sincerely repents, actively returns the proceeds of crime, seriously attempts to reduce and compensate the loss, and the victim is satisfied with compensation;
(5) the juvenile offender is not the principal offender of a jointly committed crime or the chief element in a crime group;
(6) the juvenile offender has not yet reached the age of 16, or is still a school student;
(7) other substantial circumstances which justify alternatives to pre-trial detention.

Judging from statistics in the 'White Paper on Juvenile Prosecution Work 2014–2019' released by the SPP in 2020,[7] since the revision of the CPL in 2012, investigative agencies across China have submitted for review a total of 284,569 pre-trial detention applications in juvenile criminal cases. Out of these, the procuratorates approved 194,082 (accounting for 68.2 per cent of the applications forwarded by investigative agencies) and imposed pre-trial detention. Some 88,953 applications were not approved (amounting to 31.4 per cent of the applications). In its 2020 report, the SPP stated that the rate of non-approval is higher than the rate of non-approval in case of adult criminal suspects. However, while the rate of pre-trial detention of juvenile offenders seems to be on the decline in recent years, the fact that two-thirds of juvenile suspects are detained prior to trial is certainly not in line with the general principle of strictly limiting pre-trial detention and thus reducing its adverse impact on children.

Although the CPL, in line with the provisions of the UN Convention on the Rights of the Child, Article 37, orders juvenile suspects who are arrested and detained prior to trial to be separated from adult suspects (Article 280 CPL), minors should be considered to be particularly vulnerable to the well-known risks of being separated from their families, the weakening of social bonds and exposure to prison subculture. Under the current legal framework, the rate of pre-trial detention in juvenile cases could certainly be further reduced through effective implementation of the strict limitation principle and the provision of other alternatives. In future law reforms, besides widening the range of measures as alternatives to pre-trial detention, conditions of pre-trial detention should be introduced which are narrowly defined and emphasise the risks of absconding, obstruction of justice and relapse into serious crime.

[7] SPP, 'White Paper on Juvenile Prosecution Work 2014–2019', www.legaldaily.com.cn, 1 June 2020.

iii. Conditional Non-Prosecution Policy for Juvenile Offenders

In the 2012 CPL revision, legislators incorporated a provision inspired by Article 153a of the German criminal procedural law, and introduced the possibility of finalising criminal proceedings through a decision of conditional non-prosecution. Conditional non-prosecution is only applicable in juvenile criminal proceedings. Article 282 of the CPL establishes several restrictions on the scope of conditional non-prosecution. First, conditional non-prosecution may only be applied in cases involving criminal offences covered by Chapter 4 (violent crime, including sexual violence), Chapter 5 (property offences) and Chapter 6 (covering a wide range of criminal offences, including public order offences, drug offences, pornography, prostitution, illegal immigration etc). While the range of offences in which conditional non-prosecution may be applied is certainly rather wide and covers in particular crimes where juveniles are mostly involved (assault, theft), the second restriction introduces the eligibility of a juvenile offender to a maximum prison sentence of one year. There is some doubt about whether the one-year maximum refers to the maximum sentence carried by a particular offence, or whether it refers to the individual sentence which would be imposed after adjudication. If it were the former option, this would significantly reduce the scope of conditional non-prosecution, as in Chapters 4, 5 and 6 only two criminal offence statutes are found which carry a maximum sentence of one year. The SPP did not elaborate on this controversial point in its Regulations on the implementation of the CPL. However, the legislator has since explained that the 'possible sentence of one year's imprisonment' mentioned in the law refers to the penalty that would be applied in individual cases. This corresponds to the opinion shared by Chinese legal scholars.[8]

A third restriction is established through Article 282, which requires the consent of juveniles and their legal representatives. Article 282(3) states that the consequences of a conditional dismissal (placement under supervision and probation) must be voluntarily accepted:

> Where the juvenile criminal suspect or his or her legal representative raise any objection to the conditional non-prosecution decision of the people's procuratorate, the people's procuratorate shall make a decision to initiate a public prosecution.

Article 283 of the CPL lists the obligations to be observed by a juvenile while on probation for a period between six months and a year (emphasising compliance with the instructions of the supervisory agency) and Article 284 defines the grounds under which a decision of non-prosecution may be revoked and regular prosecution proceedings may be initiated (relapse into crime and/or serious

[8] Lang Sheng (ed), *Criminal Procedure Law Amendment and Application* (Beijing, China Legal Publishing House, 2012) 472.

non-compliance with instructions). After the probation period has elapsed without relevant incident, the prosecutor will issue a decision of non-prosecution and terminate proceedings.

Although prosecutors in general accept the value of conditional non-prosecution for juvenile delinquents, in practice the application rate is low. According to empirical research conducted by scholars in a province in central China, from 2013 to 2018, only 1,534 juvenile suspects have been diverted from a full trial through conditional non-prosecution. This accounts for 15 per cent of the total number of juvenile cases reviewed for prosecution.[9] The reasons for the low rate of conditional non-prosecution are found in practical problems and an institutional framework which does not lend itself to diversionary practices (or community sanctions in general). If prosecutors intend to finalise a case through conditional non-prosecution, they need to conduct an investigation into the juvenile's social and developmental background. If conditional non-prosecution is applied, a juvenile offender is to be placed on probation for a period between six months and a year (Article 283 CPL). In China, probation services, available in Western juvenile justice systems, which could carry out social inquiry reports and supervision during the period of probation, have not been established. Social inquiry reports and supervision are tasks of the prosecutor, and increase the workload significantly. Additional work for prosecutors arises from Article 282 of the CPL, which requires the public security agency and the victim to be heard before a decision is taken to proceed with conditional non-prosecution. When police or the victim object to a non-prosecution decision, the public security agency can request reconsideration or review and the victim can file a complaint against the decision which may, in turn, delay proceedings significantly.

In future CPL reforms, practices to divert young offenders from prosecution and imprisonment should be strengthened. The current restrictions on non-prosecution, by narrowing its applicability to Chapter 4, 5 and 6 criminal offence statutes only, should be removed. More important, though, is the introduction of probation services staffed by social workers and tasked with the preparation of social inquiry reports during the investigative stage of criminal proceedings, and the supervision and guidance of juveniles placed on probation.

iv. In Camera Trials

In the 2012 CPL amendment, the ban on the public hearing of juvenile criminal cases was moved from the trial part to the special procedure part. Article 285 of the CPL now states that in camera trials shall be held, but restricts the ban on

[9] Wang Mansheng, 'Implementation and Improvement of the Conditional Non-Prosecution System for Minors' (2019) 4 *Gansu Social Sciences* 223.

public hearings to those defendants who have not attained the age of 18 at the time of trial. In the interests of a juvenile defendant and upon his consent, the law also provides for an exception:

> With the consent of the juvenile defendant or his or her legal representative, the juvenile defendant's school or a juvenile welfare organisation may send representatives to be present during the trial.

The extension of in camera proceedings to all defendants who are under the age of 18 at the time of committing the alleged offence should be considered as a possible reform.

v. Access to Juvenile Records

In accordance with the policy of educating and rehabilitating juvenile offenders, the 2012 CPL amendment added regulations on sealing the criminal records of juvenile offenders. Article 286 of the CPL states that where a juvenile has not attained the age of 18 when the crime was committed and is sentenced to anything less than five years' fixed-term imprisonment, the criminal record will be sealed. The law also provides for exceptions to this. Judicial authorities have access to sealed records when such information is necessary to handle other cases. Work place units conducting inquiries in accordance with national regulations also have access to juvenile records. No explanation of 'criminal record', however, is provided by the legislator. In subsequent explanations the legislator pointed out that 'criminal records' include various materials related to juvenile crimes generated during the process of investigation, prosecution, and trial.[10] In practice, among legal institutions the form of sealing is disputed. Most legal institutions involved in criminal proceedings seal only the paper case files, and not the electronic information. When a public security agency (police) is required to issue a certificate of criminal record, the public security agency will rely on the nationwide networked comprehensive police database. In this case then, electronic information on prior criminal convictions will sometimes be disclosed, even though the physical files are sealed. Yet another problem concerns the role of good conduct certificates, which are required when applying for certain professional positions. While Article 100(1) of the Criminal Code provides that a person enlisting in the army or applying for employment shall truthfully report to the relevant unit prior criminal convictions, Article 100(2) exempts from this obligation individuals who had received a prison sentence of less than five years for a crime committed under the age of 18. Article 100 thus expresses the goal of the legislator to reduce possible stigma and adverse effects resulting from juvenile criminal convictions. However, China has adopted special labour laws, addressing approximately a hundred occupations,

[10] Lang Sheng (ed), *Criminal Procedure Law Amendment and Application* (Beijing, China Legal Publishing House, 2012) 477.

which require as part of the application procedure a certificate of good conduct, which shows that the applicant has no prior criminal record. In practice, some legal institutions do not issue certificates of good conduct for those applicants who have been sentenced to a prison sentence of five years or less when they were still a minor. A juvenile criminal record then will effectively prevent entry into various professional fields. Although the law clearly entitles an individual to remain silent about prior juvenile criminal convictions, the right to a clean certificate of good conduct is not explicitly provided. Therefore, and based on the interest in not blocking professional opportunities (and social integration), some prosecutors have suggested that a nationwide archive of juvenile delinquency information should be established, separate from the adult register, and standards should be issued about access to information about juvenile convictions.[11] In fact, Article 100(2) of the Criminal Code calls for a law which implements the legislative goal of reducing the adverse effects of (juvenile) criminal convictions and clearly regulates not only access to prior criminal records and obligations and privileges with respect to disclosure, but also the issuing of certificates of good conduct.

II. Procedures for Reconciliation between Parties in Public Prosecution Cases

The special procedure provisions of the CPL on reconciliation between victims and offenders deal with an internationally recognised topic. In recent decades, support for the reconciliation of victims and offenders has been fuelled by the view that victims of crime do not receive adequate treatment in conventional criminal proceedings and by beliefs that mediation will lead to better results than criminal punishment.

The English words 'mediation' and 'reconciliation' correspond to Chinese terminology: 调解 (*tiaojie*) may be translated as 'mediation' and refers to procedures, and 和解 (*hejie*) may be translated as 'reconciliation' and pertains to the result of mediation proceedings in the form of an agreement or settlement.

A. The Theoretical Basis of Reconciliation in Criminal Matters

Mediation and reconciliation were provided for in the CPL as early as 1979. However, the scope of mediation and reconciliation was limited to private prosecution cases (Article 127 CPL 1979). At that time, Western approaches to

[11] 'The "formal sealing" of minor criminal records has become a stumbling block affecting minors' return to society', www.12309.gov.cn, 22 November 2019.

victim-offender reconciliation and restorative justice had not yet arrived in China. Behind the Chinese approach to mediation and reconciliation in criminal cases stood traditional Confucianism, expressed in Confucius's words 'harmony is most precious' (和为贵).[12] During recent decades, these ideas on mediation, reconciliation and harmony have contributed to changing views on criminal law and criminal procedural law. In criminological and criminal law circles the focus has moved away from retribution and punishment; now treating and restoring broken social relations receive more attention.[13] Scholars also point out that reconciliation comes with challenges for conventional criminal procedure theory. Mediation and reconciliation blur the boundary between crime and tort, and insert elements of civil litigation into the system of criminal justice and procedure. In addition, the traditional justice model is transformed from confrontational justice to cooperative justice. Finally, the purpose of criminal proceedings shifts from finding the truth and ensuring due process, to repairing distorted social relations and achieving the goal of creating a harmonious society.[14]

B. Application Conditions for Criminal Reconciliation

In the 1996 CPL reconciliation was only applicable in cases brought to court by private prosecutors. Then, in the 2012 revision, the scope of reconciliation was greatly widened to include public prosecution cases. In order to allow for the just and principled use of reconciliation, the 2012 and subsequent 2018 CPL amendments set out general conditions and limitations on the application of reconciliation.

According to Article 288 of the CPL, application is dependent on the general condition that the suspect or defendant sincerely expresses remorse and seeks forgiveness from the victim by offering compensation or an apology. Only when the victim voluntarily participates in reconciliation with the defendant may a settlement be pursued. The provision incorporates two sets of conditions which define the general scope of reconciliation in public prosecution cases:

(1) in criminal acts arising from civil disputes and falling under the offence statutes in Chapters 4 and 5 of the Criminal Code (property offences and offences against the person), reconciliation proceedings may be initiated if a criminal

[12] This refers to the principle of moral practice advocated by Confucianism. From 'The Confucian Analects of Confucius'(论语 学而): 'The use of ritual, harmony is precious' (礼之用, 和为贵). In other words, the most important function of 'Li' is to be able to be harmonious. It means that all things are handled in accordance with Li: the various relationships between people can be just right, and they can be properly mediated, so that each can be in harmony with others: https://baike.baidu.com.

[13] Chen Guoqing et al, 'The Theoretical Basis of the Criminal Reconciliation System' (2007) 4 *Journal of the National Prosecutors College* 3.

[14] ibid.

offence does not call for imprisonment of more than three years. The law does not elaborate on the definition and scope of 'civil disputes'. The explanatory part of the legislation asserts that the cause of the crime must be located in disputes between citizens related to property and personal issues, including disputes related to marriage and family in general as well as conflicts between neighbours. Furthermore, civil disputes may extend to cases triggered by ordinary conflicts. In cases of civil disputes which will result in a prison sentence of less than three years, either party may initiate reconciliation proceedings.[15] In addition, in the MPS 'Procedures for Handling Criminal Cases', six circumstances are listed which will rule out a case being treated as a civil dispute:

— hiring another person to commit an assault;
— organised crime;
— endangering public order;
— incitement to rioting;
— repeated assault;
— a general clause addresses cases that are not suitable for reconciliation.

(2) in cases involving a criminal offence carried out by negligence, other than a criminal offence of malpractice, reconciliation proceedings may be opened if the offender would be sentenced to imprisonment of less than seven years. The law adds an additional limitation which bars reconciliation for recidivists convicted for any intentional crime within the past five years.

C. Practice and Reform of Criminal Reconciliation

The CPL does not clearly stipulate at which stage the victim and the offender can conclude an agreement on reconciliation. Judging from the wording of Article 288, either party may initiate a settlement agreement at any stage of criminal proceedings (investigation, prosecution and trial). If a case is settled by the parties during the investigation stage, the public security organ and the procuratorates may recommend a lenient penalty. The prosecutor, furthermore, is authorised to dismiss a case after a settlement if the crime is minor and does not require punishment. Upon a settlement agreement, the court may impose a lenient penalty (Article 290 CPL).

In practice, the number of settlements has not increased significantly since the CPL adopted the policy of reconciliation in public prosecution cases in 2012. Prosecutors have voiced the need for further reform of reconciliation proceedings. Problems are evidently associated with the implementation of reconciliation agreements. In cases where a settlement is based on compensation by instalments,

[15] Lang Sheng (ed), *Criminal Procedure Law Amendment and Application* (Beijing, China Legal Publishing House, 2012) 480.

where the procuratorate made a decision not to prosecute, or the court imposed a lenient penalty, the law does not provide for a solution if compensation is not completed. With respect to a decision not to prosecute, it is suggested that the rules on conditional non-prosecution policy should be applicable to adults as well. Procedural constraints are then proposed which would make a recommendation for leniency by the prosecutor or the imposition of a lenient sentence dependent on completion of compensation.

Another problem arises from the lack of agreed standards regarding the amount of compensation. The amount of compensation considered to be adequate varies significantly among procuratorates and courts. In addition, compensation is blamed as an opportunity to buy one's way out of punishment and as a gateway for inequality in the application of criminal law. In addition, recommendations for alternatives to imprisonment suited to express leniency have been made. Finally, although Article 289 requires public security organs, procuratorates and courts to review the voluntariness and lawfulness of reconciliation and its results, and to moderate the drafting of the reconciliation agreement, no detailed review mechanism has been introduced, and this has sometimes resulted in abusive practices.[16]

III. Procedures for Trial in Absentia

A procedure for trials in absentia was introduced in 2018. The addition of Articles 291–297 of the CPL to the part on Special Procedures raises questions with respect to an accused's right to be present at trial, affirmed by international human rights documents. Article 14(3)d of the ICCPR states that 'everyone is entitled to be tried in his presence' and the UN Human Rights Committee has described the right 'to personally attend the proceedings' as an important component of the right to a fair trial.[17] The Human Rights Committee has, though, acknowledged that there are exceptions to this right, if it is in the interest of the proper administration of justice.[18] The principal exception is in absentia trials, in which the accused person, although informed sufficiently in advance of the proceedings, declines to exercise the right to be present at the trial.[19] Through several adjudicated cases and the General Comment, the Human Rights Committee has established standards to be complied with when introducing the possibility of in absentia trials. These standards include the steps necessary to summon the accused in a timely manner and inform the accused beforehand of the charges, the date and the place of their trial and the general duty to attend.[20] If an offender has been tried in absentia

[16] Li Hongbin, 'The Status Quo and Countermeasures of Criminal Reconciliation after Entering the Law' (2014) 4 *Application of Laws* 73.

[17] *Wolf v Panama* No 289/1988, see William A Schabas, *UN International Covenant on Civil and Political Rights – Nowak's CCPR Commentary*, 3rd edn (Kiel, NP Engel, 2019) 398.

[18] *Kostin v Russia* No 2496/2014, see ibid.

[19] General Comment 32, § 36.

[20] General Comment 32, § 31.

and is later arrested, the offender has the right to a retrial in person.[21] Where an accused is unable to be present due to illness, the court should adjourn the proceedings rather than proceed in absentia, especially in cases of serious crimes.[22] The jurisprudence of the European Court of Human Rights accepts trials in absentia provided that the accused has effective knowledge of the criminal proceedings, the authorities exercised due diligence in securing the presence of the accused (including effective enforcement of the duty to attend a criminal trial), the accused is legally represented in the proceedings, with the effective assistance of a defence counsel, and has the right to retrial in his presence.[23]

Although the CPL provisions on trials in absentia deal with three types of cases which are eligible for such a procedure, from the legislator's explanation of this amendment, it can be concluded that the legislative purpose of introducing trial in absentia provisions focuses on combating corruption and pursuing criminal suspects who have fled abroad, taking their proceeds of corruption and embezzlement with them.[24] While effective investigation and prosecution of corruption certainly are important goals,[25] the regulation of trials in absentia should be systematically designed, reflect the fundamental rights of suspects and those accused, and weigh the fair trial principle carefully against the interest in the effective administration of justice.

A. Types of Cases Eligible for Trial in Absentia

According to the CPL amendment in 2018, three rather diverse types of cases are eligible for trials in absentia. These include:

(1) criminal cases involving embezzlement or bribery, and criminal cases related to seriously endangering national security or terrorist activities that require timely trial (Articles 291, 292 CPL);
(2) cases where the defendant is suffering from a serious illness that prevents appearance in court and the trial is suspended for more than six months. Here, the defendant or his legal representative or close relatives may apply for or agree to the resumption of the trial in the absence of the defendant (Article 296 CPL);
(3) the defendant has passed away before a trial can be carried out but there is evidence to prove his innocence (Article 297 CPL).

[21] *Maleki v Italy* No 699/1996.

[22] *Thomas v Tanzania* No 005/013, a judgment of the African Court on Human and People's Rights applying Article 14(3)d; see William A Schabas, *UN International Covenant on Civil and Political Rights – Nowak's CCPR Commentary*, 3rd edn (Kiel, NP Engel, 2019) 398.

[23] *European Court of Human Rights, Guide* on Article 6 of the European Convention on Human Rights (Strasbourg, 2020) 53–55.

[24] Shen Chunyao, 'Explanation on the Draft Amendment to the Criminal Procedure Law of the PRC', 25 April 2018, www.npc.gov.cn.

[25] Xinlin Peng, 'The Reform of Criminal Procedure of Corruption Cases in China' (2019) 3 *International Journal of Legal Discourse* 33.

The first category is considered the most important exception to the general rule that a defendant must be present at the trial. In the first draft of the amendment, in fact, only embezzlement and bribery had been made eligible for trials in absentia. While the Chinese legislator evidently aimed to strengthen the ongoing anti-corruption campaign by allowing in absentia trials against fugitives in corruption cases, the regulation of trials in absentia should have been based on a systematic and principled approach, focusing on legitimate grounds for allowing criminal trials in the absence of the accused.

The question of trials in absentia may be triggered with respect to the following situations:

(1) a criminal suspect is fugitive, an accused – although summoned correctly – does not show up for a trial, or an accused absconds after attending parts of the trial;
(2) an accused is unfit to stand trial because of illness or mental health issues (unfitness caused deliberately would create a separate situation);
(3) an accused disrupts trial proceedings to an extent which impairs the proper administration of justice;
(4) a confrontation in open courtroom between the accused and the victims/witnesses would result in significant adverse effects on the latter.

The 2018 CPL amendment addresses the first situation, by selecting particularly corruption and embezzlement cases for in absentia trials, although in principle it would have possible to draft rules of a general nature. The second situation is dealt with by Article 296, which addresses unfitness to attend a trial (through no fault of the accused). The other situations are not mentioned in the in absentia trial chapter. Article 297 allows for an in absentia trial if a defendant is deceased. However, the CPL in Article 16(5) already provided for a general (and internationally consented) rule for this situation, whereby proceedings against a deceased suspect or accused shall simply be terminated. The legislator, however, evidently in the interest of justice and the interest of clearing the reputation of a wrongly accused person, allows a case to be continued if evidence of innocence can be provided. This situation certainly deserves serious consideration. But, it should be dealt with in the context of Article 16(5) of the CPL and not in the chapter on trial in absentia.

B. Procedural Issues for Trials in Absentia

The conditions under which trial in absentia proceedings may be opened differ with respect to the three categories of cases covered by the in absentia provisions. For cases of the first category (in particular embezzlement and bribery) the law requires first of all that the criminal suspect or defendant 'is located outside China'. Then, the facts of the crime must be clear and evidence must be assessed to be credible and sufficient. After a review by the people's court, it may decide to hear the case in open court. However, the court has to deliver to the accused a summons to appear and the indictment, through channels of international judicial assistance. In practice, this condition poses significant problems. The SPP's Regulation (Article 505(4)) states that the procuratorate must provide evidence to court that the offender has moved outside of China. While evidence on the location of a suspect/accused abroad might be available, summoning and delivering the indictment through international judicial assistance require a valid contact address. The problem of implementing these conditions certainly explains the fact that since the 2018 amendment was enacted not one trial in absentia of a case falling into the first category has been held. Few cases of in absentia trials for defendants unfit to stand a trial have been noted either. Thus, it seems clear that significant problems with implementation have so far prevented the realisation of the legislator's goal of using trial in absentia to combat corruption.[26]

Article 293 of the CPL states that the absent defendant must be represented by a defence counsel. A defence counsel may be mandated by the defendant or by close relatives. Where a defendant or close relatives have not retained a defender, the court must give a notice to a legal aid agency to designate a lawyer to defend the absent accused (Article 293 CPL). Concerns have been raised that an adequate defence will be difficult to achieve, as there will be very limited possibilities for contact between the defence counsel and client.

The law requires the trial court to serve the written judgment on the defendant, close relatives and the defender. Furthermore, the absent adjudicated defendant has the right to appeal. And, unlike ordinary appeal rules, where only the legal representatives have a direct right to appeal (Article 227 CPL), in trial in absentia cases, a defendant's close relatives also have the right to appeal. The defence counsel may file an appeal with the consent of the defendant or his close relatives (Article 294 CPL).

If a defendant voluntarily surrenders himself or is captured during an ongoing trial in absentia, the court shall try the case again. If an offender appears before the court after a case has been decided, the court shall start enforcement proceedings. Before doing so, the court shall inform the convicted person that he has the right to raise an objection to the judgment or ruling. If objections are raised, then the trial shall be reopened.

In general, China's criminal trial in absentia procedures have been criticised by scholars as displaying significant deficits.[27] In future procedural law reform, a systematic approach to the question of 'absence' of defendants as outlined above should be considered. Different situations require different answers. Unfitness to stand trial cases should be dealt with separately, as should those cases where the

[26] Bian Jianlin and Wu Siyuan, 'Criminal Trial in Absentia – Legislative Reflection and Practical Trends' (2020) 5 *Seeking Truth* 85.

[27] Bu Yangyang, 'On the Typology of Criminal Trials in Absentia in China' (2020) 4 *Political and Law Forum* 182.

absence of the defendant is due to deliberate disruption of proceedings or to avoid an adverse impact on victims/witnesses. Then, the law should give a clear definition of 'absence'.[28] While all criminal cases falling within this concept should be treated alike, the procedural rules should be included in the part which deals with regular trial proceedings, and not dealt with separately in the part on special procedures. Finally, in cases involving fugitive suspects, justice should be sought through carrying out a regular criminal trial in the presence of the accused. This corresponds to both the right and the duty of defendants to attend a trial. However, the emphasis should be placed on enforcing the duty of defendants to participate at trial proceedings. Criminal proceedings in absentia then can be restricted to the securing of evidence and procedural steps preventing limitation.[29] Exceptions to the general rule of trials in the presence of the accused and a full criminal trial in absentia should be restricted to minor criminal cases and placed under the condition that a defendant waives voluntarily the right to be present at the trial.[30]

IV. Procedures for Confiscating the Proceeds of Crime in Cases Where the Accused has Absconded or Died

In the 2012 CPL revision, a stand-alone confiscation of proceeds of crime was introduced, which has also become part of the special procedures chapter. Adoption of a stand-alone confiscation of proceeds of crime was also prompted by the goal of combating corruption, terrorist crimes or other serious crimes (Article 298 CPL). However, Article 298 does not restrict the stand-alone procedure to corruption and terrorist crimes but mentions these offences as examples for major crimes in general. Confiscation procedures are applicable in cases where a suspect/defendant cannot be brought to court for at least 12 months or has passed away. The procuratorate then may apply to the court for initiation of the procedure to confiscate the illegal proceeds. The confiscation procedure was introduced at a time (2012) when the procedural rules on trials in absentia had not yet been drafted. The main basis for the legislation was Article 54 of the UN Convention against Corruption. Article 54 1c requires a State Party to take:

> such measures as may be necessary to allow confiscation of such property without a criminal conviction in cases in which the offender cannot be prosecuted by reason of death, flight or absence or in other appropriate cases.

[28] For example, Article 276 of the German Criminal Procedure Code states that: 'An accused person shall be deemed to be absent if his whereabouts are unknown or if he is abroad and it does not appear feasible or reasonable that he can be brought before the competent court'.

[29] See Article 285 of German Criminal Procedure Code: (1) No main hearing shall be held in respect of a person who is absent. Proceedings instituted against an absent person shall serve the purpose of securing evidence in anticipation of his future presence in court.

[30] Ben Emmerson et al, *Human Rights and Criminal Justice*, 3rd edn (London, Sweet & Maxwell, 2012) 577–78.

In the 2018 CPL amendment, the procedure for trials in absentia was added, which, according to Article 292 CPL, may also deal with proceeds of crime. While criminal offences falling under these special procedures are similar (although the wording of Article 298 (major crimes) seems to be wider than the wording used in Article 291), the procedures are different in some ways. These differences manifest themselves in the goals to be achieved and the very nature of the procedures. The stand-alone procedure for confiscation of proceeds of crime does not deal with the issue of criminal liability, but aims to determine whether assets are proceeds of a 'major crime' and how to confiscate those proceeds. Similar to a subsidiary civil lawsuit, some jurisdictions make this a civil procedure. The procedure of trial in absentia involves the recovery of illegal property after a finding of criminal liability. However, at the point of confiscation, the functions of the two procedures overlap. The second difference lies in the scope and conditions of application. Article 298 of the CPL states that:

> Where in a case regarding a major crime such as embezzlement, bribery, or terrorist activities, a criminal suspect or defendant escapes and cannot be brought to court after being wanted for a year, or a criminal suspect or defendant has passed away, if his or her illegal income and other property involved in the case shall be recovered according to criminal law, a people's procuratorate may file an application with the people's court for confiscation of illegal income.

In Article 298 the words 'escape and hide' (逃匿, *tao ni*) are used. Article 3 of the 'Provisions of the SPC and the SPP on Several Issues concerning the Application of the Confiscation Procedures for Illegal Income in a Case Where a Criminal Suspect or Defendant Escapes or Dies' (Provisions on Confiscation)[31] explains the meaning of 'escape and hide': 'a criminal suspect or defendant absconded or escaped during criminal proceedings and subsequently hides in order to evade investigation and prosecution'. On the basis of this interpretation, it can be inferred that 'escape and hide' includes not only fleeing abroad, but also covers cases where fugitive offenders are hiding in China. The trial in absentia can only apply to cases where criminal suspects or defendants have escaped abroad. In the second paragraph of Article 3 of the Provisions on Confiscation, a new condition was added:

> Where a criminal suspect or defendant whose whereabouts have been unknown for at least two years because of an accident, or whose whereabouts are unknown because of an accident and is impossible to survive, as the relevant department proves, such cases shall be conducted pursuant to the provisions of the preceding paragraph.

The trial in absentia procedure cannot be applied to cases where a criminal suspect or defendant has died or disappeared when overseas.

On the basis of the CPL, the Provisions on Confiscation set out more detailed procedural rules. Under normal circumstances, investigations aimed at the confiscation of illegal gains should be carried out by the public security agency (Article 298,

[31] Promulgated and implemented on 5 January 2017.

paragraph 2). During the investigation phase, the public security agency may issue a wanted order in China, or the Ministry of Public Security may issue a Red International Notice through Interpol. This notice can be defined as a 'wanted' notice under Article 298(1) of the CPL. When the public security agency finds that the case complies with the conditions set out in Article 298 of the CPL, an opinion on the confiscation of criminal proceeds should be written. The opinion should refer to the specific content listed in the Provisions on Confiscation. When transferring this opinion to the procuratorate, the public security agency must also submit evidence related to crime facts and proceeds in accordance with the law, and specify the type, quantity and location of the property, as well as the conditions of seizure or freezing (Article 298(2), (3)).

Article 299 of the CPL stipulates that the trial of cases of confiscation of illegal proceeds should be held by the intermediate court at the place of the crime or the residence of the suspect or defendant, and must be based on the application of the procuratorate. After accepting an application, the court will issue a public announcement. Article 12 of the Provisions on Confiscation elaborates on the specific use and methods of a public announcement. The announcement period runs for six months (Article 299(2)). After accepting the case, the court may seal, seize, or freeze the property requested for confiscation when necessary (Article 298(3)).

The court which accepts a case involving confiscation of illegal gains must form a collegiate panel to hear the case after the public announcement period has expired. The criminal suspect, the defendant's close relatives and other interested parties have the right to apply to participate in the proceedings, and may also mandate an 'agent ad litem' to participate in the proceedings. Article 7 of the Provisions on Confiscation explains that:

> other interested parties refer to criminal suspects, close relatives of the defendant, and other natural persons and entities claiming rights to the property that is subject to confiscation.

When interested parties participate in the procedure, the court must hold a public hearing (Article 299(3) of the CPL).

After hearing the case, the court has two options. The court may confirm that the property qualifies as illegal income and order confiscation, except property which is to be returned to the victim in accordance with the law. If the court finds that property does not qualify as crime proceeds, the application should be rejected and sealing, seizure, and freezing measures will be suspended (Article 300(1) of the CPL). The suspect, the close relatives of the defendant, and other interested parties, as well as the procuratorate, may appeal the decision (Article 300(2)).

Future reforms of the CPL should consider improving the integration of trials in absentia and confiscation procedures. Where there is evidence proving that the criminal suspect or defendant is still alive, the in absentia procedure should apply; a standalone confiscation procedure should be only applicable in cases where there is proof or a valid declaration of death of the suspect or defendant.

V. Compulsory Medical Treatment Procedures for Mentally Ill Offenders Who are Exempt from Criminal Liability

In the 2012 CPL revision, a compulsory treatment procedure was added for mentally ill offenders who are not criminally liable according to law. This revision coincided with the adoption of the first comprehensive Mental Health Law in China.[32] In fact, the 1997 amendment of the Criminal Code had introduced the possibility of imposing compulsory medical treatment after a finding that an accused was exempt from criminal responsibility. However, the provisions of the Criminal Code are general and do not extend to specific implementation procedures. Article 18 of the Criminal Code simply states that the family of an offender found to be mentally ill and exempt from criminal responsibility shall be ordered to subject the mentally ill person to strict surveillance and arrange for medical treatment. When necessary, Article 18 continues, the government will provide for compulsory medical treatment. In practice, when relatives cannot effectively take care of mentally ill offenders who are exempt from criminal responsibility, a security risk may be the consequence. For cases where the government responds to such a risk by imposing compulsory medical treatment, a statutory basis of a procedure must be available which clearly and in detail spells out the conditions under which a mentally ill offender may be committed to forensic psychiatry. Such proceedings must balance the interests of the mentally ill offender in freedom with the interest of society in the containment of dangers which may be the result of untreated mental illness.

Article 302 of the CPL defines the conditions which may result in compulsory medical treatment. Compulsory medical treatment may be ordered by a court where a person has stood trial for crimes of violence which have endangered public security or the personal safety of citizens but has been exempt from criminal responsibility due to mental illness, confirmed on the basis of an expert evaluation, and is assessed as continuing to be dangerous. Article 302 of the CPL adopts a rather narrow approach to compulsory criminal commitment to forensic hospitals compared with the rather wide conception of Article 18 of the Criminal Code. Only crimes of violence justify the initiation of commitment procedures.[33] However, neither the Criminal Code nor the CPL provide for a definition of mental illness.[34]

[32] For a comprehensive analysis see Zhiyuan Guo and Floyd Feeney, 'The New Chinese Mental Health Laws' (2018) 17(2) *Washington University Global Studies Law Review* 411.

[33] Yang Shao and Bin Xie, 'Approaches to Involuntary Admission of the Mentally Ill in the People's Republic of China: Changes in Legislation From 2002 to 2012' (2015) 43(1) *The Journal of the American Academy of Psychiatry and the Law* 35, 36.

[34] Li Naling, 'Judicial formulation of "mental patient" in criminal compulsory medical procedures' (2016) 8 *Law Journal* 116.

Furthermore, criminal law remains silent with respect to the disposition of offenders who exhibit mental health problems but who are not exempt from criminal responsibility. Article 18(2) of the Criminal Code addresses offenders with a mental illness of an intermittent nature, and Article 18(3) deals with diminished criminal responsibility due to mental illness. For offenders with a mental disease of an intermittent nature, criminal responsibility is to be established and criminal punishment imposed if a criminal offence was committed when the offender was in a normal mental state. According to Article 18(3) of the Criminal Code, a mental illness which does not completely exclude but diminishes criminal responsibility will result in mitigation of criminal punishment. This might result in mentally ill offenders being sentenced to imprisonment and ultimately serving prison sentences, though they need psychiatric treatment. In addition, Article 302 sets as a condition of compulsory medical treatment the continuing danger of a mentally ill offender. The assessment of continued danger caused by mental illness poses significant problems.[35] National standards have not yet been fully developed to guide the practices of establishing mental illness, continuing danger, and involuntary commitment to forensic hospitals. Local developments have been noted and the city of Shanghai seems to be leading in this field.

According to Article 303(2) of the CPL, public security organs, procuratorates and courts have the right to initiate compulsory medical procedures for mentally ill offenders. However, in practice, it is usually public security organs who initiate them. In addition to the CPL, other laws and regulations also provide rules on the involuntary commitment of mentally ill persons assessed to endanger public security or personal safety. The People's Police Law (PPL), the Mental Health Law, and the Public Security and Administrative Punishment Law authorise compulsory medical treatment of the mentally ill. This situation calls for coordination and guidance on the relationship between criminal, administrative and civil commitment to forensic psychiatric care. Although the decision on commitment for compulsory treatment is entrusted to the courts, the law allows public security organs to impose temporary protective restraint measures on mentally ill offenders (Article 303(3) CPL).

Compulsory medical treatment procedures may be applied for by the procuratorate based on an opinion prepared by public security organs (Article 303(2), S1 CPL) on the discovery that a suspect meets the conditions of compulsory treatment during review of the case for prosecution (Article 303(2)S2 CPL). A controversial issue arises with respect to the court's power to initiate compulsory medical treatment procedures when it finds during regular trial proceedings that the defendant meets the conditions of compulsory medical treatment (Article 303(2), S3 CPL). However, the court, bearing in mind the adversarial nature of proceedings, should

[35] Yan Gu et al, 'A Review of Violence Risk Assessment for Mentally Disordered Patients in Mainland of China' (2014) 41(12) *Criminal Justice and Behavior* 1398; Wei Jianghui and Cai Weixiong, 'Compulsory Medical Treatment for Mental Patients without criminal Responsibility' (2015) 4 *Chinese Journal of Forensic Science* 102.

have the duty to terminate regular criminal trial proceedings and commence a special procedure, even where the procuratorate or defence do not forward such applications.

Upon the decision to carry out a compulsory treatment procedure, a collegial panel must be established to conduct the hearing, which the defendant and the legal representative shall be summoned to attend (Article 304 CPL). If the defendant has not yet retained a defence lawyer, the court must notify a legal aid agency to assign a lawyer to provide legal assistance for him. Legal assistance provided by a lawyer is of particular relevance, as mentally ill persons – due to behavioural problems – will sometimes be excluded from attending the hearing.

After a hearing has been completed the case should be decided with four weeks. A decision to impose compulsory medical treatment may be reviewed by the court at the next level, on application by the defendant, victim, or the legal representative or close relatives (Article 305(2) of the CPL).

Enforcement of compulsory medical treatment takes place in specialised psychiatric institutions and is supervised by the procuratorate (Article 307 CPL). Psychiatric institutions must periodically examine mental patients in order to determine whether the conditions of compulsory treatment (dangerousness) still apply. Neither the CPL nor the CPL Interpretations 2021 fix time intervals for these periodical examinations. The CPL Interpretations 2021, however, state that an application for release from a psychiatric institution by a patient or his close relatives according to Article 306(2) of the CPL may be re-introduced (if not successful) after six months (Article 645(2) SPC Interpretations). This may be interpreted as requiring short time intervals between examinations to establish the continuing danger of a patient, and reflects concern for the right to freedom. Psychiatric institutions which find that a mental patient is no longer a danger have a duty to submit a release opinion to the court, which then may issue a release order (Article 306 CPL; Article 647 SPC Interpretations). A decision of the court to continue compulsory treatment is final. There is no remedy against a decision not to release.

Comparable to the situation in Western criminal justice systems, detailed statistics on forensic psychiatric institutions and the implementation of compulsory medical treatment are not available in China. In 2016, 5.1 million mentally ill patients were counted. Approximately 10,000 cases relating to mental ill patients are processed each year, and one third of these cases pertain to serious violence.[36] A 2010 study reported that there were 225 forensic psychiatric institutions and more than 2,000 forensic psychiatric experts.[37] While China certainly recognises mental illness in the context of criminal justice as an outstanding issue, confirmed by

[36] *Southern Weekend*, 'We must speed up the process of control of mental patients' committing of crimes', 8 March 2017.

[37] Li Xue et al, 'Chinese Forensic Psychiatry: History, Development and Challenges' (2015) 1 *Journal of Forensic Science and Medicine* 61.

its adoption of the UN Convention on the Rights of Persons with Disabilities in 2008, there remains room for further improvement of the procedural law which guides decisions on compulsory medical treatment. Here, the legislator should consider the introduction of full first instance trial proceedings, aimed not at answering the question of guilt and a guilt-appropriate sentence but at the question of whether a mentally ill offender displays a degree of dangerousness which under the rule of proportionality justifies detention in a forensic psychiatric hospital.

INDEX